MW00462610

Baseball's Other All-Stars

Also by William F. McNeil
and from McFarland

Ruth, Maris, McGwire and Sosa:
Baseball's Single Season Home Run Champions (2000)

The King of Swat: An Analysis of Baseball's Home Run Hitters
from the Major, Minor, Negro and Japanese Leagues (1997)

Baseball's Other All-Stars

The Greatest Players from the
Negro Leagues, the Japanese Leagues,
the Mexican League, and the
Pre–1960 Winter Leagues in Cuba,
Puerto Rico and the Dominican Republic

by
WILLIAM F. MCNEIL

McFarland & Company, Inc., Publishers
Jefferson, North Carolina, and London

Cover image: Alejandro Oms. *(Photograph courtesy of Yuyo Ruiz.)*

Library of Congress Cataloguing-in-Publication Data

McNeil, William F., 1932–
    Baseball's other all-stars : the greatest players from the Negro
Leagues, the Japanese leagues, the Mexican League, and the
pre–1960 winter leagues in Cuba, Puerto Rico, and the Dominican
Republic / by William F. McNeil.
        p.   cm.
    Includes bibliographical references (p.) and index.
    ISBN 0-7864-0784-0 (softcover : 50# alkaline paper) ∞
    1. Baseball players — Biography.   2. Baseball players — Statistics.
3. Baseball — History.   I. Title.
GV865.A1M378   2000
796.357'092'2 — dc21   99-59170
[B]

British Library Cataloguing-in-Publication data are available

Manufactured in the United States of America

*McFarland & Company, Inc., Publishers
    Box 611, Jefferson, North Carolina 28640
    www.mcfarlandpub.com*

This book is dedicated to the memories
of the legendary baseball players who were denied
the opportunity to play in the major leagues because
of their color, and to the great baseball players in the
Japanese Leagues and the Mexican League.

Acknowledgments

I would like to thank the following people and organizations who assisted me in this project.

Dan Johnson was a major contributor to my book. He provided me with a tremendous amount of information regarding the Japanese Leagues, including player biographies, individual statistics, league history, and photographs.

Luis Alvelo was also a major contributor to this work. He supplied me with a significant amount of personal information about the early Puerto Rican Winter League, its players and its teams, as well as providing me with photographs and All-Star team selections.

Jorge S. Figueredo went out of his way to provide me with valuable statistics from the Cuban Winter Leagues. He researched the major league players who played in the CWL during the 20th century, as well as a number of key Cuban natives whose statistics were not readily available. He also selected three Cuban Winter League All-Star teams, representing three different eras in CWL history.

James R. Madden, Jr., spent most of one week making the rounds of spring training camps in Arizona to obtain badly needed photographs for the book. His efforts were above and beyond the call of duty.

I would also like to thank Yuyo Ruiz, John B. Holway, Ralph Maya, Thomas E. Van Hyning, John Thorn, Angel Torres, Larry Lester, Dick Clark, Jose Jesus Jiminez, Masaru Madate and the Office of the Japan Baseball Commissioner, James A. Riley, Robert Peterson, Fumihiro Fujisawa, Ron Vesely and the Chicago White Sox, the Boston Red Sox, the Minnesota Twins, Patricia Kelly at the National Baseball Library, Mr. and Mrs. Victor Navarro, Todd Bolton, Jerry Malloy, L. Robert Davids, Gary Engel of Prestige Collectibles, Craig Davidson of Refocus Productions, Leo W. Banks, Sonny Rosenberg, Bob Hoie, Richard Bak, Carlos Bauer, and Juan Filizola and the Salon de la Fama del Beisbol Profesional de Mexico.

Contents

Introduction

Ever since the first baseball game was played on Elysian Field in 1845, fans have been arguing over which players were the best at their position. Almost as soon as the first box score was printed in a newspaper, enthusiastic fans began trying to determine the best first baseman, the best shortstop and so on.

Before long, all-star team selections were appearing in the nation's tabloids. The selection of an all-star team is a lot of fun in many respects, because it generates spirited discussion between fans of all ages and of both sexes. In some cases, heated arguments ensue. Unfortunately, more than a few past arguments ended with a serious injury to one participant or the other. In rare situations, fatalities have occurred.

In the vast majority of cases, however, discussions of the relative merits of individual ballplayers are kept on a friendly note, with both sides putting forth their arguments as to why one player or another deserves (or does not deserve) a place on the team.

Since baseball is an American sport — developed and perfected within the borders of the United States, if not actually invented here — the selection of an all-star team has always consisted of players from the American major leagues. In 1969, a survey of baseball fans, reporters, and writers, as presented by Gerald Secor Couzens in his fine book *Baseball Album,* produced the following all-time, all-star team: *Catcher* Mickey Cochrane; *Pitcher* Walter Johnson (right hander), Lefty Grove (left hander); *First Base* Lou Gehrig; *Second Base* Rogers Hornsby; *Shortstop* Honus Wagner; *Third Base* Pie Traynor; *Right Field* Ty Cobb; *Center Field* Babe Ruth; *Left Field* Joe Dimaggio; *Manager* John McGraw.

At a glance, we would have to admit that the above lineup consists of some of the finest baseball players ever to set foot on a diamond. It would be difficult for any of us to select a better group of players. On closer inspection, however, there are several glaring problems with the team. To begin with, it is all white. No blacks are represented on the starting nine. To be sure, four of the 27 finalists in

1

the survey were black: Jackie Robinson, Ernie Banks, Roy Campanella, and Willie Mays. But none of them made the final cut.

More importantly, only the American major leagues were considered when the poll was taken. We now know that the American major leagues are only one segment of a vast professional baseball network that encircles the globe. The "great American pastime" is actually enjoyed in dozens of countries around the world, including Japan, Cuba, Mexico, Puerto Rico, Venezuela, and the Dominican Republic. In Cuba, for example, professional baseball goes back to the nineteenth century, with the first professional championship being awarded to the Havana club in 1878. The Japanese League began operations in 1936, and two years later, the Puerto Rican Winter League completed its first season.

Even in the United States, some professional baseball leagues were forced to operate outside the umbrella of organized baseball, ostracized by the major league's unwritten whites-only policy. Rube Foster, one of black baseball's legendary pioneers, founded the Negro National League in 1920. Several other black leagues followed, with the Negro American League being organized in 1937.

Over the years, tens of thousands of baseball players plied their trade in the misty world of these unrecognized professional leagues. The Negro leagues gave their fans some of the most exciting baseball seen in the United States during the first half of the twentieth century. Larger-than-life heroes like Satchel Paige, Josh Gibson, "Cool Papa" Bell, and Buck Leonard put on hitting and pitching demonstrations equal to, and in some cases superior to, those being staged in the major leagues. Great strikeout pitchers, like "Smokey Joe" Williams, "Cannonball Dick" Redding, and "Bullet Joe" Rogan, mesmerized crowds from coast to coast with their extraordinary ball handling skills. Williams, in exhibition games against white major leaguers, piled up a convincing 22–7 pitching record during his career, including a 10 inning no-hitter against the world champion New York Giants. Josh Gibson, the powerful catcher of the Homestead Grays, is still the only man to hit a fair ball out of Yankee Stadium. These legendary Negro league players were obviously qualified to play in the major leagues. It was only the color of their skin that prevented them from playing alongside the likes of Babe Ruth, Ty Cobb, and Walter Johnson.

Since the pioneering efforts of Jackie Robinson destroyed the color barrier in 1946, some effort has been made on the part of the establishment to recognize these great players. To date, 16 former Negro league players, including Paige, Gibson, and Leonard, have been inducted into the National Baseball Hall of Fame in Cooperstown, New York. Other deserving players, like "Mule" Suttles and Turkey Stearnes, are still waiting their turn. They have been waiting for over half a century now.

Cuba has produced its own baseball heroes, including Jose Mendez, Alejandro Oms, Bernardo Baro, and Cristobal Torriente. These players also competed on an equal basis with their major league counterparts in hundreds of exhibition games over the decades. John McGraw, the manager of the New York Giants, after his team faced Mendez in several exhibition games in Cuba, called him the greatest pitcher in baseball. Mendez, and many of his countrymen, also wait to be recognized by the Cooperstown museum. One Cuban player, pitcher/ second baseman/outfielder Martin Dihigo, is one of the 16 Negro league players presently in the Hall. The versatile Dihigo, in fact, is the only baseball player to be enshrined in the baseball Hall of Fame in four different countries, having been so honored in the United States, Cuba, Venezuela, and Mexico. Josh Gibson is enshrined in the United States, Mexico, and Puerto Rico.

Some Cubans of Latin extraction, like Adolfo Luque, Rafael Almeida, and Armando Marsans, enjoyed extensive major league careers in the early twentieth century, but their dark-skinned compatriots were relegated to the Negro leagues and the various Caribbean winter leagues.

Puerto Rico has produced some of the major leagues' most outstanding performers over the past 50 years. Hall of Famer Roberto Clemente thrilled American fans with his clutch hitting capabilities and his outstanding defensive skills during the 1960s. Orlando "The Baby Bull" Cepeda terrorized National League pitchers for 17 long years with his powerful bat. Fireballing southpaw Juan Pizzaro won 131 games during a successful 18-year major league career. Long before Clemente, Cepeda, or Pizzaro stepped on a diamond, however, heroic ballplayers were dazzling crowds from San Juan to Pittsburgh in the *other* professional leagues.

One of the first great Puerto Rican baseball players was Orlando Cepeda's father, Perucho, an all-star shortstop for more than twenty years. The elder Cepeda was the first Puerto Rican Winter League batting champion, winning the title in 1938-39 with an average of .365, and repeating the following year with an average of .386. Another illustrious Puerto Rican player was the fabled Francisco "Pancho" Coimbre, perhaps the island's most celebrated athlete. Coimbre, a five-point player, captured two PRWL batting championships, retiring in 1951, with a career average of .337, the second highest career batting average in Puerto Rican Winter League history.

Across the big pond, in Japan, professional baseball has been played for over half a century. The caliber of play in the Japanese leagues has gradually improved to the point where they are now close to the major league level. Many of their players could compete in the major leagues now. In fact, one of their star pitchers, Hideo Nomo, did jump to the National League in 1995, with the Los Angeles Dodgers. Nomo pitched Tommy Lasorda's club to the western division title, piling up a 13–6 won-loss record, leading the league with 236 strikeouts, and running away with Rookie of the Year honors en route. Other players, like world home run champion Sadaharu Oh, third baseman Shigeo Nagashima, and catcher Katsuya Nomura, were world class performers who would have earned a place in Cooperstown had they spent their careers in the major leagues instead of in the Japanese leagues.

The major league all-star team, as noted above, may indeed consist of the greatest baseball players in the history of the game. On the other hand, it may well be that some of the greatest players in the history of the game were excluded because they did not belong to the right club. Where do legendary performers like Josh Gibson, "Smokey Joe" Williams, Sadaharu Oh, Shigeo Nagashima, Francisco "Pancho" Coimbre, "Perucho" Cepeda, Jose Mendez, and Alejandro Oms fit in? Do they belong on the all-time baseball all-star team, alongside DiMaggio and Ruth? Can they compete on an equal footing with players like Mickey Cochrane and Pie Traynor?

This book will investigate the greatest baseball players ever to play the game outside the major leagues. The top professional leagues in the world will be compared, one against another. The procedure will be similar to that used in my book on the greatest home run hitters in baseball history, *The King of Swat*. The major leagues will be used as the base point. The other professional leagues, such as the Japanese leagues, the Cuban Winter League, the Puerto Rican Winter League, and the Negro leagues, will be adjusted to the major league base point.

The great baseball players will be evaluated on an equal basis, position by position. In the end, one all-star team will be selected; one team composed of the greatest players of all time, from the *other* professional leagues around the world. It may truly be the world's greatest all-time, all-star baseball team. At least, it should be able to compete on an equal footing with the major leagues' best.

The players who are selected for the final all-world all-star team will have competed against, and beaten, some of the greatest players in history. Whatever the makeup of the final team, baseball fans everywhere will come to know there are literally hundreds of great baseball players who never stepped onto a major league field — players with names like Oh, Mendez, and Coimbre. One hopes that these men, and many more like them, will then begin to get the recognition they so dearly deserve.

It should be noted that this book constitutes an initial study of the various professional baseball players around the world. It is intended to introduce the general public to the quality of baseball that was played outside the doors of the major leagues during the first half of the twentieth century, and to the professional leagues that are still operating in countries beyond the borders of the United States. The study is also intended to determine the approximate relationship between the various leagues, and to provide some insight into the level of competitiveness within each league. The reported differences between the leagues is only an estimate, based on a small population. However, I believe that the relative positions of the leagues are basically correct.

This is a book for the serious baseball fan.

Baseball in the Nineteenth Century

Baseball was not invented from scratch. Games such as Rounders, One Old Cat, and Club Ball, date centuries back in England. In fact, ball games were popular in ancient civilizations as long ago as 2000 B.C., according to murals on temple walls in Egypt. The British Museum has in its possession a 4000-year-old ball found in Egypt.

Baseball evolved from these early games. It is, as we know it, an American innovation. It grew piece by piece from the eighteenth century to the middle nineteenth century, when organized touring teams began to popularize the game. From that modest beginning, it evolved into the game we know today.

The period from 1845 until 1893 was a time of continual adjustment in our national pastime. The myriad of changes that took place in the game of baseball during this period were discussed in detail in my book on the great home run hitters in baseball history. Some of these changes are:

• In the beginning, all baseball diamonds were open fields. There were no fences; therefore all home runs had to be "legged out." The fastest baserunners accumulated the most triples and home runs. The big, cumbersome sluggers had to content themselves with long singles and doubles.

• The baseball was hand made and poorly constructed. Only one ball was used in a game. As the game progressed, the ball became softer and more misshapen, making it difficult to hit a long distance.

• There were no specifications on bats until 1893.

• The current four-ball, three-strike rule did not take effect until 1888.

• Gloves were not worn until the 1880s. Some hardened veterans didn't accept the hand coverings until the nineties. A few diehards never wore a glove.

• Pitchers had to pitch underhand until 1883. They were then allowed to pitch sidearm, up to shoulder height. The overhand delivery was made legal in 1884.

• The pitching distance to home plate was 45 feet until 1881, when it was increased to 50 feet. The present pitching distance of 60'6" was established in 1893.

• A batter could request a high or low pitch from the pitcher until 1886.

During the last half of the nineteenth century, the American game was exported around the world. Nemesio Guillot, a Cuban citizen, who had attended college in the United States and played baseball there, brought the game back to his homeland in 1866. Within fifteen years professional teams were flourishing in and around Havana.

Cuban refugees from the Ten Years War carried the game to the Dominican Republic during the 1870s, where it grew to become the island's most popular sport. Traveling Cuban baseball teams also introduced the sport to many other countries along the Caribbean highway, including Venezuela, Puerto Rico, and Mexico.

There were a number of legendary Cuban baseball players who showcased their talents in the Cuban League over the last two decades of the nineteenth century. Among them were Antonio Garcia, Adolfo Lujan, Jose Pastoriza, and Carlos Royer. Their careers will be reviewed in a later chapter.

An American professor who was teaching school in Japan introduced the game there in 1873. Several years later, sailors from American ships visiting the country engaged in a number of baseball games against local club teams. The game took hold immediately, and quickly spread to the schools around the island. By 1915, annual national high school baseball tournaments were being held. Ten years later, college tournaments were underway, and by 1935, professional baseball was being played in Japan.

Back in the United States, Irish immigrants by the dozens took up the game of professional baseball, simply because of the tenor of the times. Hundreds of thousands of Irish had come to the United States during the middle of the nineteenth century, primarily as a result of the great potato famine that swept their homeland. They were discriminated against in America, as minorities have been since the country was first founded. The Irish could find work only in the most menial jobs; domestic servants, laborers on the railroads and roads, and coal miners. Restaurants often displayed signs in their windows, saying "Help wanted. Irish need not apply."

Baseball, at the time, was not considered to be an honorable profession by the majority of Americans, so jobs were open to any person with good athletic ability. Irish men flocked to the sport in droves, finding it preferable to working on the railroads or in the mines. Some of the greatest players of the nineteenth century were Irish, including:

Cy Young

Cy Young

• Michael J. "King" Kelly, a flamboyant catcher and outfielder for the Chicago White Stockings and Boston Beaneaters, from 1878 to 1893. He retired with a lifetime batting average of .313.

• Cy Young, the greatest pitcher of the nineteenth century, setting many records that will probably never be broken, such as:

Most victories	511
Most losses	316
Most games started	815
Most complete games	749
Most innings pitched	7356

• James F. "Pud" Galvin, a tireless worker who piled up 361 victories during the 1880s. From 1879 to 1884, he pitched in 70 percent of his team's 543 games.

• Tim Keefe and "Smiling Mickey" Welch of the New York Metropolitans, an unbeatable duo during the mid 1880s. Keefe won 342 games during a 14-year career, while Welch racked up 307 wins in 13 years. Between them they won 324 games in five years, from 1885 to 1889.

• Big Dan Brouthers, the epitome of the nineteenth century slugger. The 6'2" 200 pound superstar rapped the ball at a .342 clip from 1879 to 1896. He pounded out 106 home runs during his career, and his .519 slugging percentage is the highest in the nineteenth century and is still #9 all-time.

• Roger Connor, the home run king of the nineteenth century, with 137 career home runs. The left handed slugger compiled a .325 career batting average, with 2535 base hits in 18 years.

Other outstanding Irish major league players of the nineteenth century included pitcher Tony "The Count" Mullane, shortstop Hughie "Ee-Yah" Jennings, third basemen John "Little Napoleon" McGraw and Denny Lyons, and outfielders "Big Ed" Delahanty, Sam Thompson, Harry Stovey, and Wee Willie Keeler who "Hit 'em where they ain't."

In the early twentieth century, other immigrants found similar discrimination when they sought work. Italians, Jews, Poles, and Catholics of all nationalities had to struggle to realize the American dream. Many of them gravitated to the game of baseball as a viable escape. Some took up boxing as a means of support.

Harry Stovey. (National Baseball Library and Archive, Cooperstown, N.Y.)

Blacks had their own unique problems. Since they were also a minority in the nineteenth century, they gravitated to baseball, along with the Irish. But they had an even bigger mountain to climb. They were held in less esteem than the Irish and other white minorities. The color of their skin made their job much more difficult.

They also had the Ku Klux Klan to contend with. The KKK was originally organized in 1867 to prevent blacks from voting and to harass white sympathizers. It gradually expanded its operations to take action against any "uppity blacks," or troublesome Catholics, Jews, and other minorities. Frequently the white robed, hooded men burned fiery crosses on people's lawns as a warning. At other times, they lynched their helpless victims.

John McGraw

In the United States, there were numerous black players on professional baseball rosters during the 1870s and 1880s. Some of them were members of organized ball until 1893, when baseball's unofficial segregation policy finally closed the door on them. These players, as well as black players who were members of traveling Negro teams, or "outlaw" leagues outside organized baseball, contributed to the development of our National Pastime.

A cross section of some of the outstanding nineteenth century black professional baseball players in the United States includes:

• Moses Fleetwood Walker, the first black to play major league baseball. The 26-year-old catcher was a member of the Toledo team of the American Association in 1884, hitting a respectable .263. His brother, Welday, also played for Toledo in 1884, hitting a paltry .222 in five games.

• Ulysses F. "Frank" Grant, an outstanding second baseman of the period, who was never allowed to play major league baseball. He was black, probably the greatest black baseball player of the nineteenth century, and maybe the best at the position, black or white. According to existing records, the Pittsfield, Massachusetts, native was quick defensively, with outstanding range, sure hands, and a strong throwing arm.

Grant compiled a solid .337 batting average over six minor league seasons, with nine home runs a year. His aspirations to play in the major leagues were scuttled, however, when, in 1887, major league owners began to put their "whites only" policy into effect. The black infielder barnstormed with the Cuban Giants throughout the '90s, and finished his baseball career with the black Philadelphia Giants in 1903. Based on comparative numbers between leagues, and between the dead ball era and the lively ball era, it is conceivable that Frank Grant would have excelled in the major leagues, both offensively and defensively. In addition to his unsurpassed fielding prowess, Frank Grant was projected to hit .303 in the majors, with an average of 23 home runs a year (later chapters will explain how batting averages and home runs in the dead ball era, were adjusted, to bring them into agreement with the statistics from the lively ball era).

• John W. (Bud) Fowler, another black second baseman who was penalized by the discriminating policies of professional baseball. Fowler, the first black player in organized baseball, played in the minor leagues from 1878 to 1890, before finally falling victim to segregation. He starred in several high minor leagues over that period, including the Western League, where he hit .309 for Topeka and led the league with 12 triples. He pounded the ball at a .350 clip for Binghamton of the International League in 1887.

After his departure from organized ball, he played for several Negro teams until 1899. He organized the Page Fence Giants, a powerful black team in Adrian, Michigan, that included such legendary black players as Grant "Home Run" Johnson and Sol White.

Bud Fowler's minor league statistics for his ten year career show a solid .308 batting average, with 190 stolen bases in 466 games.

• Solomon "Sol" White, another black infielder of the day. The 5'9", 170 pound speedster was the top black batsman of the nineteenth century, terrorizing opposing pitchers with a hefty .356 batting average for five years in organized baseball. He played for six different teams, never hitting less than .308 for any team. Included in his averages were .371 for Wheeling in the Ohio State League and .356 for the York Colored Giants of the Eastern Interstate League.

White also played for several black teams like the Page Fence Giants, the Cuban Giants, and the Philadelphia Giants, which he helped organize in 1902.

• George W. Stovey, a southpaw curveball artist, who played parts of six seasons in organized baseball. He compiled a record of 16–15 for Jersey City in the Eastern League as a 20-year-old phenom in 1886. The next year he went 34–14 for the Newark entry in the International League, the greatest season ever by an International League hurler. The Pennsylvania pitcher was destined for greatness but, before he could display his wares in the National League, he was singled out for "special attention" by Cap Anson, the influential manager of the Chicago White Stockings. Stovey was black, and Anson, whose White Stockings were scheduled to play an exhibition game against Newark, said his team would not take the field against the Bears if Stovey played. As a result of Anson's complaints, the Negro southpaw was subsequently banned from the league, paving the way for the heinous segregation policy that would bar blacks from organized baseball for over 50 years.

George Stovey ended his minor league career with a record of 60–40, and a fine 2.17 earned run average. The only nineteenth century major league pitcher who had a better ERA than Stovey was John Montgomery Ward, who put together a 2.10 ERA with Providence and New York of the National League between 1878 and 1884. Stovey continued pitching in the Negro leagues, with the New York Gorhams and the Cuban X Giants, until 1896. After leaving the professional ranks, he played amateur baseball around his home town of Williamsport, Pennsylvania, into his early fifties.

• William Selden, another potential major league star pitcher who was denied the chance to play in the major leagues because of his color. He played minor league baseball for three years, compiling a 40–11 record, a dazzling .784 winning percentage. In 1889, pitching for the Cuban Giants who represented Trenton in the Middle States League, he racked up a 23–6 record. Unfortunately, like Stovey, he was drummed out of the league the following year. He spent the next nine years touring with various black teams such as the New York Gorhams and the Cuban X Giants.

• William T. "Billy" Whyte, one of the top pitchers of the nineteenth century. He played with William Selden on the Trenton team in the Middle States League in 1889, and won 26 games against only five losses, for a brilliant .839 winning percentage. In all, he was 37–11, .771, during his three years of minor league ball. He also held his own in exhibition games against major league teams. Whyte pitched for the Cuban Giants for seven years, retiring in 1894.

An Overview of Baseball, 1900–1950

This book is primarily concerned with the great professional baseball players who displayed their talents, day in and day out, in the shadowy world of "outlaw" baseball — outside the control of organized baseball. However, before reviewing the various professional leagues that spanned the globe — from the American Negro leagues, to leagues in Mexico and Japan — in this century, it is important to present a brief overview of organized baseball, since the rules, regulations, and equipment that existed in organized ball trickled down to the other leagues. The players who starred in the big leagues during that same time span are the players the All-World All-Stars will be measured against, and it is important to know the competition.

By the time the twentieth century dawned, the modern game of baseball was in full swing. The American League joined the National League as a major league in 1901. Although baseball was a segregated sport at the time, there were still baseball people who admired the talents of the black players, and who tried to recruit them to play in the major leagues. A case in point is Charlie Grant. Grant was a smooth fielding, hard hitting second baseman on a Negro team when he was discovered by Baltimore Orioles manager, John McGraw, in 1901. McGraw tried to hire the black infielder, by disguising him as an Indian named Chief Tokohama, supposedly a full blooded Cherokee. Unfortunately, the ruse was exposed by Chicago White Sox owner Charles Comiskey, and Grant went back to playing in the Negro leagues.

Other owners such as Connie Mack and Clark Griffith were interested in hiring black players over the years, but they didn't want to buck the system, so their desires went unfulfilled.

The period from 1900 to 1919 was an anomaly of the twentieth century. It was the only period when the "dead ball" was in use. The position players were,

Christy Mathewson

for the most part, skilled defensive practitioners of the sport, with good foot speed and a keen batting eye that produced few strikeouts and fewer home runs. They were contact hitters who sprayed the field with singles, doubles, and triples.

Runs were difficult to come by during the 1900–20 period, and home runs were few and far between. The league home run leader, from 1900 through 1919,

"Home-Run" Baker

averaged only 13 home runs a year. Batting averages hovered around the .255 mark, and the average team scored less than 600 runs per year.

The most significant change made in the game after 1900 came about in 1920 with the advent of the so-called "lively ball." The cork-centered baseball, introduced in 1910, was made even more skitterish by the use of a new, tighter yarn and an improved manufacturing process. Simultaneous with these changes was the banning of trick pitches, such as shine balls, spit balls, and emory balls.

There was one exception, however. Eighteen major league pitchers, who relied on the spit ball for their livelihood, were allowed to continue throwing it throughout their careers. Burleigh Grimes, the last of the legal spitballers, retired in 1934.

The changes in the construction of the baseball and the restrictions imposed on the types of pitches a pitcher could throw all favored the batter. Hitting replaced pitching as the dominant factor in the game. A quick scan of the all-time leaders in career earned run average reflects the changing situation. The all-time career leader in earned run average is "Big Ed" Walsh, who pitched for the Chicago White Sox from 1904 through 1917. He retired with a career earned run average of 1.82. He is followed by Addie Joss (1902–10) and Mordecai Brown (1903–16). The first 29 pitchers on the all-time list did the bulk of their pitching prior to 1920. Fifty-six of the first 57 pitchers on the list were from the "old school." Only Hoyt Wilhelm, who pitched from 1952 through 1972, could break into the top 30. The next modern pitcher to make the list is Whitey Ford of the New York Yankees, who did his mound work between 1950 and 1967. He is #58. Sandy Koufax is #62.

The game changed drastically in 1920, when the "rabbit ball" was put into play. During the '20s, while earned run averages skyrocketed, batting averages increased by approximately 29 points, and home runs more than doubled. The pendulum had swung from one side to the other, from pitching to hitting.

The Babe Ruth era, which peaked in the 1926–50 period, revolutionized the game. It actually began in 1920, when the Bambino launched an unbelievable 54 home runs in American League parks, but it was several years before the "slugger's mentality" caught on with other long ball hitters.

Players from the 1900–25 era averaged less than 10 home runs a year, with the exception of Rogers Hornsby and Harry "The Horse" Heilmann, who averaged 20 and 13 home runs respectively. Both players were transition players, whose careers peaked with the advent of the lively ball era, between 1921 and 1930.

Outside organized baseball, the game circled the globe in the early twentieth century. The American Negro leagues joined the ranks of the professionals, with the formation of the Negro National League, in 1920. The NNL was joined by the Eastern Colored League in 1923 and, between the two leagues, they developed such immense talents as Satchel Paige, Oscar Charleston, Chino Smith, Turkey Stearnes, Cool Papa Bell, "Bullet Joe" Rogan, and "Smokey Joe" Williams.

Their progress followed in the same footsteps as for the major leagues. The Negro leagues converted over to the lively ball in the early 1920s, and the big sluggers took on added prestige, as offense became the order of the day. Mule Suttles unloaded 26 round trippers in just 342 at-bats for the St. Louis Stars in 1926. Turkey Stearnes hit 65 home runs in 924 at-bats for the Detroit Stars, between 1926 and 1928. Chino Smith banged out 23 homers in 245 at-bats for the Lincoln Giants in 1929.

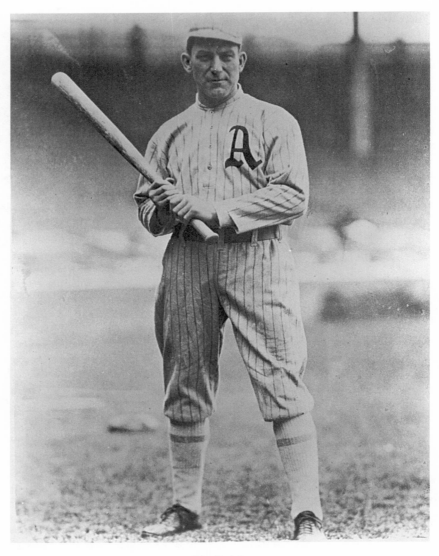

Nap Lajoie

Winter leagues also flourished in America during the first quarter of the twentieth century. Florida's prestigious hotels, like the Royal Poinciana and the Breakers in Palm Beach, fielded professional teams made up of players from the Negro leagues. Some of the great black players who participated in the Hotel League included Rube Foster, Pete Hill, Grant "Home Run" Johnson, Spot Poles, Pop Lloyd, "Cannonball Dick" Redding, and Louis "Big Bertha" Santop. Other hotels fielded squads of white players from the major leagues. Competition was spirited, as the teams fought for bragging rights.

Across the country, another winter league, this one in California, also drew large contingents of players from both the Negro leagues and the major leagues. The California League, however, was an integrated circuit, presenting direct comparisons between the black players and their major league counterparts. Black stars like Biz Mackey, Cool Papa Bell, Satchel Paige, and Josh Gibson played with, and competed against, such big leaguers as Babe Ruth, Dizzy Dean, Babe Herman, and Jimmie Foxx.

In Cuba, winter and summer leagues showcased both local talent and American major leaguers. The Cuban Winter League in the early 1920s was one of the first integrated professional leagues in the world, pairing such Negro league legends as Oscar Charleston and Cristobal Torriente with major leagues stars like Charlie Dressen and Hank DeBerry.

Cuba was also the scene of dozens of exhibition games between Cuban teams and visiting major league teams, like John McGraw's Giants and Connie Mack's A's. The Cuban teams, with homegrown players like Antonio Garcia, Jose Mendez, Eustaquio Pedroso, and Julian Castillo, along with Negro league stars like John Henry Lloyd, Louis Santop, and Grant Johnson, held the cocky major leaguers to a draw in over 60 contests.

Other winter leagues flourished throughout Central and South America and the Caribbean region. Some of the countries playing baseball from the 1930s on included Mexico, Puerto Rico, Venezuela, the Dominican Republic, Panama, and Colombia. The peripatetic American Negro leaguers wintered all over the Caribbean basin during the first half of the twentieth century, mixing business with pleasure. Unlike their treatment in the United States which, at best was discriminatory, and at worst bestial, they were treated like heroes in Cuba, Mexico, Puerto Rico, and the Dominican Republic. As Willie Wells once said regarding his life in Mexico, "Here they treat me like a man."

The quarter century from 1926 through 1950 was a dynamic period in organized baseball history. The game evolved from a pitcher's game to a hitter's game, with individual club home run records being set on a regular basis. Babe Ruth, the Sultan of Swat, set the season home run record at 60 in 1927. It remained one of baseball's most untouchable records until 1961, when Roger Maris of the New York Yankees slammed 61 round trippers out of various American League parks, 31 of them coming on the road (Maris' record was broken, in 1998, by Mark McGwire, who homered an amazing 70 times in National League's stadiums).

Batting averages skyrocketed with the introduction of the rabbit ball in 1920, reaching a peak in 1930 when the National League, as a league, hit .303. The American League was close behind at .288. The baseball, it seems, was the culprit for the 1930 blip on the batting average chart. A change in the manufacturing process had produced a baseball with recessed seams as opposed to the raised seams on a regulation ball. The recessed seams prevented pitchers from gripping the ball properly — for instance, when throwing a curveball. As a result, pitched balls, in 1930, had very little movement and, as we know, batters love to hit straight balls, regardless of the speed. They just laid back and teed off. The situation was corrected the following year, and batting averages returned to their pre–1930 levels.

Overall, the game became more offensive-minded during the second quarter of the century. More players hit for higher batting averages than ever before. Home run totals tripled previous levels, as more batters gripped the bat at the end, à la Babe Ruth, and swung for the fences. Run production skyrocketed, and offense dominated the game.

When the rabbit ball was introduced in 1920, the average major league team hit just under 40 home runs in a season. In 1926, the first year of the second quarter, teams averaged 54 homers a year. By 1930, the average was up to almost 100 home runs a year. The Babe Ruth–dominated New York Yankees were the first major league team to hit more than 100 home runs in a single season, pounding out 115 of them in 1920. In 1929, seven major league clubs hit over 100 home runs, and by the end of the second quarter, in 1950, 13 of 16 teams surpassed the century mark.

Long ball hitting went on a sabbatical during the early '40s, as World War II stripped organized ball of most of its able bodied players. Beginning in 1946, baseball began to return to normal, although with the heavy loss of life in the war, the talent pool was greatly decimated. It took several years before things were as they had been before the great conflict.

Ralph Kiner raised home run hitting to a new level in the late 1940s. After leading the National League with 23 home runs in his rookie season, the New Mexico slugger, assisted by the construction of the famous "Kiner's Korner" in Pittsburgh's Forbes Field, jacked 51 balls out of National League parks in 1947. His famous quote, "Singles hitters drive Chevys. Home run hitters drive Cadillacs," encouraged a new generation of sluggers to forgo bat control and swing from the heels.

Home run levels reached a new all-time high as the second quarter of the century came to an end. Sixteen major league teams averaged 130 home runs each in 1950.

In the "Outlaw" leagues, the Negro American League, which came into existence in 1937, combined with the Negro National League to produce celebrated players like Josh Gibson, Satchel Paige, Leon Day, Ray Dandridge, Willie Wells, and "Double Duty" Radcliffe. During the 1920s and '30s, the black baseball players were the ambassadors of the sport around the world. They traveled to the Far East several times over a 15 year period, bringing the American Game to dozens of venues, including Hawaii, the Philippines, and Japan. They were particularly revered in Japan, where they not only played numerous games against Japanese college and professional all-star teams, but they also took the time to work with the Japanese teams, to teach them the finer points of the game, as well as the fundamentals. Players like Biz Mackey and "Bullet Joe" Rogan worked with the Japanese players on their batting technique and their fielding, as well as instructing them in the strategy of the game.

Baseball grew in popularity by leaps and bounds in Japan during the first half of the twentieth century. The first professional team was formed in 1935 and, a year later, the Japanese League began play. Unlike some of the other leagues around the world, the Japanese League did not adopt the lively ball until after World War II. No one hit more than ten home runs in a season until 1946, when Hiroshi Oshita socked the unbelievable total of 20. Shigeya Iijima, with 12, was the only other player in the league to break the magic 10 barrier.

Some of the early Japanese baseball legends included Victor Starffin, a Russian refugee who was Japan's first 300 game winner; Tetsuharu Kawakami, Japan's first batting champion, who retired in 1958 with a career average of .313, at that time the highest average in the Japanese professional leagues; and Shigeru Chiba, a Japanese Hall of Fame second baseman.

A summer professional baseball league was organized in the Dominican Republic in the early 1930s, but it lasted only a short time. The most extraordinary league in the world was the Dominican Summer League of 1937. The four presidential candidates each supported one of the teams in the league, creating a nerve-wracking political campaign, as well as a tension-filled season. General Rafael Trujillo, the notorious Dominican dictator, who backed one of the teams, kept his Negro league players, like Satchel Paige and Josh Gibson, under armed guard at night to prevent them from partying. Needless to say, as soon as they had clinched the pennant, the Negro leaguers caught the first plane home.

Professional baseball got underway in earnest in Puerto Rico in 1937 with the organization of a winter league. In addition to Puerto Rican legends like Pancho Coimbre and Perucho Cepeda, the league attracted many Negro league players, like Paige, Gibson, Roy Campanella, Buck Leonard, Willard Brown, and Bob Thurman.

Perhaps the most historical event of the second quarter of the twentieth century in organized baseball was the collapse of the reprehensible color barrier. Branch Rickey, the courageous general manager of the Brooklyn Dodgers, with the support of the equally brave Commissioner of Baseball, Albert B. "Happy" Chandler, signed Jackie Robinson, a Negro, to a minor league contract in 1945. Robinson, a graduate of the Negro leagues, went on to star in the major leagues for ten years, helping the Dodgers to six National League flags and one World Championship. The great Negro trailblazer opened the door for blacks to compete in organized baseball on an equal basis with whites. He was elected to the baseball Hall of Fame in 1962.

Robinson was followed into the majors by more than 100 talented Negro league players over the next ten years. The caliber of play in the major leagues was elevated to a new level by this influx of Negro league professionals. Many baseball experts consider the late forties to be the beginning of the golden age of baseball. It continued through the fifties until expansion once again diluted the talent pool.

It may be that the major league home run surge, beginning in the late '40s, was the result of the integration of organized baseball, with the subsequent arrival in the major leagues of dozens of Negro league sluggers rather than the result of the so-called "Kiner Influence." It may also be that the surge was just the natural evolution of the "Babe Ruth syndrome" that was born in the 1920s. It was probably a combination of all three.

When the lively ball first came into play, and the home run became an important part of the game, those players who were already long ball hitters gained the benefit of it — players like Ruth, Tilly Walker, Ken Williams, and Cy Williams. Most veteran hitters, however, like Ty Cobb, George Sisler, Tris Speaker, Bobby Veach, and Edd Roush, refused to change their batting style in the middle of a successful career. The full effect of the change in batting philosophy wasn't felt for a full generation, when the kids of the '20s and '30s, who emulated the Bambino's batting grip, became the major leaguers of the late '30s and early '40s. Statistics support that theory as home run levels gradually increased year after year through the '20s and '30s and new sluggers entered the professional ranks. The trend was temporarily interrupted in the early '40s because of World War II, but it was back on track again as the second quarter came to an end.

There were still great pitchers in the majors during the second quarter of the twentieth century, but their earned run averages were no longer sub–2.00. They were now 3.00+, for the most part. Robert Moses "Lefty" Grove, perhaps the greatest southpaw pitcher in major league history, compiled a 3.06 ERA during the '20s and 30s. His southpaw counterparts who pitched during the first decade of the century — Rube Waddell and Eddie Plank — had much lower earned-run-averages (2.16 and 2.35 respectively), but the difference was due to changes in the playing environment and not in the skill of the participants. The top pitchers of the day still racked up their 20-win seasons, with an occasional 30-win season thrown in, but the days of a pitcher winning 40 games in a season were over.

The period from 1925 to 1950 produced some of the greatest major league players yet seen across America. Compared with the players of the 1900–25 era, the 1926–50 contingent was more of an offensive machine. The position players were still defensive stalwarts, but they could also propel the ball long distances with monotonous regularity. Most of the outstanding players had career batting averages over .300.

A few of the major league legends of the first fifty years of the twentieth century are familiar names to fans of the game:

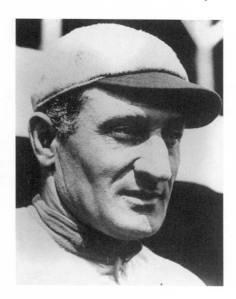

Honus Wagner

• Shortstop John Peter "Honus" Wagner, known as The Flying Dutchman, could do it all. He could hit, hit with power, run, field, and throw. Branch Rickey called him the greatest ballplayer he had ever seen. Standing 5'11" tall and tipping the scales at a rugged 200 pounds, the man called the "Octopus" had no peers defensively. Although ungainly in appearance, the big, bowlegged, barrel chested infielder captured everything within his reach. He had outstanding range, sure hands, and a strong throwing arm. He led the league in fielding average three times and showed the way in putouts twice.

Wagner rolled up a .329 batting average over a glorious 21 year career. The right handed slugger hit over .300 his first 17 years in the National League, with a league record eight batting titles.

• Ty Cobb, the man people loved to hate, may have been the greatest hitter of all time. His .367 career batting average is the highest of all time and is one of baseball's most untouchable records. Cobb holds a barrel-full of records. He led the league in hitting an unprecedented nine times. He led in runs scored five times, hits eight times, doubles three times, triples four times, home runs once, and runs batted in four times. The 6'1", 175 pound outfielder's 892 career stolen bases were the highest total of the twentieth century before Lou Brock surpassed him in 1977.

• "Shoeless Joe" Jackson, the illiterate country boy from South Carolina, who was a victim of the infamous Black Sox scandal, may well have been baseball's most natural hitter. Babe Ruth patterned his batting stance after Jackson's.

Shoeless Joe burst upon the major league baseball scene like a meteor, smashing the ball at a torrid .408 clip as a rookie for the Cleveland Indians in 1911 (Cobb hit .420). The smooth swinging lefty piled up a .356 career batting average over a 13-year career, a figure exceeded only by Ty Cobb (.367) and Rogers Hornsby (.358). His average of 19 triples for every 550 at-bats is the highest average in major league history.

• Walter "The Big Train" Johnson is considered by many baseball experts to be the greatest pitcher in baseball history. Johnson had the misfortune to pitch for second division ballclubs most of his career, yet he still managed to pile up 416 victories in 21 years. His record included 12 years of 20 or more

"Shoeless Joe" Jackson

victories and two years of more than 30 wins. His 110 career shutouts may never be topped.

    • Lou Gehrig was a tireless worker who loved playing baseball. He set a major league record by playing in 2130 consecutive games from 1925 to 1939. Cal Ripken of the Baltimore Orioles broke his record in 1995.

    At the plate, he was awesome. His .340 lifetime batting average included 12 successive .300 seasons. He batted in more than 100 runs in a season 13 times, setting an American League record of 184 RBIs in 1931. He led the league in RBIs five times, batting average once, runs scored four times, doubles twice,

Ty Cobb

triples once, and home runs three times. His 0.92 runs batted in per game is #2 all-time (behind Sam Thompson) and #1 in the twentieth century.

• James Emory "Jimmie" Foxx, a brawny farm boy from Sudlersville, Maryland, came up to the major leagues with the Philadelphia Athletics at the age of 17, and stayed around for 20 years. The Beast, as he was called, was the strongest man in baseball. He packed 190 pounds of solid muscle on his stocky 5'11" frame, with bulging biceps and a massive chest.

He led the league in home runs four times, runs batted in four times, and batting average twice. He hit 30 or more home runs for 12 successive years, topping the 40 mark five times and hitting 50 or more twice. His enormous power produced 13 seasons of more than 100 RBIs. He knocked in over 150 runs on four occasions, with a high of 175 in 1938. When he retired in 1945, he left behind

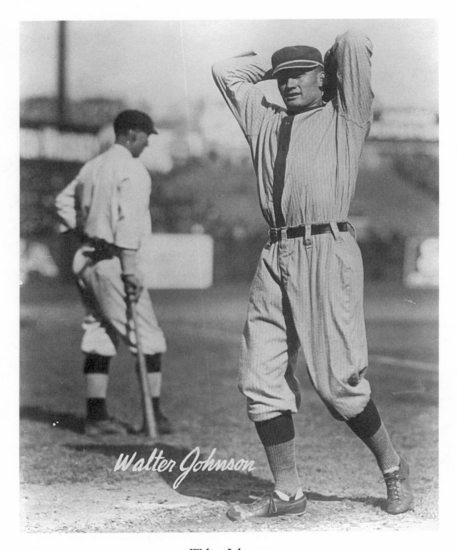

Walter Johnson

a career batting average of .325, with 534 home runs, 1921 RBIs, and 2646 base hits.

• Babe Ruth, as everyone knows, was the American League's premier south-paw pitcher before he was converted to an outfielder to take advantage of his explosive bat. Ruth enjoyed two 20 victory seasons on the mound and, in 1916, led all junior circuit hurlers with an earned run average of 1.75. His career pitching totals were 94–46, with a sparkling 2.28 earned run average (#10 all-time).

But it was at the plate where George Herman Ruth became a legend. Babe Ruth hit the ball farther, and more frequently, than any other hitter in the annals of major league baseball. The 6'2", 215 pound, left handed slugger rescued baseball after the notorious Black Sox scandal. His 54 home runs in 1920 almost doubled his own major league record of 29, set the previous year. His total also exceeded the home run total of every other major league team, with the exception of the Philadelphia Phillies, who hit 64. In 1927, when he established the season record of 60 home runs, he accounted for 14 percent of all the home runs hit in the American League that year. To put that in perspective, Roger Maris would have had to hit the astounding total of 210 home runs in 1961 to equal the Babe's feat.

When Ruth retired, he was #7 in batting average (.342), #1 in home runs (714), #2 in runs scored, #1 in runs-batted-in, and #1 in slugging average. He was among the first group of six players selected for the Hall of Fame in 1936.

• "Joltin' Joe" DiMaggio is considered by many baseball experts to be the greatest all-around baseball player of the twentieth century. Joltin' Joe was a true superstar, excelling in all five phases of the game. At the plate, he had no equal as a clutch hitter. He led New York to ten American League flags and nine World Championships in 13 years, an unparalleled accomplishment. He compiled a .325 career batting average with 361 home runs and 1537 RBIs. His 56-game consecutive game hitting streak in 1941 remains one of the game's untouchable records.

• Theodore Samuel Williams may well be the greatest hitter in baseball history. He is certainly the greatest hitter in the last sixty years. Only Ty Cobb, Shoeless Joe Jackson, and Rogers Hornsby have higher career averages than the Splendid Splinter's .344 — and they achieved their averages in the 1910s and 1920s against the dead ball.

The big left fielder of the Boston Red Sox was the last .400 hitter in major league baseball, finishing with a .406 mark in 1941. Williams' manager offered to let him sit out the season-ending doubleheader to protect his .400 average. But Ted would have none of it. Instead, he went out with a flourish, pounding out six hits in eight trips to the plate.

Ted Williams accumulated 521 home runs, 1839 runs batted in, and 2019 bases on balls during his 19–year career. He might well have challenged the career leaders in all those categories if he hadn't missed almost five seasons because of military service.

• Lefty Grove, the 6'3", 204 pound southpaw, threw B-Bs at opposing batters over a legendary 17-year career. As a member of Connie Mack's Philadelphia Athletics, Grove led the American League in strikeouts his first seven years in the league. He also led the league in victories four times and earned run average nine times.

Over one four-year period, the fireballing Grove won 103 games against only 23 losses for a spectacular .817 winning percentage. In 1930, the "Year of the Hitter," Connie Mack's ace went 28–5, with a sparkling 2.54 ERA, a full 2.11 runs per game below the league average. The following year, he did even better. He compiled a 31–4 record, with a 2.06 earned-run-average, less than half the league average.

Lefty Grove retired in 1941, leaving behind an enviable 300–141 won-loss record. His .680 career winning percentage is exceeded by only three other hurlers in baseball history.

An Overview of Baseball,
1951–2000

The period from 1950 through 1960 is considered by many baseball experts to be the "Golden Age" of major league baseball. Many significant changes took place in major league baseball from 1946 through 1959, altering the face of the game forever.

The most momentous event was the integration of professional baseball by Jackie Robinson in 1946. Integration was not completed overnight, however, as a number of teams fought it to the bitter end. It was finally put to rest once and for all when Pumpsie Green was promoted to the Boston Red Sox roster in 1959.

The quality of play in the major leagues reached an all-time high during the '50s as black players from throughout the western hemisphere replaced white journeymen players on big league rosters. At the same time, major league scouts actively recruited black players from high schools, colleges, and sandlots all across the country, uncovering such future stars as Richie Allen, Willie Davis, Bob Gibson, Vada Pinson, Frank Robinson, and Willie McCovey. They also scoured Central and South America, as well as countries throughout the Carribean basin, bringing back future Hall of Fame candidates Roberto Clemente, Orlando Cepeda, Tony Perez, Luis Tiant, Felipe Alou, Manny Mota, and Juan Marichal. The 1960s saw the blossoming of black stars like Lou Brock, Joe Morgan, Willie Stargell, Ferguson Jenkins, Tony Oliva, and Billy Williams.

Baseball did indeed reach its zenith during the 1950s through integration. Unfortunately, as integration became a way of life in professional baseball, it destroyed an historic piece of Americana. The Negro leagues fell victim to the unrelenting advance of progress. Negro league teams, like the Kansas City Monarchs and the Newark Eagles, could no longer attract highly skilled players, who opted for the opportunities of organized ball instead. By the end of the decade, the unique Negro leagues no longer existed. Teams like the Homestead Grays,

Baltimore Elite Giants, and Pittsburgh Crawfords became mere memories. With equality came sadness at the loss of an era.

Integration had a profound effect on other leagues in the western hemisphere also, particularly the leagues in Cuba and Puerto Rico. From 1920 to 1945, 35 players from Mexico, Central America and South America had played major league baseball, with 26 of them coming from Cuba. Four came from Mexico, two from Venezuela, two from Puerto Rico, and one from Colombia. They were white, partly white, or could pass for white. In the days before integration, foreign-born players were seldom seen in the major leagues. The Washington Senators were the lone major league team scouting foreign players. Their Cuban contingent numbered 14 players between 1920 and 1945. Players like Roberto Estalella, Mike Guerra, and Roberto Ortiz were considered curiosities by other big league clubs.

From 1945 to 1960, 90 players of all colors from around the western hemisphere played in the big leagues, including 48 from Cuba, 16 from Puerto Rico, seven from the Dominican Republic, five from Panama, five from Venezuela, and eight from Mexico. By 1998, more than 600 foreign players had graced major league diamonds.

The Cuban leagues suffered more than most countries after Jackie Robinson opened the door for blacks to play in organized baseball. Not only did Cuba lose the support of the great Negro league players, but black Cubans like Minnie Minoso and Sandy Amoros (of World Series fame) traveled north to make their fortunes. The rise to power of Fidel Castro in 1960 ended the Cuban Winter League once and for all.

Cuba, unlike other countries outside the United States, had provided the major leagues with ballplayers as early as 1871 when Esteban Bellan strutted his stuff for the Troy Haymakers. By the time integration opened the gates to black ballplayers, 39 Cuban natives had played major league baseball. The more notable players included Adolfo Luque, who won 194 games over a 20 year career; Mike Gonzalez, a 17-year major league veteran; and Roberto Estalella and Mike Guerra, both of whom played in the American League for nine years.

After Castro slammed the door on freedom in his country, Cuban citizens were prevented from leaving the island nation, and the flow of baseball players into major league baseball came to a standstill until the 1990s, except for Cuban-born citizens who fled the country at the time of the communist takeover.

In the 1990s a number of Cuban athletes, including many baseball players, defected from their country in pursuit of a better life and more opportunities in the United States. Pitcher Rene Arocha was the first baseball player to defect. He was followed by pitchers Livan Hernandez in 1995, Rolando Arrojo, a 121-game winner in Cuba, in 1996, and Orlando "El Duque" Hernandez, Livan's half-brother, who fled the island on a small raft in 1998.

The Puerto Rican Winter League was initially hurt by integration as some of their greatest players headed north to major league stardom. There were no white Puerto Ricans in the major leagues until 1941 when Hiram Bithorn pitched for the Chicago Cubs. The right hander's four-year 34–31 record was highlighted by an 18–12 season in 1943. Luis Olmo played major league ball for six years between 1943 and 1951, compiling a respectable .281 batting average.

After 1946, most of the Negro league players who had helped make the Puerto Rican Winter League a high level professional league entered organized baseball, leaving the PRWL decimated of its best players. They were joined by black Puerto Rican players who had previously been banned from organized ball. Over the past 42 years, more than 150 Puerto Rican natives have enjoyed major league success: early arrivals included Vic Power, Roberto Clemente, Orlando Cepeda, and Juan Pizzaro.

The league rebounded handsomely, however, to become one of the highest rated leagues in the world, somewhere between major league caliber and AAA caliber. The league was strengthened by the influx of minor league players sent by their major league owners to Puerto Rico during the winter months to fine tune their game. It was further strengthened by the return of Puerto Rican major leaguers who showcased their talents before the home fans from November to February.

Baseball in Mexico did not suffer as much as in other countries after integration became the law of the land in the United States because most of the players in the Mexican League were native-born Mexicans who were not affected by the color problem. The first Mexican professional league, which was formed in 1937, did attract a number of Negro league players like Roy Campanella, Willie Wells, Bill Wright, and Ray Dandridge, and that source of talent dried up after Jackie Robinson buried Jim Crow. The league also recruited some of the great Cuban stars, such as Martin Dihigo, Lazaro Salazar, Silvio Garcia, Ramon Bragana, and Cocaina Garcia, and after 1946 the Cuban contingent also headed north to display their wares in organized baseball in the United States. But these players were in the minority in Mexico. Most of the Mexican League players were homegrown products.

After World War II, Jorge Pascual, a Mexican entrepreneur, raided the major leagues for players and came away with stars like Sal "The Barber" Maglie of the New York Giants, Max Lanier of the St. Louis Cardinals, and Luis Olmo of the Brooklyn Dodgers. Baseball officials in the United States and Mexico soon realized this type of activity could cause chaos in both countries, so they sat down together and drew up an agreement of mutual respect.

The Mexican League joined organized baseball in 1955 and has operated as a recognized minor league ever since. For several years, it operated as a AA league. Then from 1968 to 1992 it enjoyed AAA status. And for the past six years, it has been an independent league.

At the present time, Mexico has more than a dozen players in the major leagues, but most players still prefer to play at home. Mexican players seem more comfortable in their own country, where they are idolized as heroes. Also, some players encountered discrimination in the United States, which discouraged them from playing there. Hector Espino, Mexico's career home run king, was recruited by a major league team in 1964 and spent part of the season in Jacksonville, Florida. Although he batted .300 in 32 International League games, he was so upset at the discrimination he encountered, he returned to Mexico to finish out his career. Other great Mexican baseball players who spent most, or all, of their careers in their native land include Ramon Arano (334 victories), Alfredo Ortiz (255 wins), Andres Mora (419 home runs), and Orlando Sanchez (.344 batting average).

Japan was unaffected by the goings-on in the United States. The Japanese League, which was organized in 1936, was canceled in 1945 due to the war, but American occupation administrators supported reactivation of the league in 1946, as a way to restore the morale of the country. By 1949, the game was thriving and, thanks to a new lively ball, home runs were clearing the fences in record numbers.

Beginning in the early 1950s, some American players, most of whom did not have the talent to become major leaguers, began to take advantage of the opportunity to earn a good living by playing ball in Japan. Leo Kiely, a left handed pitcher, played in Japan in 1953, going 6–0 with a 1.80 earned run average. Pitcher Glenn Mickens and journeyman infielder Larry Raines followed Kiely to the Land of the Rising Sun. Over the next 45 years, more than 500 American professionals — some minor leaguers, some major league journeymen, and some major league veterans trying to squeeze one more payday out of their fading careers — made the trip across the Pacific Ocean.

The style of play in the major leagues changed after integration was introduced, partly due to the Negro league batting philosophy, and partly the result of the Babe Ruth and Ralph Kiner syndromes. Home run production in the majors exploded during the late 1940s. It had been gradually increasing prior to World War II as a new generation of ballplayers, emulating the colorful and exciting Sultan of Swat, gripped their bats down at the end and swung for the fences. Ruth's longball-hitting contemporaries like Lou Gehrig, Mel Ott, and Jimmie Foxx gave way to a new generation of sluggers like Joe DiMaggio, Ted Williams, Hank Greenberg, and Johnny Mize. By 1940, prior to the entrance of the United States into the global holocaust, home run production reached a new high of 98 home runs per team per year.

In 1946, following the wartime hiatus, the long ball onslaught resumed, led by a young slugger from Santa Rita, New Mexico. Ralph Kiner, a muscular 6'2", 195 pound right handed bomber, returned from the war and immediately found a spot on the roster of the lowly Pittsburgh Pirates. He proceeded to lead the National League in home runs his first seven years in the league. His home run totals, from 1947 through 1951, were 51, 40, 54, 47, and 42 — an average of 47 homers a year. Soon, big league rosters were crammed with fuzzy cheeked sluggers like Mickey Mantle, Duke Snider, Eddie Mathews, Ted Kluszewski, Gus Zernial, and Al Rosen.

These long ball hitters were ably supported by the big bombers from the Negro leagues — Hank Thompson (20 home runs per year), Luke Easter (28 HRs), Larry Doby (25 HRs), and Roy Campanella (31 HRs). Sam Jethroe chipped in with 18, Monte Irvin with 15, and Jackie Robinson with 14. The Negro league philosophy, for years, had been one of controlled power hitting. A study of the most prominent Negro league players who made the jump to the major leagues showed they hit approximately 27 percent more home runs in the majors than they had in the Negro leagues (see appendix).

The result of the Negro league philosophy, coupled with the Ruth and Kiner syndromes, was that the home run totals of major league teams reached 130 home runs per team by 1950, an increase of 33 percent in ten years. This level of home run activity was sustained throughout the 1950s and '60s, before tailing off slightly during the following two decades.

Baseball, which had been isolated in the upper northeast quadrant of the country for 100 years, became a national sport in the 1950s as, first the Braves relocated from Boston to Milwaukee, then the Dodgers and Giants left their Brooklyn and New York homes for sunny California. In 1961, after 60 years of relative stability, major league owners voted to expand the number of teams in the major leagues from 16 to 20. Washington and Los Angeles joined the American League in 1961, and Houston and New York became members of the National League a year later. By 1975, there were a total of 24 major league teams.

The last quarter of the twentieth century has been one of turmoil and transition for major league baseball. The first sign of trouble reared its ugly head on December 23, 1975, when Peter Seitz, the chairman of a three-man mediation panel, ruled that players who perform one year without a signed contract automatically become free agents. Los Angeles Dodger pitcher Andy Messersmith took advantage of that ruling by jumping ship after the 1975 season and signing a multi-year contract with the Atlanta Braves for a whopping $1.75 million. Over the next year, 24 other players took advantage of the new ruling to move to other teams, with lucrative new contracts. Reggie Jackson topped the list, by signing a five year deal with the New York Yankees for a record $3,000,000.

Outrageous player salaries were only one of the problems affecting major league baseball in the '70s, '80s, and '90s. Labor relations, in general, went from bad to worse. Player strikes and lockouts, and the threat of the same, has dominated the baseball scene for the past 20 years. In 1981, a 50-day player strike forced a split season, with first-half winners playing second-half winners to determine division champions. The infamous 1994 players' strike was much worse. The eight-month unholy war, from August 12, 1994, through early April 1995, caused the cancellation of the World Series and brought the wrath of the fans down upon the baseball empire. Attendance plummeted 20 percent in the two years following the strike, as alienated fans refused to contribute to the corruption of major league players and owners.

Continued expansion is also weakening major league baseball. The dilution of talent significantly reduced the overall quality of play by the 1970s. It decreased even further in the 1990s as the number of teams increased to 30. Until 1961, the 16 major league teams had a total complement of 400 players. By 1998, there were 750 major league players, an increase of 88 percent. Over the same period, the population of the country increased only 25 percent.

Even that increase might have been absorbed with only a minimum loss of quality if all other things remained equal. But other things didn't remain equal. Professional football and professional basketball suddenly exploded about 1950, as television beamed their games into every living room in the country. Over the past 50 years, these sports have competed with professional baseball for the hearts and souls of talented young athletes.

Free agency, soaring salaries, expansion, poor labor relations, competition from other sports — all these things have impacted the quality of major league baseball. In addition, the fascination with home runs, brought about by Ruth and Kiner, has resulted in a dramatic increase in strikeouts over the past 35 years. At one time, Babe Ruth was the major league all-time strikeout king, fanning 1330 times in 22 years, an average of 87 times for every 550 at-bats. Today, Ruth ranks no better than 31st on the all-time list, far behind Reggie Jackson's 2597 (Mr. October struck out an average of 144 times a year for 21 years). Other big name "whiffers" included Willie Stargell, Tony Perez, Mike Schmidt, Dave Kingman, Bobby Bonds, Mickey Mantle, Lou Brock, and Lee May, all of whom fanned over 1500 times.

The above named players represent a new breed of hitter, the so-called "guess hitter," who tries to out-think the pitcher by guessing where the ball will be thrown, and what kind of a pitch it will be. The guess hitter believes that if he swings hard in the right area, he will hit more home runs. That theory doesn't hold up under close scrutiny, however. From 1950 through 1993, strikeouts shot up by 63 percent. At the same time, home runs rose only 7 percent, and batting averages remained relatively constant. Guess hitting has proven to be a no-brainer that has weakened the sport of baseball.

In the power department, home runs increased at a steady rate after the introduction of the lively ball, finally leveling off between 1960 and 1993. Then in 1994 they jumped up by 22 percent, causing some baseball purists to scream about a "juiced up" ball. Home runs have stayed at that elevated level for the past four years.

The increase in home runs, however, is at least partially due to the size of the players. Certainly today's players are bigger and stronger than their counterparts of 50 years ago, thanks, in part, to the rigid weight training that many of them practice year round. It is obvious that a player's size impacts his home run totals, but there are many other factors that also contribute to his long distance hitting. These include his swing (balance, stride, wrist snap, etc.) and his hand-eye coordination.

There has also been an increase in the number of "homer friendly" stadiums that have been built in recent years. Fulton County Stadium in Atlanta, known as "The Launching Pad," produced 43 percent more home runs than the average major league park from 1966 to 1997. Denver's Mile High Stadium (5,176 feet above sea level) recorded 70 percent more homers than other major league parks. The Rockies' newest park, Coors Field, is yielding home runs at an equally fantastic pace. In 1995, 65 percent more home runs sailed out of Coors Field than in the average major league stadium — and 133 percent more than Dodger Stadium.

Pitching reached an all-time low in the 90s, partly as a result of expansion, but also because of other factors such as five man pitching rotations and pitch counts. In the old days (before free agency), four man pitching staffs were common. After free agency, management became overly protective of their high salaried investments. They added a fifth starter to the rotation. They also instituted a pitch count of slightly over 100 pitches per game — a mysterious number that appeared out of the woodwork several years ago. Now, when a starting pitcher reaches the magic number, he can retire to the comfort of the clubhouse. In the old days, when men were men and pitching a complete game was a matter of pride, a pitcher averaged about 135 pitches in a game. Some pitchers threw as many as 150–200 pitches a game. Now, when they hit 100 pitches they're gone.

The new philosophy, however, has not reduced arm miseries, as owners hoped it would. In fact, the opposite may be true. There are indications that there are more arm problems now than there were 20 to 30 years ago. Every team had one or more pitchers on the disabled list during 1997, 1998, and 1999. By actual count, on July 25, 1998, there were 77 pitchers on the disabled list, 32 in the American League and 45 in the National League. And on April 11, 1999, only five days into the new season, 53 pitchers, including 32 from the National League, were on the DL.

The only thing the new philosophy has done is reduce the accomplishments of the individual pitchers. Today, a pitcher pitches fewer innings, throws fewer complete games, tosses fewer shutouts, and wins fewer games than his predecessors. Today, a pitcher is considered a quality pitcher if he can go six innings. Under these conditions, it will be difficult for these and future pitchers to be compared with the likes of Walter Johnson, Sandy Koufax, or Bob Feller, pitchers who hurled 300+ innings a year, won 25–30 games, and tossed 20 or more complete games. It will be even more difficult for pitchers to win 300 or more games in a career. Greg Maddux and Roger Clemens are the only active pitchers who appear to have a chance to reach that rarefied environment.

As 1998 dawned, dire predictions were being made about the future of major league baseball. Then, the game suddenly rose from the ashes like a twentieth century phoenix and regained much of its lost magic and many of its fans, thanks to two genuine heroes. Mark McGwire of the St. Louis Cardinals and Sammy Sosa of the Chicago Cubs made bold and exciting assaults on Roger

Frank Thomas, "The Big Hurt," has batted in 100 or more runs in each of his first eight years in the majors. He is a lifetime .321 hitter. (Ron Vesely/Chicago White Sox.)

Maris' 38-year-old single season home run record: both eclipsed the 1961 mark of 61 round-trippers.

Each player had pounded out 66 homers as the final weekend of the season got underway but, while Sosa went homerless, McGwire launched four dingers to close out baseball's most exhilarating recent season with a heretofore unheard of 70 home runs.

Roger Clemens won his fifth Cy Young award in 1998. His 247–134 record is the best of all active pitchers. (Courtesy Boston Red Sox.)

At the present time, major league baseball is still trying to recover from the sins of the past 40 years. Only time will tell if the flame of fan interest can be rekindled permanently. With all the problems the major leagues have experienced however, there are still players who have transcended the sport in which they participated. Some of the following players saw their careers peak before the advent of todays permissive atmosphere. Others are the product of today's game.

 • Roy Campanella, a nine-year veteran of the Negro leagues, and three-time National League most valuable player, was a slugger of world class proportions.

Kirby Puckett had the second highest career batting average since 1963 (.318) when eye problems forced him to retire. (Courtesy Minnesota Twins.)

He was also an excellent defensive catcher, who was unsurpassed at handling pitchers, was quick as a cat behind the plate, and often outran runners to first base when backing up a play. His rifle arm shot down 64 percent of all would-be base stealers during his first two years in Brooklyn. He once went 51 games without allowing a stolen base.

• Mark McGwire broke into major league baseball with 49 home runs in 1987. After several years of personal problems and injuries, the 6'5" 250 pound behemoth exploded in 1996 with 52 home runs. He followed that up with 58 homers in 1997 and a mind boggling 70 in 1998. At age 35, the right handed superstar could break the 700 career home run barrier before he retires — if he stays healthy.

• Jackie Robinson was a franchise player. The Negro pioneer could do it all. In the field, he had better than average range, a sure glove, and an accurate arm. At the plate, the .311 batter provided power and excitement. A right handed hitter, he could swing for the fences or lay down a bunt, as the situation warranted. He was most valuable once on base. His daring leads and constant dancing upset pitchers from New York to St. Louis, causing them to lose concentration and to make bad pitches to succeeding batters.

• Mickey Mantle was a true superstar. He could do it all — field, run, throw, hit, and hit with power. He was the greatest switch hitter ever to play the game, and one of the most powerful batters ever to send a ball into orbit. The handsome blonde bomber hit tape measure home runs in most American League parks, several times exceeding the 550-foot mark. He captured the triple crown in 1956, hitting 52 home runs, driving in 130 runners, and batting a strong .353. Mantle might have established an all-time career home run record if he had

Mark McGwire's 70 home runs in 1998 made him a legend. He still has a shot at 700 career homers if he can stay healthy for another five to six years. (W. McNeil.)

stayed healthy. He hit 404 round trippers by the time he was 30 years old (Hank Aaron had 366), but bad knees and other ailments held him to just 132 homers thereafter.

• Willie Mays, the "Say-Hey Kid," was a superstar like Mantle, but was flashier than the Yankee speedster. Mays, a graduate of the Negro leagues, starred with the New York–San Francisco Giants from 1951 through 1972. Unlike Mantle, Mays was not bothered by health problems, allowing him to play major league baseball until he was 42 years old. He had hit 319 home runs by the time he was 30 years old (compared with Mantle's 404), but he was able to launch another 341 homers before he retired.

Over the course of his memorable career, Mays slugged 660 home runs (#3 all-time), scored 2062 runs (#5), batted in 1903 runs (#7), and swatted 3283 hits (#9). He had a lifetime batting average of .302. He is considered by many baseball experts to be the greatest all-around player of all time.

• Sandy Koufax is the greatest left handed pitcher of the last 50 years and is arguably the greatest pitcher, left or right handed, in major league history. Koufax, in his prime, was unhittable. Not only did he possess the liveliest fastball in baseball, he also possessed the most devastating curveball in the majors. And he coupled those weapons with pinpoint control. He led the league in victories three times during his last five years in the league, and showed the way in earned run average all five years. His 111–34 record and 1.86 earned run average, during that time, stamped him as one of the greatest. He also tossed four no-hitters, including a perfect game.

• Mike Schmidt is unquestionably the best third baseman of his time. A solid defensive player, the powerful right handed slugger launched 548 balls into orbit during an outstanding 18-year career. He led the National League in home runs eight times, slugging percentage five times, and runs batted in four times. He was a three-time National League MVP, winning the award in 1980, 1981, and 1986. The 11-time Gold Glove winner led all third basemen in assists five times, total chances six times, and double plays six times. He stands #3 all-time in both career assists and double plays. Mike Schmidt joined the immortals in Cooperstown in 1995.

• Tony Gwynn is baseball's most prolific hitter over the past 37 years. His 17-year average, through 1998, is a lofty .339 (#14 all-time and #2 since 1936). The left handed hitter strikes out an average of only 26 times a year, while punching line drives to all fields. In his younger days, he was also a stolen base threat, swiping 56 sacks in 1987 and 40 more in 1989. The pudgy, 200 pound right fielder plays a solid defense, with good range, a dependable glove and an accurate throwing arm. He joined the 3000-hit club in 1999.

• Dennis Eckersley is one of baseball's most extraordinary talents, a first-rate starting pitcher who became the major leagues' premier closer. The lanky Californian was a starter during his first 12 years in the majors. He no-hit the California Angels in 1977, won 20 games the following year, and won ten or more games, nine times, en route to a 152–133 won-loss record. Ten years into his career, at the age of 34, he was converted to a relief pitcher. Since that time, he racked up 390 saves, including 36 in 1997 at the age of 43. Eckersley won both the Most Valuable Player award and the Cy Young Award in 1992, as he pitched Oakland to the Western Division title, with 51 saves and a sparkling 1.91 ERA. His 24-year career shows a major league record 1071 games pitched, 197 victories, and 171 losses.

Other players who *could* be all-stars when their careers end include Ken Griffey, Jr., Alex Rodriguez, Cal Ripken, Jr., Greg Maddux, Sammy Sosa, Roger Clemens, and Mike Piazza.

Ken Griffey, Jr., is in the midst of a superstar career. His 398 career home runs at age 29 have him on track to break the magic 800 barrier before he retires. (James R. Madden, Jr.)

While the major leagues have wallowed in their self-inflicted wounds in recent years, baseball outside the United States has thrived. Some changes in the game have made their way from the majors to other professional leagues around the world, including the lively ball, bat design, and bigger gloves. Fortunately, the negative aspects of the big league game, such as the bad attitude of some players, lackadaisical play, guess hitting (with the associated high frequency of strikeouts), high salaries, free agency, and pitch counts, have for the most part not infected the game outside the United States.

Beginning in the 1950s and continuing to the present time, the winter leagues in Puerto Rico and the Dominican Republic have showcased not only the brightest native major leaguers but also promising minor league players who were sent to the southern climes by their major league clubs for further seasoning. The citizens of Puerto Rico, for instance, witnessed the development of such major league talents as Cal Ripken, Jr., Mike Schmidt, Sandy Koufax, Steve Carlton, and Frank Howard. In the Dominican Republic, Billy Buckner, Steve Garvey, George Foster, Bob Gibson, and Orel Hershiser put the final touches on their baseball maturation.

Cal Ripken, Jr., played 2632 consecutive games between 1982 and 1998, an all-time major league record. (W. McNeil.)

New winter leagues popped up around the western hemisphere in the 1950s, '60s and '70s. The Mexican Pacific League began operations in 1947. Venezuela started its own winter league in 1966. Three years later, Mexico, the Dominican Republic, Puerto Rico, and Venezuela revived the Caribbean World Series, which had been inactive since Castro's Cuba withdrew from professional competition in 1960. The first true World Series was held in Venezuela, and the home team, Magallanes, walked off with the trophy. The series has been a spirited and competitive one for the last 29 years. Over that time, the Dominican Republic has held the upper hand 11 times, Puerto Rico has brought the cup home 9 times, Venezuela 6, and Mexico 3.

In other parts of the world, baseball grew in popularity. Australia and Hawaii joined the winter league festivities in 1989 and 1993 respectively. The great Japanese batting sensation, Ichiro Suzuki, perfected his stroke in the Hawaii Winter League. New summer leagues also blossomed. The Dominican Summer League joined organized baseball in 1985. Venezuela started its own summer league to screen new young talent the same year. In the Far East, the Korea Baseball Organization successfully completed its first year in 1998. Taiwan had two summer leagues: the Chinese Professional Baseball League, founded in 1996, and the Taiwan Major League, founded in 1997. Both leagues attracted a number of American minor leaguers, as well as players from other countries in the western hemisphere. Baseball also spread to dozens of other countries, including China, Russia, Italy, Spain, South Africa, and the Netherlands. The National Pastime was rapidly becoming a global pastime.

The Japanese and American leagues began working closely together in the 1990s to prevent the type of player raids that caused havoc in America in the

Alex Rodriguez is a potential superstar. He was the first infielder to hit 40 or more home runs (42) and steal 40 or more bases (46) in the same season. The 23-year-old shortstop has a .308 batting average for six years in the majors. (James R. Madden, Jr.)

late nineteenth century. The two countries agreed to respect each other's player contracts and free agency policies. Players could not move from one league to the other unless they were sold or traded by their parent club or had become free agents. In 1995, after becoming a free agent, Hideo Nomo signed a contract to play for the Los Angeles Dodgers in the United States' National League. Two years later, the San Diego Padres obtained the rights to Hideki Irabu from the Chiba Lotte Orions of the Japan Pacific League. In 1999, Japan's greatest batter, Ichiro Suzuki, visited the Seattle Mariners' spring training camp in Arizona to observe American conditioning practices. There are rumors that the Orix Blue Wave will sell Ichiro to a major league team after the 1999 season.

The resurgence of professional baseball around the world was not limited to the free world. It even made inroads into Fidel Castro's communist Cuba, where on March 29, 1999, the Baltimore Orioles marched onto the field at Estadio Latinoamericano in Havana to do battle with the Cuban All-Stars. It was the first game to feature a major league team on Cuban soil since Sandy Koufax of the Los Angeles Dodgers beat the Cincinnati Reds 2–1 in 1959.

The Cuban team included Omar Linares, the big third baseman, who has averaged .455 with 87 home runs for every 550 at-bats in International competition over the past 15 years. He is considered to be Cuba's greatest modern player. The game was an epic struggle, with Cuban right hander Jose Contreras emerging as the player of the game. His eight shutout innings, liberally sprinkled with 10 strikeouts, kept Cuba in the game, but the O's rallied for a run in the top of the 11th off relief pitcher Pedro Lazo, to pull out a hard fought 3–2 victory.

Contreras' outstanding pitching performance brought back memories of the pitching gems of Eustaquio Pedroso and Jose Mendez, whose Cuban teams battled touring major league teams such as John McGraw's Giants and Connie Mack's Athletics to a standstill over decades of head to head competition between 1890 and 1920.

With the arrival of the new millennium baseball is on a fast track around the world. At its present pace, it is only a matter of time before the major leagues expand into Mexico and perhaps other Western Hemisphere countries. In fact, the major leagues did open their 1999 season in Monterrey, Mexico, with the San Diego Padres hosting the Colorado Rockies on April 4. The Rockies walloped the Padres 8–2 before 27,104 screaming fans. The Baltimore Orioles also have a game scheduled in Mexico during the 1999 season. And next year, the Orioles hope to open their season in Japan.

The time may also be approaching when a bona fide World Series will be held, matching the best professional team from North America against the best teams from Asia, Europe, Africa, South America, and Australia.

Negro League All-Star Team, 1900–1925

The previous chapters have presented a brief overview of baseball during the twentieth century, with an emphasis on the American major leagues. The remaining chapters of this book will discuss the other professional baseball leagues around the world that were in existence during the same period, but operated outside the umbrella of organized baseball. There were, in fact, other professional baseball leagues in operation, side by side with the major leagues in the United States, in such cities as New York, St. Louis, and Chicago. They were called the Negro leagues.

When baseball was first played in the United States, in the 1850s and 1860s, it was somewhat of an integrated sport. Blacks and whites occasionally played on the same team. During the Civil War, there is photographic evidence that blacks and whites played together in prisoner of war camps in both the North and South. When the first professional baseball league was formed, The National Association of Professional Baseball Players, in 1871, players of both colors were eligible to participate.

The first recorded black professional baseball player was John W. "Bud" Fowler, who starred at second base for a number of teams in organized baseball over a period of 18 years. Fowler was born in Fort Plain, New York, on March 16, 1858, and began his professional career with the Lynn, Massachusetts, Live Oaks in 1878. In addition to being a superior defensive player, Fowler was a consistent .300 hitter, leaving behind a .309 career average.

There were 100 or so black players in organized ball in the 1880s, including Sol White, Frank Grant, George Stovey, William Selden, Fleetwood Walker, and Welday Walker, as noted earlier. When club owners, spurred on by Adrian "Cap" Anson, the manager of the Chicago White Stockings, decided to bar blacks from organized baseball in 1888, most of the players gravitated toward the many barnstorming black teams. Blacks continued to play in the minor leagues for a number of years, although little by little, they were weeded out.

Several all-black baseball teams participated in the minor leagues from 1889 through 1898, including the first recorded black professional baseball team, the Cuban Giants. The Giants competed in the Mid-States League in 1889, along with another black team, the New York Gorhams. In 1890, the Giants were members of the Eastern Interstate League, and the following year they joined the Connecticut State League. The last all-black team in organized ball was the Celeron, New York, team in the Iron & Oil League in 1898. In 1899, a curtain descended over organized baseball, as the odious segregation policy became the law of the land in professional baseball. For the next 46 years, organized baseball went through its most shameful period.

The Cuban Giants, however, along with numerous other black teams such as the Gorhams, the Page Fence Giants, the Atlantic City Bacharach Giants, the Philadelphia Giants, the Indianapolis ABC's, the Brooklyn Royal Giants, the Chicago American Giants, J.L. Wilkinson's All-Nations team, and the Cuban X Giants, carried on the baseball spirit in the black community, bringing the game to thousands of fans across the country thanks to a hectic traveling schedule.

In the fall, after the major league season was over, the big leaguers and the Negro leaguers often met in exhibition games. The Negro leaguers more than held their own. In fact, over a period of 50 years, according to John B. Holway in *Blackball Stars*, the Negro leaguers won 268 of the documented 436 games played between the two groups, a winning percentage of 61 percent.

The exclusive Poinciana and Breakers hotels in Palm Beach, Florida, hired the best black baseball players in the country to represent them in the Florida Hotel League during the winter months, just after the turn of the century. The rosters of the two hotels were a veritable who's who in black baseball, from about 1905 to 1915. Some of the legendary players who wore Poinciana or Breakers colors, included "Cannonball Dick" Redding, Spotswood Poles, Pete Hill, Louis Santop, Smokey Joe Williams, Rube Foster, Grant "Home Run" Johnson, and John Henry Lloyd. Pete Hill, for one, played in the Hotel League for more than ten years.

During this same period, a California Winter League attracted both Negro league players and major league players. Baseball fans on the West Coast were isolated from major league baseball, which was concentrated in the eastern half of the country. Since most fans couldn't go east to see big time baseball, some enterprising promoters, seizing the opportunity, brought big time baseball to them.

The California Winter League was an integrated league, probably the first integrated league in the United States in the twentieth century. Some of the major league players who participated in the winter sport included Babe Ruth, Al Simmons, Jimmie Foxx, Irish Meusel, Bob Meusel, and Charlie Root. Negro leaguers included "Bullet Joe" Rogan, "Smokey Joe" Williams, Dobie Moore, Biz Mackey, Newt Allen, and Tank Carr. The league continued well into the thirties, with "Cool Papa" Bell, Turkey Stearnes, Willie Wells, and Satchel Paige making the westward trek over the Rockies. According to Holway, Paige went 18–1 in California in 1933.

Many of the Negro leaguers played baseball 12 months a year, either because they loved the sport, or because they needed the money — probably a combination of the two. In addition to the fall exhibitions with the major leaguers, and the opportunities in Florida and California, a number of black players headed further south, to the friendly and beautiful island of Cuba, where they participated in the Cuban Winter League. John Henry Lloyd played ball in Cuba for 27 years, from 1906 through 1932. Other early Negro leaguers who made the Caribbean island a winter vacation stop were Spotswood Poles, Pete Hill, Bruce Petway, Louis Santop, "Home Run" Johnson, Bill Monroe, and Rube Foster.

Numerous major league teams visited Cuba during the winter to play exhibition games against highly rated Cuban Winter League teams. Once again, the Negro leaguers, in combination with their Cuban counterparts, fought the big leaguers to a standstill. In 1908, Cuban teams embarrassed the Cincinnati Reds, beating them seven times in eleven games, capped off by Jose Mendez's brilliant 1–0, one hitter. The following year, right handed fireballer Eustaquio Pedroso tossed a no-hitter at the Detroit Tigers, winning 2–1 in eleven innings. Hughie Jennings' tamed tabbys limped back to the States after losing 8 of 12 games to the Cubans.

In 1910, the Detroit Tigers returned to play a 12 game series against the Havana Reds, with Lloyd, Petway, and Johnson. Although the Tigers won the series 7 games to 4, the Reds gave the major leaguers something to remember them by. Catcher Bruce Petway gunned down the immortal Ty Cobb stealing, three out of three. Not only that, the great Detroit outfielder, fresh off a sensational American League season in which he tattooed the ball at a league leading .385 clip, was outhit by three black players. His .371 batting average was fourth behind Lloyd (.500), "Home Run" Johnson (.412), and Petway (.390), according to Robert Peterson in his excellent history of black baseball prior to the Jackie Robinson era, *Only the Ball Was White*. Cobb was so incensed at being humiliated by the American blacks that he vowed never to play against Negroes again — and he never did.

Connie Mack next brought his Philadelphia Athletics to the island nation to do battle with the talented warriors. After facing the likes of Mendez, Lloyd, Pedroso, and Johnson, the A's manager was happy to escape with a split in eight games.

Eventually, the Cuban Winter League (CWL) became an integrated league, probably the first integrated professional league in the twentieth century, not counting the California league. The 1922-23 rosters, as shown in *The Negro Leagues Book*, edited by Dick Clark and Larry Lester, revealed a potpourri of races on the various teams. The Marianao club included Brooklyn Dodger players "Glass Arm" Eddie Brown, Hank DeBerry, and Jesse Petty, as well as Negro leaguer Cristobal Torriente. Havana had Adolpho Luque, Edgar Wesley, and John Henry Lloyd, while Almendares sported CWL and Negro league star Valentin Dreke alongside Mike Herrera of the Boston Red Sox, and Santa Clara fielded the likes of Dobie Moore, Oscar Charleston, and Pedro Dibut. Dibut, in fact, touched all the bases. In addition to playing in the Cuban Winter League, he also played with the Cuban Stars in the Negro league, and with the Cincinnati Reds in the National League.

In truth, the Negro league baseball players were the founding fathers of international baseball. Their travels carried them to all parts of the globe over the years. They colonized most of the western hemisphere from 1900 to 1961. Negro leaguers played in professional leagues in Cuba, the Dominican Republic, Colombia, Venezuela, Panama, Puerto Rico, Nicaragua, and Mexico. During the twenties, they made several junkets across the Pacific, making friends wherever they went. The Royal Giants, fresh from the California Winter League, visited Hawaii and the Philippines in 1927, then went on to Japan, where they entertained and impressed the local populace. The team consisting of "Bullet Joe" Rogan, Biz Mackey, Rap Dixon, Newt Allen, and Crush Holloway, finished with a perfect 23–0–1 record. They repeated the feat five years later, running up a convincing 23–1 mark. Although the Negro leaguers dominated the home islanders, they made numerous friends on the tour, as they spent many hours teaching the Japanese players the finer points of the game.

While the great Negro league players, like John Henry Lloyd, "Smokey Joe" Williams, "Cannonball Dick" Redding, Louis Santop, Spotswood Poles, Pete Hill, and Grant "Home Run" Johnson were virtually unknown in the white community in the United States, they were legendary figures in Cuba during the first two decades of the century. Later, players like Josh Gibson, Satchel Paige, "Cool Papa" Bell, and Buck Leonard were known and admired throughout the western hemisphere.

In the United States, Negro league baseball operated in a haphazard manner from the late 1800s until 1920. There were many outstanding black baseball clubs traveling the country during that time, as noted before, but no one was able to organize them into a stable league, with definite playing schedules, player contracts, and associated administrative and promotional functions.

The talent was there, but no one was able to pull it together. The nucleus of a professional black baseball league existed in teams like the Brooklyn Royal Giants, Philadelphia Giants, Chicago Leland Giants, and J.L. Wilkinson's All-Nations team, which was composed of players of many races, including Negroes, Cubans, Mexicans, Orientals — and one girl. Each of these teams operated independently, moving from town to town across the country, scheduling games wherever they could find them. They played each other, they played white professional all-star teams, they played major league teams, they played semi-pro teams, and they played town teams. Wherever there was a team ready to take them on, and fans ready to pay to see them play, the itinerant black teams went. As long as they could pay their expenses, and have a few bucks left over for pocket money, the players were content. They were playing a game they loved, and they were getting paid for it. The team owners were kept occupied by the day to day concerns of survival. They were careless about keeping playing statistics or won-loss records. Still, the two teams generally regarded as the best during a particular season often faced each other in an unofficial World Series in the fall.

Into this den of confusion came the man who would be known as the father of Negro baseball. His name was Andrew "Rube" Foster. Foster was born in Calvert, Texas, on September 17, 1879, the son of an elder in the AME Church. By the time he was 18, Foster was pitching on local semi-pro baseball teams. Within five years, he had graduated to the black major leagues, joining the Chicago Union Giants in 1902.

The 6'2", 200 pound righthander was an immediate success in the big time. He was blazing fast, and possessed a full arsenal of pitches, including a deadly screwball. Some accounts credit Foster with teaching the screwball to Christy Mathewson of the New York Giants. In any event, the big Texan made his mark on Negro league baseball. Although statistics are lacking, he is considered to be one of the great Negro league pitchers of the first quarter of the twentieth century, often winning forty to fifty games a year against all competition, from semi-pro teams to major league teams. He is said to have beaten the great Rube Waddell in 1902, after Waddell had gone 25–7 with the American League champion Philadelphia Athletics. That victory gained Mr. Foster a nickname. He was known as Rube from that day on.

Incomplete records developed by Bob Hoie and Carlos Bauer in *The Historical Register* credit Foster with a record of 135–42, for a magnificent .763 winning percentage, against the top Negro and Cuban professional teams.

Rube Foster became a player-manager in 1907 when he took over the reins of the Leland Giants. As the years passed, Foster became less of a player and more of an administrator. He became part owner of the Giants in 1909 and, over the next ten years, he put together some of the greatest teams in Negro league history. His 1910 Giant team, starring himself, Pete Hill, "Home Run" Johnson, and John Henry Lloyd, is often called the greatest team ever assembled. Their record of 123 wins against only six losses is an all-time professional record.

By 1919, however, chaos reigned in the Negro leagues. Player contracts were not honored, as players jumped from one team to another for more money. As player's salaries skyrocketed, clubs began experiencing severe financial difficulties, with several teams forced to close down operations.

Rube Foster took matters into his own hands. He called all the owners of teams in the Midwest together for a meeting at the Kansas City YMCA on February 13, 1920. It was at that meeting that the Negro National League was formed.

It consisted of eight teams: Foster's American Giants, the Indianapolis ABC's, the Chicago Giants, the Cuban Stars, the Detroit Stars, the St. Louis Stars, the Kansas City Monarchs, and the Dayton Marcos.

This was the beginning of organized baseball in the black community. The Eastern Colored League was formed in 1923, and the first bonafide World Series was held between the two leagues in 1924. The Kansas City Monarchs, with "Bullet Joe" Rogan and Jose Mendez winning two games apiece, defeated the Hilldale club five games to four.

Rube Foster essentially gave his life for his new league. The strain of working 18-hour days finally took its toll on the hardy pioneer, and he was stricken with a fatal mental disorder in 1926. Rube Foster died in a mental institution on December 9, 1930. The Negro leagues of the 1930s and 1940s were his legacy — the integration of the major leagues his reward.

Andrew "Rube" Foster was elected to baseball's Hall of Fame in Cooperstown, New York, in 1981.

It was not easy selecting a Negro league all-star team for the first quarter of the twentieth century, since statistics were severely lacking for most of the players. In many cases, the choices were made based on the testimony of the players' contemporaries, as reported by the trail blazing Negro league historians, John Holway, Robert Peterson, Dick Clark, Larry Lester, James A. Riley, and others. It was also based on the, so far, incomplete statistics unearthed by the above mentioned researchers.

CATCHER:

• The #1 catcher on the 1900–25 Negro league all-star team is the big, burly slugger of the Hilltop Daisies, Louis "Big Bertha" Santop. The 6'4", 240 pound right handed slugger was named after the long distance cannon used by the German army in the first world war.

The German's Big Bertha sent projectiles screaming into the sky over long distances. The Daisies' Big Bertha did likewise. He was the foremost slugger of his day in the Negro leagues, averaging 10 home runs a year in the era of the dead ball when home runs were a rarity. He was also a consistent .300 hitter, with a career average in the mid–.350 range.

In addition to his offensive strengths, Santop was a rock on defense. He reportedly had a strong throwing arm that discouraged would-be base thieves.

• Bruce Petway was Santop's backup. Petway was a superior defensive catcher, with the strongest throwing arm in professional baseball during the first quarter of the century (just ask Ty Cobb). At 5'7" tall and 170 pounds, the native of Nashville, Tennessee, was exceptionally fast. He was death on bunts, and frequently beat baserunners to first base on infield grounders.

Petway was an outstanding baserunner and base stealer himself. He led the Cuban Winter League in stolen bases in 1912, an unusual feat for a backstop.

Petway's weakness was his proficiency with the bat. He had occasional big years where he pounded the ball at a .300+ clip, but overall he lacked consistency. His career numbers reflected only a .254 batting average in the Negro leagues and .210 in Cuba.

PITCHER:

• "Smokey Joe" Williams is the ace of the pitching staff. A poll of Negro league experts in the 1950s voted Williams the most outstanding pitcher in Negro league history, edging out Satchel Paige by a single vote.

Williams, known as "Cyclone" in his early days, threw nothing but smoke. His career spanned 28 years, from 1905 to 1932, winter and summer. Williams, like many of his contemporaries, played Negro league baseball during the summer, then followed the tour to California, Florida, and Cuba.

The 6'5" hurler pitched against major league teams 31 times in exhibition matches.

Louis Santop. (Noir Tech Research, Inc.)

He emerged victorious on 22 occasions, with two ties. He lost only seven games to the big leaguers. In one game against John McGraw's New York Giants, in 1917, Smokey Joe pitched a 10 inning no-hitter, sprinkled with 20 strikeouts, but lost 1–0 on infield errors.

Smokey Joe was finally admitted into the Baseball Hall of Fame in Cooperstown, New York, in 1999.

• "Cannonball Dick" Redding was another flamethrower in the Williams mold. He was a big, likable guy, who stood 6'4" tall, with long arms and enormous hands. Unfortunately, like his contemporary Smokey Joe, his career statistics are still fragmentary. His accomplishments have been passed on by word of mouth, and by occasional newspaper articles and box scores.

John Holway reported on some of Redding's pitching achievements in his classic biographies of 25 Negro league players and executives in *Blackball Stars*. According to Holway, the "Cannonball" ran off 17 straight victories in his rookie year of 1911. In 1912, he compiled a record of 43–12, against all opposition, amateur as well as professional. In 1914, Redding's home record was 12–3. His road record is unknown. In 1915, he once again had a sustained winning streak, running off 20 wins in a row, including several wins against white professional teams.

Dick Redding is generally considered one of the four greatest pitchers in Negro league history, along with Joe Williams, Satchel Paige, and "Bullet Joe" Rogan.

• Jose Mendez was a small man, 5'8" tall, and weighing only 155 pounds. But on the mound, he was a giant. He was big and muscular through the shoulders and upper arms, the result of countless hours of hacking sugar cane in the fields, and he fired B-Bs at opposing batters over a spectacular 20-year career, beginning in 1908. Generally regarded as the greatest pitcher in Cuban baseball history, "El Diamante Negro" (the Black Diamond), as he was called, dazzled Negro leaguers and major leaguers alike.

Pitching primarily in Cuba his first seven years, he led the Cuban Winter League in pitching five times, with records of 9–0, 15–6, 7–0, 11–2, and 10–0. Arm problems curtailed his pitching activities after 1914, leaving his final Cuban stats at 74–25.

Over that same period, he had equal success against major league teams in exhibition games. In 1908, he blanked the Cincinnati Reds 1–0 on a one-hitter. He out-pitched the A's Eddie Plank twice, by scores of 5–2 and 7–5, and he split two decisions with Christy Mathewson.

Mendez continued to play ball in the States until 1927, primarily with the Kansas City Monarchs. Playing shortstop and managing the team, he led the Monarchs to three Negro National League pennants. Taking an occasional turn on the mound, the crafty Cuban won 20 games against only four losses to close out his career.

• Andrew "Rube" Foster was a big, burly Texan, with a blazing fastball and a sharp breaking curve. He also had a devastating screwball that tied batters in knots. And he prided himself on his pinpoint control, walking less than two batters for every nine innings.

Foster was born in Calvert, Texas, in 1879, and began his baseball career with the Fort Worth Yellow Jackets 17 years later. During the first decade of the twentieth century, he piled up 40 to 50 wins a year, playing year-round.

As his career progressed, he pitched less and less. He first became a field manager, then a club owner. In 1920, he founded the Negro National League, and became its first president.

Foster's pitching statistics are incomplete, but do show a 26–11 record in the Cuban Winter League, and a 111–31 record against Negro professional teams from 1903 to 1917. According to contemporary accounts, and eyewitness testimony, the 6'4", 240 pound right hander was one of the greatest pitchers in Negro baseball. He was voted into the Baseball Hall of Fame in 1981.

• John Donaldson, a tall, slender southpaw, is considered to be the top left hander of the first quarter century. Born in 1892 in Glasgow, Missouri, Donaldson starred for J.L. Wilkinson's All-Nations team from 1913 through 1917. He ran up

Rube Foster

impressive won-loss records against mostly semi-pro opposition across the Midwest. According to Larry Lester in *The Ballplayers*, edited by Mike Shatzkin, "Donaldson was reported to have struck out more than 240 batters over a 12 game span in 1916. In one 18 inning game, he struck out 35; in a 12 inning contest, he fanned 27 more. He threw three consecutive no-hitters against semi-pro teams."

Donaldson also befuddled the top Negro league teams in the country, beating Rube Foster's Chicago American Giants twice, and the Indianapolis ABC's three times. He finished his career with the Kansas City Monarchs in 1923.

• Frank Wickware, a fireballing right hander, starred for various Negro league teams from 1910 to 1925. Known as "The Red Ant" Wickware compiled a 30–16 record in box scores located thus far. He was the ace of Foster's Chicago American Giants for several years, once going 18–1. In 1914, he tossed two no-hitters, one against the Indianapolis ABC's, the other against the Cuban Stars. He also starred in the Cuban Winter League for two years, leading the league with 10 victories in 1912. Proving he could hold his own with the best, Wickare outpitched the great Walter Johnson twice in three meetings, one a 1–0 shut-out.

• Bill "Plunk" Drake, was a 6', 205 pound curveball artist who earned his nickname by plunking opposing batters in the ribs from time to time. Drake was a fun loving jokester off the field, often entertaining players on the bench when he wasn't pitching. But, on the mound, he was mean. According to George Sweatt, in John Holway's fine collection of Negro league player interviews, *Voices from the Great Black Baseball Leagues*, "He liked to throw at people.... He'd throw three balls — one at your foot, one at your head, one behind you. Then he'd pitch. You didn't know what he was going to do, he was so crazy."

Drake starred in the Negro leagues from 1915 to 1930. Fragmentary records credit him with 80 wins against 62 losses during that period. In 1921, the cocky right hander compiled a 20–10 record, one of only six pitchers to win 20 games in the short Negro league season.

FIRST BASE:

• Edgar Wesley was a big power-hitting left handed batter, who starred for the Detroit Stars of the Negro National League during the '20s. Wesley teamed up with "Turkey" Stearnes to make the stars the terror of the league over that period.

Wesley was one of the first home run hitters of note in Negro league base-ball, averaging 28 homers a year, based on a 550 at-bat season. He led the Negro National League in home runs twice, smashing 11 round trippers in 1920, and 18 in 1926.

He was also a high average hitter, finishing his 14-year career with a .324 average. He led the league in batting in 1925, with a sizzling .416 mark.

The modest first baseman was also a fine defensive player, and exhibited good speed on the bases.

• Ben Taylor was a solid, all-around first baseman from 1908 to 1929. He was a powerful left handed hitter, who sent line drives to all parts of the ball-park. Batting against the dead ball, he concentrated on keeping the ball in play, rather than aiming for the fences. His .324 lifetime batting average would have included 32 doubles, eight triples, and six home runs, in an average season.

Taylor was a graceful fielder, in addition to being an outstanding hitter. He was considered to be the best defensive first baseman in the Negro leagues during the first quarter of the century.

SECOND BASE:

• William "Bill" Monroe beat out "Bingo" DeMoss for the starting posi-tion at second base on the all-star team, on the basis of a more potent bat. Although not DeMoss' equal in the field, Monroe outhit his rival by almost 100 points.

The right handed hitter stung the ball at a .300+ clip over a 19-year career. He also starred in the Cuban Winter League, hitting .333 in 1907-8. Like most Negro leaguers, Monroe moved around from team to team, following the greenbacks.

In the field, Monroe entertained the fans with his exciting brand of baseball. He often caught pop flies behind his back, and frequently talked to batters while he scooped up their ground balls.

Rube Foster claimed that Monroe was the greatest baseball player of all time, black or white.

• Elwood "Bingo" DeMoss was the backup at the keystone sack. His career spanned the years 1910–30, with such teams as the Indianapolis ABC's and the Chicago American Giants. DeMoss was noted for his defensive gymnastics, his blinding speed, and his quick hands. He made all the plays, including the impossible ones. He is generally recognized as the greatest defensive second baseman in Negro league history.

His weak bat prevented him from becoming the greatest all-around second baseman. He hit only .236 during his career, according to statistics compiled by John Holway.

SHORTSTOP:

• The greatest shortstop of all time, in the Negro leagues, and maybe the greatest of all-time in any league, was John Henry Lloyd. He was frequently compared to Honus Wagner, the greatest shortstop in major league history. In discussing the two of them, Connie Mack once said, "You could put John Henry Lloyd and Honus Wagner in a paper bag, and whichever one you pulled out, you couldn't lose."

Lloyd could do it all. He had big hands, according to Holway, and scooped up ground balls like a shovel, dirt and all. He was a graceful fielder, with exceptional range, who glided across the infield from second base to third, snatching hits away from frustrated batters.

At the plate, the Palatka, Florida, native was in his element. He pounded the ball at a .353 clip over an illustrious 26-year career. His .564 batting average for the New York Lincoln Giants in 1928 is the all-time, single season, Negro league record. He also won the batting title in 1924 with an average of .433.

Lloyd also excelled in the Cuban Winter League, where he played for 27 years, amassing a career batting average of .331. In 1909, in an exhibition series against the Detroit Tigers, Lloyd outhit Ty Cobb .500 to .371.

John Henry Lloyd joined other baseball immortals in Cooperstown in 1977.

• Dobie Moore is considered by many Negro league baseball experts to be the greatest shortstop ever. He was, like Lloyd, an outstanding all-around player. He had no weaknesses, defensively or offensively. He was particularly adept at running down balls in the hole behind third base and throwing out batters with his rifle arm.

At bat, the husky, 5'11", 230 pound infielder hit the ball consistently and with power. He led the Negro National League in batting in 1924 with a sizzling .453, the sixth highest average ever recorded in the Negro leagues. He also tied for the league lead in home runs that year, with 10. His .365 career batting average is the second highest average in the annals of Negro baseball, behind Chino Smith's .428. In an average season of 550 at-bats, the likable Moore would have accumulated 201 base hits, with 35 doubles, 15 triples, and 12 home runs. He also excelled in Cuba, where he compiled a lifetime batting average of .356.

THIRD BASE:

• Oliver "The Ghost" Marcelle was the king of third basemen during the teens and twenties and one of the greatest third basemen of all time. A native of Louisiana, the handsome Creole was a graceful fielder and a solid .300 hitter. Small at five foot nine and 160 pounds, Marcelle had exceptionally quick reflexes, snatching line drives out of the air like apples off a tree.

The Ghost could hit the old apple too. Although not a

John Henry Lloyd. (Noir Tech Research, Inc.)

power hitter, he sprayed singles all over the park, good for a .304 average, year after year. He was also a good hit-and-run man, and an outstanding baserunner.

The scrappy infielder led the Cuban Winter League in batting in 1924 with an average of .393. His career average on the island was .305 for eight years.

• Behind Marcelle was William "Brody" Francis, a tiny 5'5" pepperpot, who could field with the best of them. He had wide range, sure hands, and a strong throwing arm. He was also a smart, daring baserunner, with above average speed.

He usually batted in the number two spot in the lineup, to take advantage of his outstanding bat control, and his ability to draw bases on balls. Even though he had some strong years at the plate, with averages of .396, .344, and .324, his lifetime average hovered around the .270 mark over a 22-year career.

Dobie Moore. (Yuyo Ruiz.)

OUTFIELD:

• Negro league baseball produced some of the greatest outfielders in baseball history during the first 25 years of the twentieth century. Foremost among them was Preston "Pete" Hill, the smooth swinging left hander for Rube Foster's great Chicago American Giant teams. Hill was one of baseball's first superstars, excelling in all phases of the game. He was the Willie Mays of the dead ball era. A fast, aggressive, center fielder, he had a great glove, and a cannon for a throwing arm.

He could do it all at the plate; hit to any field, go for the long ball if necessary, or drag a bunt down the first base line to keep the infielders on their toes.

Pete Hill. (Dick Clark.)

On the bases, he played like Jackie Robinson, constantly moving, and daring the opposing pitcher to catch him.

Pete Hill enjoyed an 18 year career in the Negro leagues, finishing with a batting average in the .308–.326 range. His average in Cuba, over a six year period, was .307.

• Spotswood Poles was known as the "Black Ty Cobb" from 1909 to 1923. He was black baseball's fastest runner during his career, and may have been the fastest ever.

The 5'7", 165 pounder was an outstanding defensive center fielder, but he is best remembered for his skills at the plate and on the bases. The little, bow legged switch hitter rapped the ball with authority wherever he played. His Negro league averages, although sparse and far from complete, were generally in the .350–.450 range, with a high of .487 in 1914. James A. Riley, in his classic work, *The Biographical Encyclopedia of the Negro Baseball Leagues*, credits him with a .400+ career average. His Cuban Winter League average was .319 for four years, including .355 in 1913. Showing that those results were no flukes, Spot Poles, in ten games against major league competition, hit the big leaguers for 25 hits in 41 at-bats — an amazing .610 average.

His stolen base achievements were remembered with awe by his contemporaries. Although the statistical data has long been lost, he was credited with 41 stolen bases in 60 games in his first season with the New York Lincoln Giants, in 1911.

• Cristobal Torriente was the greatest outfielder ever to come out of Cuba. A true superstar, the chunky 5'9", 190 pound left handed batter played baseball year round from 1913 to 1932, spending his summers in the States and his winters on the island. He slugged the ball to death in both countries, walking off with two batting crowns in each place. He led the Negro National League in batting in 1920 with an average of .411 and repeated three years later with an average of .412. He took the Cuban Winter League batting crown in 1915, and again in 1920, with averages of .387 and .360. He also won two home run titles in Cuba.

When he retired, Torriente left behind a career batting average of .335 in the Negro leagues. Based on a 550 at-bat season, the Cuban strongboy would have averaged 33 doubles, 10 triples, and 13 home runs a year. In Cuba, he averaged .352 throughout his career. He also hit major league pitching well, besting such hurlers as Leon Cadore, 247-game winner Jack Quinn, and Dolph Luque, to the tune of .311 in 28 exhibition games.

Cristobal Torriente. (John B. Holway.)

Torriente was more than just a slugger, however. He had good speed, covered right field like a blanket, and had a strong, accurate throwing arm. Indianapolis ABCs manager C.I. Taylor said it best, as reported by Riley in his *Encyclopedia*, when he stated, "If I should see Torriente walking up the other side of the street, I would say, 'There walks a ballclub.'"

• Jimmy Lyons was another fleet-footed outfielder who starred in the Negro leagues for 16 years. He had great range in center field and very seldom made a bad play. On the bases, he was an intelligent and aggressive baserunner, averaging 47 stolen bases a year, based on fragmentary statistics.

At the plate, the chunky 5'8" speedster was a master with the bat. He could drag bunt if the situation warranted it, or he could hit the long ball if need be. He often batted in the leadoff position, and occasionally in the third spot. His season batting averages appear to have been in the .350–.400 range during his first ten years in the league, falling off to .250–.300 over his last five years.

* Valentin Dreke, a native of Union De Reyes, Cuba, was an outstanding all-around player in the Negro leagues for 11 years. Like Jimmy Lyons, Dreke was a stellar center fielder, with good range and a strong throwing arm. He was also a solid .300 hitter, who sprayed the ball to all fields, with an occasional drag bunt thrown in. His career batting average in the Negro leagues was .334.

John Beckwith. (Noir Tech Research, Inc.)

He played winter ball in his native Cuba for eight years, finishing with a commendable .307 average. He led the league in stolen bases in 1924.

Valentin Dreke was voted into the Cuban baseball Hall of Fame in 1945.

• Floyd "Jelly" Gardner was the right fielder for the Chicago American Giants for most of his 15-year career in the Negro leagues. The 5'6", 160 pound speedster usually batted leadoff in Rube Foster's lineup to take advantage of his sharp batting eye, outstanding bat control, and blazing speed. He was adept at drawing walks, bunting, and placing base hits into open areas of the outfield. His high on-base percentage, plus his great speed on the bases, produced bunches of runs over the years. The Giants won four Negro National League pennants in one seven year period, with Gardner igniting the attack.

UTILITY:

• John Beckwith, the "Black Bomber," was one of the most feared sluggers and baserunners in Negro league history. A capable shortstop, the rugged 230-pound Beckwith raised havoc on offense. He made contact frequently, and always hit the ball hard. Former teammates, and opponents alike insisted that Beckwith hit the ball farther than any other batter in the game, including Josh Gibson. According to John Holway, the Black Bomber hit the longest ball in Griffith Stadium history, a 460-foot shot that struck an advertising sign 40 feet above the field.

His .356 career batting average, one of the highest ever recorded in the Negro leagues, included a league leading .430 in 1930. He also captured two home run crowns, in '30 and '31. Beckwith's extra base hit output was awesome, averaging 33 doubles, eight triples, and 30 home runs for every 550 at-bats (#5 all-time). His home run average was exceeded by only two players — Gibson (48) and Mule Suttles (34).

John Beckwith ran the bases with evil intentions and with spikes flying. A moody, temperamental individual, the husky slugger was ready to fight at the drop of a hat. He did his greatest damage with the bat, however.

• The last utility spot is held down by Grant "Home Run" Johnson, another slugging shortstop. Considering the first two decades of the twentieth century showcased the likes of John Henry Lloyd, Dobie Moore, John Beckwith, and Home Run Johnson, as well as Honus Wagner, it would seem that this period was the golden age of great shortstops.

Johnson's career lasted from 1895 to 1916. He earned his nickname as a 20-year-

"Home Run" Johnson. (Refocus Productions.)

old slugger in semi-pro ball, back in his home town of Findlay, Ohio. The sobriquet was well deserved, as he continued to tattoo outfield fences all over eastern America with his powerful drives for 22 years.

Home Run Johnson was a natural hitter, who still recorded averages around the .400 level near the end of his career. Although most Negro league batting statistics are missing for Johnson, it is known that he averaged .319 during five years in Cuba. In fact, in 1909, he outhit the great Ty Cobb in a series of exhibition games in Havana, ripping the ball at a .421 clip compared to Cobb's .371.

Negro League All-Star Team, 1900–1925

Catcher	Louis Santop*
	Bruce Petway
Pitcher	Smokey Joe Williams*
	Cannonball Dick Redding
	Jose Mendez
	Rube Foster
	William Drake
	John Donaldson
	Frank Wickware
First Base	Edgar Wesley*
	Ben Taylor
Second Base	Bill Monroe*
	Bingo De Moss
Shortstop	John Henry Lloyd*
	Dobie Moore
Third Base	Oliver Marcelle*
	Brodie Francis
Outfield	Pete Hill*
	Spot Poles*
	Cristobal Torriente*
	Jimmy Lyons
	Valentin Dreke
	Floyd Gardner
Utility	John Beckwith
	Grant Johnson

Note: An asterisk denotes one of the starting nine players.

Negro League All-Star Team, 1926–1950

The Negro leaguers continued their mission as the good will ambassadors of international baseball as the second quarter of the twentieth century got underway. Negro league players were still heavily involved in the Cuban Winter League and the Mexican Winter League. They also had representatives in the Dominican Winter League, as well as leagues in Venezuela and Panama.

In 1938, they helped kick off the Puerto Rican Winter League (PRWL) with players like Tetelo Vargas, Raymond Brown, and Jimmie Crutchfield, spending the winter in San Juan and surrounding villages. Over the next couple of years, Puerto Rican fans were treated to some of the greatest baseball of the twentieth century, as Negro league greats such as Satchel Paige, Josh Gibson, Leon Day, Roy Campanella, and Monte Irvin, all made the trek south.

Luis Alvelo, Puerto Rico's foremost Winter League historian, particularly during the Negro League period in the late '30s and early '40s, claims this was the Golden Age of baseball on the island. According to Alvelo, the Negro league players were more than great ballplayers. They were outstanding representatives of their sport and their country. In addition to playing in the league, which operated only on weekends, the Negro leaguers spent considerable time during the week teaching interested Puerto Rican players the finer points of the game. They also spent many hours socializing with the Puerto Rican players and fans at the park and in town. They visited fans in their homes. They took toys to children in the hospitals. They were, in fact, heroes to the citizens of the tiny Insular Commonwealth of the United States.

On the field, the Negro league players mesmerized the fans with eye-popping feats of incredible strength and heroic skill. Satchel Paige sparked the Guayama club to the 1939-40 pennant by winning an all-time league record 19 games over a short, 56-game season. He also set the all-time league strikeout mark by fanning 208 batters in 205 innings. If his numbers were adjusted to a major league schedule of 154 games, Paige would have racked up an amazing 52 victories, with 572 strikeouts in 564 innings pitched. Naturally, he was voted the league's Most Valuable Player. Two years later, Josh Gibson established a batting record that will probably last forever. He tattooed the ball at an astronomical .480 clip in 123 at-bats, led the league in home runs with 13, and walked off with his own MVP trophy. Buck Leonard batted .390, and led the league in doubles and home runs during his one year stint on the island. Willard Brown, a Negro league Hall of Famer, was known as "Ese Hombre" (That Man) in Puerto Rico, because of his almost mythical prowess with the bat. Brown holds the PRWL single season home run record with 27 round trippers in 234 at-bats during the 1947-48 season when he was 36 years old. He also owns the PRWL's highest career batting average with a ten-year mark of .350 (Roberto Clemente and Orlando Cepeda averaged .323).

Back home, as the second quarter of the twentieth century got underway, the Negro leaguers were entering a Golden Age of their own. The Negro National League, founded by Rube Foster, flourished. Other Negro leagues, such as the Eastern Colored League, which operated between 1923 and 1928, and the Negro American League, which came into existence in 1937, stimulated interest in the game, competition between the leagues and between different areas of the country. It also provided a format for a genuine World Series between the champions of the two leagues.

Legendary players graced the rosters of the various teams; Josh Gibson with the Homestead Grays, Satchel Paige with the Pittsburgh Crawfords, and later the Kansas City Monarchs, "Bullet Joe" Rogan with the Monarchs, Buck Leonard with the Homestead Grays, and Ray Dandridge, Larry Doby, and Monte Irvin, with the Newark Eagles.

As was noted earlier, Negro league players barnstormed around the country with their major league counterparts after the season ended in October, and they more than held their own, winning an estimated 61 percent of the contests between the two groups. Major league stars, like Dizzy Dean, Bob Feller, Jimmie Foxx, and Babe Ruth regularly locked horns with Negro league stars "Cool Papa" Bell, Oscar Charleston, Turkey Stearnes, Satchel Paige, Josh Gibson, and others, and they came away impressed. The general consensus of the big leaguers was that the Negro leaguers were of equal skill, and belonged in the major leagues.

Baseball was headed in the direction of an integrated organization as early as the 1920s, but it was still on a slow track. It would take until 1945 to actually accomplish the inevitable. The major stumbling block to the historic merger was one of courage. Many major league owners, like Clark Griffith of the Washington Senators, would have loved to have had some Negro league players on their roster, but they shied away from challenging the still bigoted establishment.

It wasn't until Branch Rickey came along, a man with the courage of his convictions, that baseball entered a new, historic phase. Rickey had been an enemy of prejudice and bigotry his entire life. As a young college coach in Michigan, the fervent Methodist was appalled at the treatment of blacks by local restaurants and hotels. He vowed, even then, to do whatever he could to correct such injustices.

Early in his major league career, "The Mahatma," as he was called, was unable to attack the racial discrimination that ran rampant through organized baseball, primarily because baseball commissioner Kenesaw Mountain Landis was a staunch advocate of segregated baseball leagues. On the death of Landis in 1944, the major league baseball owners elected Albert B. "Happy" Chandler, a former governor of Kentucky and U.S. senator, to the post of baseball commissioner. Branch Rickey finally had an ally.

Chandler, after witnessing the heroic efforts of black soldiers, sailors, and airmen during World War II, staunchly believed that blacks deserved to share the American dream on an equal plane with whites. When Rickey approached him in the spring of 1945 with his plan to integrate organized baseball, Chandler gave him his wholehearted support. Even though most club owners were still against integration, they could no longer prevent the inevitable.

The sports world was rocked to its core on October 23, 1945, when General Manager Branch Rickey of the Brooklyn Dodgers announced the club had signed a Negro, Jackie Robinson, to a professional baseball contract. Initially, the road was rocky for Jackie, as racists, on the field and off, taunted him with the vilest insults and threats. But Jackie persevered, eventually winning a National League batting championship, capturing a league Most Valuable Player trophy, helping the Dodgers win six National League pennants in ten years, and finally, in 1962, joining the other baseball immortals in the Hall of Fame, in Cooperstown, New York.

Jackie Robinson's courageous achievement opened the door for other blacks to play major league baseball. It also, sadly, sounded the death knell for the Negro leagues. Robinson was followed into the majors by a flood of more than 100 talented Negro league players, including pitchers Satchel Paige, Don Newcombe, Joe Black, and "Toothpick" Sam Jones. World class sluggers like Willie Mays, Ernie Banks, Hank Aaron, Monte Irvin, Roy Campanella, Luke Easter, and Larry Doby began their careers as well. The Negro leagues struggled on for another dozen years or so, but with their talent reduced to a lower minor league level, they eventually closed up shop for good.

The major leagues, on the other hand, prospered. The caliber of play was elevated to a new level by the influx of Negro league talent. Many baseball experts consider the late forties to be the beginning of the golden age of major league baseball, continuing through the fifties.

Negro league baseball had come full circle during the second quarter of the twentieth century. From a chaotic existence during the first two decades of the century, the Negro leagues produced a stable and more visible environment during the '20s, '30s, and '40s. They showcased dozens of superstars in Negro league cities from New York to Kansas City, and from Chicago to Birmingham. They attracted thousands of white fans to their games, and they competed with whites on an equal basis in exhibition games year after year.

The Negro leagues did their job well. So well, in fact, they put themselves out of business. By the end of the second quarter of the century, blacks had achieved their goal: admission into organized baseball. It was, at once, satisfying yet sad. An era had ended. The glorious and romantic journey of Negro league baseball faded into the mist. It became only a memory — and there are still those who pine for its return.

The final quarter century of Negro league baseball produced some of the game's most skillful and exciting baseball players. Choosing an all-star team from this celebrated group is most difficult. In reviewing the selections, it must be remembered that there are dozens more who could have been chosen without losing a step.

CATCHER:

• The Negro leagues were blessed with one of the greatest catchers ever to play the game. Josh Gibson towered over his contemporaries. He is considered one of the two greatest hitters in Negro league history — the other being Chino Smith. Gibson starred in the Negro leagues for 17 years, averaging .362 during that time. His awesome power, which was legendary throughout the land, produced an average of 48 home runs for every 550 at-bats, a figure (outside of Babe Ruth) unmatched in baseball annals. He led the Negro leagues in home runs nine times.

Josh Gibson not only excelled in the United States; he was also a superstar in Mexico and the Caribbean region. He averaged .373 with 54 homers in Mexico, .355 with 27 homers in Puerto Rico, and .353 with 31 homers in Cuba. He won home run titles in all three countries. He also slugged white major leaguers for a .426 average in exhibition games, smashing five home runs in 61 at-bats. He was elected to baseball's Hall of Fame in 1972.

• Gibson's backup on the all-star team is the incomparable Biz Mackey. Mackey excelled in all phases of the game. He was unquestionably the Negro league's greatest defensive catcher, famed for his powerful and accurate throwing arm. It was Mackey who taught the youthful Roy Campanella the fine points of defensive play.

Biz Mackey was also an offensive threat. He compiled a .322 batting average during a celebrated 28-year career, averaging 41 extra base hits a year, including 11 home runs.

PITCHER:

• Satchel Paige is the leading pitcher on the all-star team. He was a legend in his own time, the idol of three continents. The talented and eccentric satchel-man dazzled fans from New York to Havana with his skills and with his theatrics. His legendary pitching repertoire included his famous hesitation pitch, as well as other unique deliveries, such as his be-ball, his bat-dodger, and his step-n-pitch-it.

The tall, lanky Paige was more than an entertainer, however. He was one of the most gifted pitchers in baseball history — black or white. He starred in the Negro leagues for 21 years, primarily with the Pittsburgh Crawfords and the Kansas City Monarchs. His Negro league pitching slate showed 123 victories against 79 losses during the abbreviated Negro league season. If all his pitching victories were counted — those in Puerto Rico (including the 19 games he won in the 1939-40 Winter League), the Cuban Winter League, the California Winter League, the exhibition games against the white major leaguers, and his sojourns into the Dominican Republic and Mexico — his victory total might well have exceeded the 511 victories posted by Cy Young.

Satchel Paige did have the opportunity of pitching in the major leagues, although he was at the advanced baseball age of 42 when Bill Veeck signed him to a Cleveland Indians contract in 1948. Still, he helped pitch the Indians to the American league pennant, winning six games against a single loss. He gave the young major leaguers a pitching lesson along the way, tossing a 5–0 complete game shutout at the Chicago White Sox on August 13, then coming back seven days later to blank the same team by the score of 1–0.

Paige pitched in the majors for six years, compiling a 28–31 record. He spent three more years with the Miami Marlins of the International League, racking up a 31–22 record, with a 2.73 ERA. He was 52 years old at the time.

In a fitting finale, the ageless one returned to the major leagues one more time. Pitching for the Kansas City Athletics in 1965, the 59-year-old Paige blanked the Boston Red Sox for three innings.

Satchel Paige walked through the front door of the Hall of Fame in Cooperstown, New York, in 1971 to hang his plaque on the wall alongside his buddies, Bob Feller and Dizzy Dean. It was a memorable moment in Negro league history.

• "Bullet Joe" Rogan may have been the greatest all-around player in Negro league history. The Oklahoma native was arguably one of the three best pitchers the Negro leagues ever produced. His winning percentage of .715, based on 113 victories against only 34 losses, is #2 all-time. He had all the pitches, including a moving fastball, a curveball, a palmball, and a forkball. The chunky, 5'7" right hander also pitched intelligently, keeping the batters off balance by mixing pitches, speeds, and locations. He even teased the batter with a spitter from time to time.

Joe Rogan was also a brilliant fielder and generally regarded as the best fielding pitcher in Negro league baseball. He played center field and second base when not pitching, and excelled at both positions.

He was more than just a pitcher and a fielder, however. He was a powerful hitter who usually batted in the cleanup slot in the awesome Kansas City batting

Satchel Paige. (Yuyo Ruiz.)

order. When he retired in 1930 after a brilliant 11-year career, he left behind a .343 batting average which included 30 doubles, 15 triples, and 15 home runs per year.

The Negro league superstar was voted into Cooperstown in 1998.

• Willie Foster, a stylish southpaw, beat Rogan into Cooperstown, being elected to the elite assemblage in 1996. Foster, the brother of Rube Foster, pitched in the Negro National League from 1923 to 1938. His 137 career victories are the most ever recorded in the Negro leagues. In 1927, when the Chicago American Giants of the Negro National League played a 46-game schedule, Willie led the league with a 21–3 record. He was one of only seven pitchers to win 20 or more games during the short Negro league season. He also holds the record for most career shutouts, with 34.

Foster possessed a wide assortment of pitches, which included, according to James A. Riley, "a blazing fast ball, a slider, a fast-breaking drop, a sidearm curve, and a masterful change of pace." He pitched the Giants to three pennants and, in 1926, with his team needing to win both ends of a season-closing doubleheader, Foster outpitched Bullet Joe Rogan in both ends of the twin bill, winning 1–0 and 5–0. As an encore, he won two more games against the Bacharach Giants in the World Series, taking the clincher 1–0. In all, he won 12 post-season games, more than any other Negro league pitcher.

• Leon Day was the ace of the Newark Eagles staff from 1936 to 1946. Partial statistics credit him with a 67–29 record during his Negro league career. Although he stood only 5'7" tall and weighed a scant 170 pounds, his fastball blazed plateward at an estimated 90–95 mph.

Day holds the Negro league single game strikeout record, fanning 18 Baltimore Elite batters in 1942. He struck out the great Roy Campanella three times that day. In 1946, just back from three years of military service in World War II, the hard-throwing right hander tossed an opening day no-hitter at the Philadelphia Stars, winning 2–0.

Leon Day played ball year-round, traveling to Venezuela, Puerto Rico, Cuba, and Mexico during the winter months. Like Joe Rogan before him, Day was an all-around player, who played in the infield or outfield when not pitching. He was an outstanding fielder and a solid .300 hitter with good power.

By the way, he went 3–0 in head-to-head battles against the great Satchel Paige. He entered Cooperstown in 1996.

• Ray Brown holds the all-time Negro league career winning percentage record (.762), based on 109 victories against 34 losses over a 19-year career. Brown also holds the single season pitching record, compiling a mark of 24–4 with a 2.09 total run average in 1940. The Homestead Grays' ace led the league in pitching on two other occasions, going 11–6 in 1941, and 12–4 with a 2.83 TRA in 1942. He added a third TRA title in 1938, with a minuscule 0.75.

The 6'1", 195 pound right hander threw a perfect game against the Chicago American Giants in 1945, winning 7–0.

Ray Brown added another 138 or more victories to his list, pitching in Cuba, Mexico, and Puerto Rico. He led the Cuban Winter League in pitching twice. In 1936-37, he went 21–4, with a no-hitter. The following year, he topped the league with a 12–5 mark. He led the Puerto Rican Winter League in ERA

Leon Day

twice, with 1.05 in 1940-41, and 1.80 in 1941-42.

Brown was a true iron man. He had a rubber arm, thanks to an effortless knuckleball. This allowed him to pitch frequently, including doubleheaders, if necessary. He could also play a good outfield, and a respectable infield. Like many Negro league pitchers, he was a good hitter — a Negro league asset that has become lost on most contemporary major league pitchers.

• Ted Trent pitched in the Negro leagues for 13 years, running up a 93–49 record. The tall, skinny right hander used a big, roundhouse curveball as his out pitch. He also threw a deadly drop and a big-time fastball. Trent's best year was 1928, when he ran up a brilliant 21–3 record.

He once fanned the New York Giants great first baseman, Bill Terry, four times in an exhibition game.

• Jesse "Nip" Winters was a big southpaw, who stood 6'5" tall and weighed 225 pounds. He starred in the Negro leagues for 14 years, from 1920 to 1933, mixing a good fastball with a sharp curve to compile a 95–54 career record. He was considered to be the best pitcher in the Eastern Colored League.

He led the league in winning percentage four times, including 21–10 in 1925.

He also led in total run average four times, as he pitched the Hilldale Daisies to three consecutive pennants.

FIRST BASE:

• Walter "Buck" Leonard was the greatest first baseman in Negro league history. Over a ten-year period, Leonard teamed with Josh Gibson to give the Homestead Grays a 1–2 batting punch comparable to the great Yankee combo of Ruth and Gehrig. Leonard and Gibson, known as the "Thunder Twins," sparked the Grays to a record nine consecutive Negro National League pennants, between 1937 and 1946.

Ray Brown. (Yuyo Ruiz.)

Leonard was a smooth swinging, left handed hitter, who hit for both average and distance. He banged out 29 home runs a year, to go along with a .336 batting average, during a memorable 17-year career. In post season play, he was devastating, crushing the ball at a .419 clip.

Buck Leonard played baseball 12 months a year, traveling the western hemisphere in search of a game. In addition to the California Winter League, Leonard made annual treks to Cuba, Puerto Rico, Mexico, and Venezuela. In the 1941 Puerto Rican Winter League, Leonard rapped the ball at a .390 gait, with a league-leading eight home runs in 118 at-bats.

The native of Rocky Mount, N.C., finally made it into organized baseball, playing ten games with Portsmouth in the Piedmont League in 1953. The 45-year-old graybeard cracked 11 hits in 33 at-bats, for a .333 average. He was elected to baseball's Hall of Fame in 1972.

• George "Mule" Suttles was one of the Negro league's most colorful players from 1918 to 1944. He was not the graceful fielder that Buck Leonard was, but he got the job done. At the plate, however, he was explosive. He hit the ball higher and longer than any other man in the game, Gibson included. When Suttles stepped to the plate, the crowd would invariably root him on with the chant, "Kick Mule, kick." And more often than not, the powerful right handed slugger would kick one into the distant left field stands.

Suttles is the #1 all-time career home run hitter in Negro league baseball, with 190 circuit blows to his credit. His average of 34 round trippers a year trails only Josh Gibson's 48 in the Negro league record book.

Mule Suttles is one of the legends of the game.

SECOND BASE:

• The second base-man on the 1926–50 all-star team is the slick fielding Sammy T. Hughes. The 6'3", 190 pounder had all the attributes of a defen-sive genius. He had a wide range, a sure glove, and a strong throwing arm. His pivot on a double play was poetry in motion.

According to James A. Riley, "In addition to his picture-perfect work afield, he was also a good base runner and a solid hitter. A thinking man's player, Hughes was a con-sistent contact hitter who excelled on the hit-and-run play and was a good bunter...."

Sammy T. was a life-time .300 hitter, from 1931 to 1946, who put together occasional season averages as high as .355.

• Newt "Colt" Allen was the premier second baseman of the 1920s. He was small and quick (5'8", 160 pounds), agile in the field, and a streak on the basepaths. The switch hit-

Buck Leonard

ter was also a consistent contact hitter, who left behind a career average of .298. He batted second in the powerful Kansas City Monarchs lineup, for 23 years, setting the table for the likes of Dobie Moore and Bullet Rogan.

SHORTSTOP:

• Willie Wells was one of the most outstanding shortstops in Negro league history. He had exceptional range, sure hands, and got a great jump on the ball.

His only weakness was a mediocre throwing arm, but he offset that by intelligent positioning and by playing shallow.

He was a terror at bat, as well. His .328 career average included 61 extra base hits a year, with 20 dingers. Wells, whose 26-year career included annual junkets to Cuba, Mexico, and Puerto Rico, was a hero in those southern countries. In Mexico, he was lovingly known as "El Diablo"—the Devil—because of his defensive capabilities. Opposing fans often admonished their team with cries of "Don't hit it to shortstop. That's where The Devil plays." The Devil was elected to the Hall of Fame in 1997.

Willie Wells

• Richard Lundy, King Richard to the fans, was one of the four greatest shortstops in the annals of Negro league baseball. The others were Lloyd, Dobie Moore, and Wells. King Richard didn't take a back seat to any of them.

The 5'11", 180 pounder, whose career spanned 24 years, from 1916 to 1939, anchored the sensational Bacharach Giant defense for 12 years. The graceful infielder had all the tools, including a strong, accurate throwing arm. His .324 career batting average compared with Wells', but his power was slightly less, with 21 doubles, five triples, and 12 home runs a year. He dazzled the fans in Cuba over an extended career, fielding like a gazelle, and rapping the ball to the tune of .341, one of the highest career averages in Cuban baseball history.

THIRD BASE:

• Third base, like the other positions of the all-star team, is a toss-up. Ray Dandridge and Judy Johnson were equally outstanding. Dandridge won the starting job on the basis of a more potent bat. The squat, bowlegged, 170 pound third sacker was a flashy fielder, with sure hands and a gun for an arm. He, Willie Wells, Dick Seay, and Mule Suttles formed the famed "million dollar infield" of the Newark Eagles during the 1930s.

Dandridge was a solid hitter who sprayed base hits all over the ballpark. He led the Negro National League in batting in 1934, with a mark of .436, on his way to a .322 career average. Hooks, as he was called, spanked the ball with authority wherever he played —.282 in Cuba, .347 in Mexico, and .318 in AAA minor league ball.

Ray Dandridge deserved to play major league baseball before he retired, but in 1949, when he arrived at the New York Giants farm team in Minneapolis, he was a well-traveled 35-year-old veteran, considered by many to be over the hill. In spite of leading the American Association in batting with an average of .369, he was ignored by the big club the following year. It was the biggest disappointment of his life.

That slight was finally forgotten in 1987, when he was elected to the Hall of Fame.

• Judy Johnson, another Hall of Famer (1975), was a complete ballplayer. He excelled both defensively and offensively. He was often called the smartest third baseman that ever played the game. According to teammate Jimmy Crutchfield, in John B. Holway's *Blackball Stars*, Johnson "was like a rock ... a steadying influence on the club. He had a great brain, could anticipate a play, knew what his opponents were going to do." Willie Wells added, "He had intelligence and finesse."

Judy Johnson starred for the Hilldale Daisies for ten years, before finishing his 20-year career with the Pittsburgh Crawfords. He left behind a .322 career average in the Negro leagues. In the winter, he ripped Cuban League pitching for a .331 average.

OUTFIELD:

The outfield on the Negro league all-star team consists of some of the finest players ever to walk on a ballfield. The starting group of Oscar Charleston, "Cool Papa" Bell, and Chino Smith bring with them three of the most devastating bats in the game.

• Oscar Charleston was the top center fielder in Negro league history. He was often called the "Black Cobb" because of his aggressive style of play and his slashing, powerful baserunning. He did hit the ball with authority, like Cobb (a .350 career average), but he also hit for distance, as attested to by his 28 home runs a year. Charleston's .365 career average in Cuba is exceeded only by Jud Wilson.

Charleston was famous for his blinding speed in the outfield. He played a shallow center field, but could run down anything hit in his direction.

He was elected to the baseball Hall of Fame in Cooperstown, New York, in 1976.

• Charles "Chino" Smith has been called the greatest hitter the Negro leagues ever produced. Certainly his statistics back up that claim. His .428 career batting average is 63 points higher than the #2 man, Dobie Moore. Smith, a slightly built, 5'6", 168 pound outfielder was deceptively powerful, with lightning-fast wrists and split-second timing.

The little left hander was a cocky contact hitter who rarely struck out. His hit parade included almost 80 extra base hits a year, with 50 doubles, eight triples, and 21 home runs. In his first game in Yankee Stadium, in 1930, he belted out two homers and a triple, in three at-bats.

Chino was disdainful of opposing pitchers, often watching two pitches go by, and frequently spitting at them as they passed the plate; then sending the next pitch on a line, back through the box, forcing the pitcher to duck as the ball whistled past him on its way to center field.

Chino Smith's career was, unfortunately, much too brief. He contracted yellow fever in Cuba during the winter of 1931, and died shortly thereafter. He was not yet 31 years old. His Negro league career totaled only seven years,

Judy Johnson

but in three of those years, he batted over .400. Pitchers could never get little Chino out. It took the grim reaper to do that.

• James "Cool Papa" Bell was the fastest man ever to play in the Negro leagues. His base running feats are legendary, such as scoring the winning run in the 1934 Negro league all-star game when he raced home from second on an infield out. He routinely flew from first to third on sacrifice bunts, scored from second on fly balls, and scored from first on singles.

Cool Papa could do it all. He was a center fielder extraordinaire, combining blazing speed with outstanding anticipation, a sure glove, and an accurate throwing arm. At the plate, the 6', 160 pound switch hitter was always a threat to bunt, but he could also hit with power if necessary. He averaged 29 doubles, 10 triples and 10 home runs a year in the tough Negro leagues.

Bell played ball, winter and summer, for 25 years. When he retired, he left behind a batting average of .338 in the Negro leagues. He also hit .316 in Cuba and .376 in Mexico. Proving his greatness, the sleek greyhound tattooed major league pitchers like Dizzy Dean, Bob Feller, and Johnny Vander Meer at a .383 clip in 41 exhibition games.

James Cool Papa Bell carried his plaque into the Baseball Hall of Fame in 1974.

• Norman "Turkey" Stearnes was a man whose greatness has long been overlooked by the baseball establishment. He was one of the most magnificent ballplayers in Negro league history — a true superstar. He should have been in the Hall of Fame years ago.

Turkey Stearnes was an extraordinary center fielder, with outstanding speed and range. He was the equal of Oscar Charleston and Cool Papa Bell in the outfield. He was also a hard, aggressive baserunner, who was near the top of the league in stolen bases, year after year.

At the plate, the left handed pull hitter was a one man wrecking crew. His .352 lifetime batting average included 33 doubles, 18 triples, and 30 home runs, a year. His extra base hit output is exceeded only by Josh Gibson. His home run average is #3 all-time, behind Gibson and Mule Suttles.

Turkey Stearnes sent high fly balls out of major league parks on a regular basis, leading the Negro leagues in home runs seven times in 14 years. He was also a consistent hitter, batting over .300 thirteen times. He led the league in batting in 1935, with an average of .430. In post-season play, he stung the ball at a .474 pace. Against the major leaguers, he compiled a solid .351 average.

• Monte Irvin starred for the Newark Eagles for ten years, with three years out for military service, before getting his chance at the big time with the New York Giants in 1949. Irvin was a superstar in the Negro leagues, playing short-stop, second base, and center field with equal skill. The big, righthanded hitter was one of the premier batsmen in the league, piling up a .345 average during his career. He led the league in home runs twice, batting average once, and runs batted in three times.

When he finally got his chance in the majors, he was already 30 years old, but he still put together an outstanding big league career. He sparked the Giants to the 1951 National League pennant, hitting .312 with 24 home runs, and leading the league in runs batted in with 121.

Over the course of an eight-year major league career, Irvin hit .293, with 731 base hits, and 99 home runs, in 2499 at-bats. He was elected to the Hall of Fame in 1973.

• Willard Brown was another heroic ballplayer who just missed his chance at major league stardom. When he finally got the call in 1947 he was already 36 years old, with 13 years in the Negro leagues behind him. Brown played only 21 games for the St. Louis Browns in the American League, hitting a paltry .179 with one home run before deciding to return to the Negro leagues. The anti-black

"Cool Papa" Bell

atmosphere that still pervaded the majors at that time probably had as much to do with his poor performance and his decision to go back to the segregated leagues as anything.

Willard Brown was, like the other outfielders on the all-star team, a super-star, who possessed the five attributes necessary to be classified as such. He could run, field, throw, hit, and hit with power. He ripped the ball at a .352 clip (#9 all-time) with 20 homers a year during 14 years in the Negro leagues. He also

Jud Wilson. (John B. Holway.)

hit the ball at a .316 pace in Mexico and, after returning to the minor leagues in 1950, at the age of 39, he went on to hit for a .309 average with 24 home runs a year for six years.

But it was in Puerto Rico where Willard Brown was a true hero. He was affectionately called "Ese Hombre"—That Man—around the island. He devastated opposing pitchers in the Puerto Rican Winter League for ten years. He led the league in hitting three times, in home runs three times, and in RBIs four times. He captured two most valuable player awards.

Willard Brown compiled the highest lifetime batting average in Puerto Rican baseball history—.350. Roberto Clemente and Orlando Cepeda both hit .323 and Tony Perez hit .308.

Brown also holds the single season home run record, banging out 27 round trippers in just 234 at-bats during the 1947-48 season, the same year he played for St. Louis. Apparently, he took out his frustration on the beleagured pitchers in Puerto Rico.

UTILITY:

• Jud Wilson was one of the most feared hitters in the Negro leagues for 24 years, from 1922 to 1945. He played third base and first base, but it was with a bat in his hand that he is best remembered. The left handed slugger hit consistently, year after year, and he hit with power. He was at his best in the clutch when the game was on the line.

He stung the ball at a .347 pace during his career, chipping in with 30 two-baggers, six triples, and 14 homers a year. He holds the all-time highest career batting average in Cuba, raking Cuban Winter League pitchers for a .372 average over six years, with 13 home runs. He continued his battering on major league pitchers, hitting .360 against them with three home runs in 86 at-bats.

Wilson was not only feared at bat. He was also feared on the bases. He was a terrifying baserunner, a stocky 5'8", 185 pound bundle of dynamite who asked no quarter and gave none. He was as famous for his brawling as for his hitting.

Martin Dihigo. (Yuyo Ruiz.)

• Martin Dihigo was one of the two greatest all-around players in the Negro leagues, along with Joe Rogan. He could play center field or second base, and excel at either position. And he was one of the most outstanding pitchers of the '20s, '30s, and '40s. He is the only player to have been elected to the baseball Hall of Fame in four countries, the United States, Cuba, Venezuela, and Mexico.

He was tall (6'3"), sturdy (190 pounds), and graceful. A native of Cuba, where he was known as "El Immortal," he traveled the western hemisphere baseball circuit for 26 years. Between the three countries, he left behind a lifetime batting mark of .304 while running up a 256–136 won-loss record on the mound.

Negro League All-Star Team, 1926–1950

Catcher	Josh Gibson*
	Biz Mackey
Pitcher	Satchel Paige*
	Bullet Joe Rogan
	Willie Foster
	Leon Day
	Ted Trent
	Ray Brown
	Nip Winters

First Base	Buck Leonard*
	Mule Suttles
Second Base	Sammy T. Hughes*
	Newt Allen
Shortstop	Willie Wells*
	Dick Lundy
Third Base	Ray Dandridge*
	Judy Johnson
Outfield	Oscar Charleston*
	Cool Papa Bell
	Chino Smith*
	Turkey Stearnes*
	Monte Irvin
	Willard Brown
Utility	Jud Wilson
	Martin Dihigo

Note: An asterisk (*) denotes one of the starting nine players.

The All-Time Negro League All-Star Team, and the Negro League Hall of Fame

Negro league baseball existed for a little more than half a century. During that time, it entertained American baseball fans, particularly black fans, with an exciting diversion from their everyday, humdrum existences. It allowed them to excel vicariously through their heroes in a high visibility activity admired by millions of people from coast to coast.

Negro league baseball was a fiercely partisan sport. The citizens of Kansas City were fanatically loyal to their Monarchs, just as the people of Hilldale were to their Daisies, or the inhabitants of Baltimore were to their Black Sox. Home town fans selfishly defended their warriors against any would-be usurper. Sunday afternoon baseball games in the black communities across eastern America were lively social events, attended by fans of both sexes. The men were nattily attired in suits and ties, while the women were decked out in their best Sunday-go-to-meeting clothes. The Negro leaguers not only brought joy and excitement to thousands of people in the United States, they also cultivated a love for the sport in dozens of far away places around the globe, from the sugar cane fields of Cuba to the sandy plateau of the Egyptian desert, and from the cricket fields of jolly old England to small baseball stadiums in the Land of the Rising Sun.

Negro league baseball during the first half of the twentieth century was an important and historic piece of Americana. Then suddenly it was gone. When Jackie Robinson tore down the barrier of segregation that separated white America from black America, he ushered in a new era in organized baseball, an era of integration and equality. The new arrangement also spelled doom for the Negro leagues. Within a decade, they were gone.

Was it all for the better? The answer is not clear. The adventure, excitement, camaraderie, and love of the game that was Negro league baseball has long
since disappeared. Today's game, the modern game of major league baseball, is
no longer about fun. It is all about money. Now, the joy of playing baseball dis-
appears as soon as a young prospect is elevated to major league status. The kid's
game that was learned on the school playground and was cultivated on dusty
little league fields and high school diamonds is quickly forgotten. Ravenous
agents, like vultures from the Kalahari, swoop down on unsuspecting children,
destroying their innocence and cultivating their greed. Modern Americans are
discovering what people have learned over five thousand years of recorded history: Money corrupts. It is a lesson that is too often learned at great personal
expense. And the young athletes of America, black and white alike, are paying
the price for fame and fortune.

While American baseball suffers through its new-found freedom, it is
important to remember the dedicated Negro league pioneers, before their names
and their deeds are washed away by the sands of time. This chapter will, first,
select an all-time Negro league all-star team, composed of the greatest 25 ball
players in the history of Negro league baseball. In addition, it will recognize those
players who deserve recognition in baseball's Hall of Fame.

The Hall of Fame selections are, admittedly, imperfect. There are probably some deserving players who have been inadvertently left off the list. Perhaps
some who are on the list should not be. The Hall of Fame selections do not
include biographies of the players unless they were selected for the all-star team —
just the names are presented. Interested readers should refer to the dedicated
researchers and writers who are far more knowledgeable about the subject than
this writer. Background material, anecdotes, and statistics on most of the players selected for the Hall of Fame can be found in the works of Robert Peterson,
John B. Holway, James A. Riley, Dick Clark, Larry Lester, Bruce Chadwick,
Janet Bruce, Richard Bak, James Bankes, Donn Rogosin, and others. Many of
their works are listed in the Bibliography.

In order to select an all-time Negro league all-star team, it is necessary to
compare the various eras on an equal basis. This is difficult because the introduction of the lively ball in 1920 produced an entirely different game than was
played from 1860 through 1919. In the early days of the sport, a single, two
stolen bases, and a sacrifice fly might produce a 1–0 victory. After 1919, home
runs became the order of the day. The overpowering pitching that dominated
the dead ball era was neutralized by the new "jackrabbit" ball.

Fortunately, there is data available that allows us to adjust the home run
production of those players who strutted their stuff in the early days of the sport
to the modern game. Table II in the later portion of the book compares the home
run production of 20 of the top major league players of the day whose careers
straddled the two eras. According to the numbers, home run production jumped
up by a factor of 2.14 after 1919. This factor is confirmed by a comparison of

the entire major leagues' home run output for the decade before 1920 to the decade from 1920 through 1929. That factor was actually 2.51.

How that factor affects the statistics of the players from the old dead ball era can best be demonstrated by reviewing the home run performances of a couple of players whose careers spanned the dead ball era. Pete Hill, one of the Negro league's first superstars, rapped nine home runs a year in the early 1900s. Using the HR conversion factor of 2.51, Hill could be expected to hit an average of 23 home runs a year in the Negro leagues after 1920. His home run production would jump up even more if converted to a major league base point. As this book's tables show, a Negro league player moving from the Negro leagues to the major leagues will lose approximately 48 points in his batting average but will hit about 27 percent more home runs.

Frank Grant, the slugging second baseman of the 1890s, would also see his home run production increase from nine home runs a year to 23 if he had played in the Negro leagues after 1920. "Big Bertha," Louis Santop, the premier slugger of the dead ball days, would bang out an average of 25 home runs a year in the modern era.

The roster of the all-time Negro league all-star team is composed of the following twenty-five players:

CATCHER:

The Negro leagues produced four of the greatest catchers in baseball history — Louis Santop, Bruce Petway, Josh Gibson, and Biz Mackey. Another legendary Negro league backstop will be profiled with the major league all-star team of 1951–1975. His name is Roy Campanella.

• The #1 catcher on the all-time Negro league all-star team is Josh Gibson, in a runaway. There may have been other catchers who outperformed Gibson with the mitt, but he more than made up for it with his explosive bat. His average of 48 round trippers a year is unmatched in Negro league annals. Mule Suttles, with 34, is a distant second, 14 homers behind.

• The number two spot on the roster is a close call, between Louis Santop and Biz Mackey. Both backstops were consistent .300 hitters. Santop had the edge from a power standpoint, while Mackey won the nod defensively. Big Bertha is the choice, by a nose.

PITCHER:

The greatest pitchers in Negro league history are generally considered to be Satchel Paige, "Smokey Joe" Williams, "Cannonball" Dick Redding, and "Bullet Joe" Rogan. These four legends anchor the formidable pitching staff of the all-star team. They are ably supported by the talented southpaw, Willie Foster,

Josh Gibson

brother of the great Rube Foster, knuckleball artist Ray Brown, and fireballing
Leon Day, the pride of Newark. This group could undoubtedly hold its own
with any pitching staff in baseball history.

FIRST BASE:

• Buck Leonard, known as the Black Lou Gehrig during his heyday, is a
clear cut winner at first base. Leonard could do it all. He was a graceful fielder
and a .300 hitter with long ball potential.

• Mule Suttles did not have Leonard's glove, but he more than made up for it at the plate. In addition to a lifetime batting average of .329, his 34 home runs for every 550 at-bats is #2 all-time in the Negro leagues.

• Edgar Wesley was an outstanding first baseman who combined a good batting eye with long ball power, speed on the bases, and a dependable glove. Mule Suttles edged him out for all-star status by the narrowest of margins.

SECOND BASE:

• Bill Monroe is the all-time Negro league second baseman. A flashy gloveman, Monroe also tattooed the ball, racking up a career average over .300 in both the United States and Cuba.

• Sammy T. Hughes was the prototypical second baseman. A tall rangy infielder, Hughes could beat you with his glove or with his bat. He was proficient with both.

• Both Newt Allen and Bingo DeMoss were superlative defensive infielders. Allen was selected as Hughes' backup. DeMoss was a notoriously weak hitter.

"Smokey Joe" Williams. (John B. Holway.)

SHORTSTOP:

• John Henry Lloyd was, by all accounts, the all-time Negro league shortstop. He may have been the greatest ever, black or white. The comparisons

Above: "Bullet Joe" Rogan. *Right:* Dobie
Moore. (Noir Tech Research, Inc.)

between him and Honus Wagner left the
two of them in a veritable deadlock. Lloyd
had no weakness, either in the field or at
the bat.

• His backup on the all-star team is Dobie Moore. Moore also excelled
both defensively and offensively. Willie Wells and Dick Lundy were worthy
competitors, but Wells' weak arm put him at a disadvantage. Additionally, Moore
outhit both Wells and Lundy by 40 points.

Left: "Cool Papa" Bell. *Above:* Ray Dandridge. (Yuyo Ruiz.)

THIRD BASE:

Third base is another tossup. Ray Dandridge and Oliver "Ghost" Marcelle both outdistanced Judy Johnson and Brodie Francis. Both Dandridge and Marcelle were magicians in the field, but Dandridge gained the #1 spot of the strength of his superior bat. Marcelle and Johnson were both .300 hitters, but the "Ghost" nosed out Johnson on the basis of superior glove work. Francis was not as consistent as any of the top three, either in the field, or at the bat.

OUTFIELD:

The Negro leagues had the luxury of numerous outstanding ballhawks. There were literally dozens of outfielders who possessed all the tools necessary for greatness. A couple of them were true superstars, who could hit, hit with power, run, field, and throw. Oscar Charleston, Turkey Stearnes, and Pete Hill fell into that category. They were ably supported on the all-star team by the flashy "Cool Papa" Bell, the cocky Chino Smith, and the lackadaisical Willard Brown. Charleston, Stearnes, Brown, and little Chino all ripped the ball at a .350+ pace during their careers, with 20 or more home runs a year. Bell hit a cool .337, with explosive speed that turned singles into doubles and doubles into triples. His greatest weapon was his baserunning ability, which often rattled opposing pitchers, much like the speed of Jackie Robinson. Pete Hill could do it all but, since he played around the turn of the century, his batting statistics are severely lacking. His reported .307 batting average was probably much higher, and his home run average of nine homers a year would have threatened the 30 mark if he had hit against the lively ball.

UTILITY:

The utility players are two of the most exceptional players on the team. Martin Dihigo was arguably the greatest all-around player in the history of the game. He excelled in center field. He was selected as the all-star second base-man on many Negro league teams. In addition, on the mound, he won over 250 games in his 26-year career. At the plate, he was a solid .319 hitter who aver-aged 25 homers a year. Dihigo is the only baseball player in history to be hon-ored in the Hall of Fame in four countries: the United States, Mexico, Cuba, and Venezuela.

John Beckwith, the moody slugger from Louisville, Kentucky, rattled the fences everywhere he played, piling up a .350 batting average, with 30 home runs a year. He played a respectable shortstop or third base, and occasionally took over the catching duties.

Jud Wilson, sadly, had to be left off the squad. Jud was a pure hitter, who spanked the ball at a .347 clip for 24 years. He had good power and was a dan-gerous clutch hitter.

All-Time Negro League All-Star Team

Catcher	Josh Gibson*
	Louis Santop
Pitcher	"Smokey Joe" Williams*
	"Bullet Joe" Rogan
	Satchel Paige
	"Cannonball Dick" Redding
	Willie Foster
	Ray Brown
	Leon Day
First Base	Buck Leonard*
	Mule Suttles
Second Base	Bill Monroe*
	Sammy T. Hughes
Shortstop	John Henry Lloyd*
	Dobie Moore
Third Base	Ray Dandridge*
	Oliver "Ghost" Marcelle
Outfield	Oscar Charleston*
	Turkey Stearnes*
	Pete Hill*

Oscar Charleston

Outfield (continued)

"Cool Papa" Bell
Chino Smith
Willard Brown

Utility

Martin Dihigo
John Beckwith

Note: An asterisk (*) denotes the starting nine players.

Left to right: **Mule Suttles, Willie Foster, Turkey Stearnes. (Robert Peterson.)**

In addition to the all-time Negro league all-star team, there were many other stars who played in relative obscurity outside the umbrella of organized baseball during the first half of the twentieth century, who were nearly as talented as those who were selected for the team.

Many of these players deserve consideration for election into baseball's Hall of Fame in Cooperstown, New York. Since the Hall was opened to Negro league players in 1971, with the admittance of Satchel Paige, a total of only 16 players have been elected.

It is likely that some well-deserving players like Turkey Stearnes and Mule Suttles will finally get their just reward, but that will still leave 10 members of the all-star team on the outside, looking in.

The author's selections for consideration for membership into the Baseball Hall of Fame in Cooperstown, New York, including those already inducted, are:

Catcher:	Josh Gibson* Louis Santop	Biz Mackey Roy Campanella*
Pitcher:	Satchel Paige* Bullet Joe Rogan* Smokey Joe Williams* Cannonball Dick Redding John Donaldson Rube Foster* Willie Foster* Leon Day* Ray Brown Rats Henderson Max Manning	Jose Mendez Chet Brewer Ted Trent Nip Winters Webster McDonald Andy Cooper Bill Byrd Hilton Smith Bill Holland Plunk Drake Dizzy Dismukes
First Base:	Buck Leonard* Mule Suttles Edgar Wesley	Ben Taylor Bob Boyd
Second Base:	Sammy Hughes Bill Monroe	Frank Grant Newt Allen
Shortstop:	John Henry Lloyd* Dobie Moore Dick Lundy Willie Wells* Sam Bankhead	John Beckwith Home Run Johnson Artie Wilson Bus Clarkson
Third Base:	Ray Dandridge* Judy Johnson* Oliver Marcelle	Jud Wilson Dave Malarcher
Outfield:	Turkey Stearnes Oscar Charleston* Cool Papa Bell* Cristobal Torriente Pete Hill	Heavy Johnson Rap Dixon Monte Irvin* Larry Doby* Bernardo Baro

	Spot Poles	Sam Jethroe
	Willard Brown	Alejandro Oms
	Chino Smith	Wild Bill Wright
Utility:	Martin Dihigo*	
	Double Duty Radcliffe	
Honorable Mention:	Buck O'Neil	Valentin Dreke
	Bruce Petway	Slim Jones
	Ed Rile	Dave Brown
	Hank Thompson	Bingo DeMoss
	Frog Redus	Jimmy Lyons
	Fats Jenkins	George Giles
	Jelly Gardner	Vic Harris
	Crush Holloway	Frank Wickware
	Sam Streeter	Jimmy Crutchfield
Manager:	Rube Foster*	C.J. Taylor
	Oscar Charleston	C.I. Taylor

Note: An asterisk (*) denotes a current member of the baseball Hall of Fame in Cooperstown, New York.

Roy Campanella was elected by the major league committee. All others were elected by the Negro leagues committee.

Cuban Winter League
All-Star Team, 1882–1960

The Cuban people began a love affair with baseball more than 130 years ago, not long after the game was popularized in the United States. According to oral history, the game was brought back to Cuba from the United States by a Cuban student, Nemesio Guillot, in 1866. The first recorded baseball game, as reported by John Thorn and Pete Palmer in *Total Baseball*, was played in Havana in June 1866, and pitted Cuban longshoremen against seamen from a visiting American cargo vessel.

The game quickly took hold, and before long baseball teams sprang up all over the tiny Spanish possession. By 1871, one Cuban player, Esteban Bellan, was playing major league baseball in the United States. Bellan held down third base for the Troy Haymakers and the New York Mutuals, from 1871 to 1873, batting .252 in 60 games. He had, in fact, played with the Haymakers as early as 1869, in their amateur days, when they held the powerful Cincinnati Redlegs, baseball's first professional team, to a 17–17 tie. It was the Reds' only blemish over an 80-game run.

The first professional baseball teams in Cuba were the Havana Baseball Club, founded in 1872, and the Matanzas Baseball Club, founded the following year. The first professional game was played on December 27, 1874, when the Havana team with Esteban Bellan routed Matanzas, 51–9.

The first professional baseball league was formed in 1878, the Liga de Beisbol Professional Cubana, a three team league, consisting of Havana, Almendares, and Matanzas. From 1878 until 1960, professional baseball flourished in the island nation, finally coming to an end when Fidel Castro took control of the country and eliminated all professional sports on the island.

In the early years of the Cuban League, Havana dominated the league. They won the first pennant in 1878, and took nine of twelve through 1892. The first big baseball star in Cuba, after Esteban Bellan, was Pablo Ronquilla, the league's first batting champion, who hit .350 in 1885, the first year batting and pitching statistics were maintained. Adolfo Lujan was the first pitching leader, going 5–0 in 1885–86. Other nineteenth century baseball luminaries included Antonio Garcia, a power hitting catcher for the Havana club during the 1880s, and pitchers Jose Pastoriza and Miguel Pratts.

During the last decade of the nineteenth century, according to Cuban historian Ralph Maya, the Spanish authorities in Cuba discouraged the people from playing baseball, feeling it was an unmanly sport. They also considered it to be an American sport, and they tried to suppress anything American, since they were involved in a dispute with the United States at the time. The authorities even cancelled the 1895-96 and '97 Cuban League seasons in an unsuccessful attempt to eliminate the sport.

In 1898, the U.S. battleship *Maine* was blown up in Havana Harbor, precipitating the Spanish-American War. The war ended less than four months later, with Spain ceding several Caribbean territories to the United States. As part of the treaty, Cuba was declared to be an independent territory, under the protection of the United States.

As the twentieth century dawned, Cuban baseball became a force to be reckoned with in the western hemisphere. Visiting American major league teams were manhandled by Cuban squads over a period of five or six years. The first team to visit Cuba was the Cincinnati Reds, with Miller Huggins and Hans Lobert, in 1908. To their chagrin, the Cubans beat them seven times in eleven games. Jose Mendez, one of Cuba's legendary hurlers, whipped John Ganzel's team three times, including a 1–0, one hitter.

The following year, the Cubans took the measure of the World Champion Detroit Tigers, seven out of 12, although the Tigers were without the services of their two best players, Ty Cobb and Sam Crawford. Hughie Jenning's boys were completely embarrassed in one game when Cuban right hander, Eustaquio Pedroso, blew his fastball past the Detroiters for eleven innings, en route to a 1–0 no-hitter.

Returning in 1910, with both Cobb and Crawford in tow, Detroit reversed the results, winning seven of twelve. When the series was finally over, however, it was discovered that three American Negro league players had out hit the mighty Ty Cobb. John Henry Lloyd slugged the ball at a .500 clip, while Grant "Home Run" Johnson (.412) and Bruce Petway (.388) all surpassed Cobb's .369 average. To add insult to injury, the fleet-footed Cobb was cut down stealing three times in three attempts by the aforementioned Petway. Cobb stormed out of Cuba in disgust, vowing never to play against blacks again. He never did.

Other major league teams visited the island over the next several years, including John McGraw's New York Giants, Connie Mack's Philadelphia Athletics, and Red Dooin's Philadelphia Phillies. When the dust cleared, the Cubans had played the major leaguers to a standstill, winning 32 of 64 games.

Jose Mendez's record in 18 games against the best the major leagues could offer was eight wins against seven losses, three shutouts including a one hitter and a two hitter, and an earned run average of about 2.50.

After an eight-year hiatus, the New York Giants returned to Cuba in 1920 for an exhibition series against the Almendares and Havana teams. The first eight games of the series ended in a 3–3–2 deadlock, with Isidro Fabre of Almendares blanking the visiting major leaguers 5–0 in the finale. At that time, a ringer arrived from the United States to grace the Giant lineup. His name was Babe Ruth, and he was coming off a sensational season with the New York Yankees. His 54 home runs had almost doubled his old major league mark of 29, established the previous year. The Giants, with Ruth, whipped the Havana and Almendares teams six times in nine games, with one tie. The Bambino batted .345 for the series, with two home runs, but he was upstaged by the Cuban slugger, Cristobal Torriente, who batted an even .400. More importantly, the Cuban strongman had demolished the Giants single-handedly in game five, smashing three home runs and a double, good for six RBIs, as Fabre and his Almendares teammates routed the New Yorkers 11–4. Although the Giants won the overall series 9-5-3, the Almendares team took their series with the New Yorkers 4-3-2.

American major league teams continued to visit the island periodically until 1960, when Castro and his people were isolated from the western world. In 1947, the Brooklyn Dodgers, who had played an exhibition series against a Cuban all-star team in 1941, moved their spring training camp to Havana in an attempt to protect rookie Jackie Robinson from the racial problems he would have encountered in Florida.

Cuba was the hub of Caribbean baseball for over 80 years, from the late 1870s until 1960. Moreover, it was the center of integrated baseball in the twentieth century, until 1945. The tiny island off the coast of Florida attracted the best baseball players from all over the Caribbean basin, Mexico, Central and South America, even the American Negro leagues. As early as 1908, black players like John Henry Lloyd made annual winter treks south to play in the Cuban Winter League. Lloyd was followed by Negro league legends like Oscar Charleston, Pete Hill, Grant "Home Run" Johnson, Chino Smith, Willie Wells, and Ray Dandridge.

In the early 1920s, the Cuban Winter League was a veritable who's who of professional baseball, both black and white. For instance, the 1922-23 Marianao club had the great Cuban and Negro league star, Cristobal Torriente, on their roster, along with white major leaguers Eddie Brown, Jess Petty, and Charlie Dressen. Almendares had Cuban and Negro league players Bernardo Baro and Valentin Dreke, plus major leaguers Jakie May and Oscar Fuhr. Not to be outdone, Havana teamed Negro leaguer John Henry Lloyd with Cuban League star Pelayo Chacon and major leaguers Adolfo Luque and John Bischoff.

It was baseball at its purest.

Almendares Park. (Yuyo Ruiz.)

Unfortunately for the great black Cuban ballplayers of the time, the American major league owners deemed them unsuitable to play alongside white players in organized ball. They did however, play everywhere else in the western hemisphere — Cuba, Mexico, Puerto Rico, the Dominican Republic, Venezuela, Colombia, Nicaragua, and Panama. They even strutted their stuff in the United States, although not in organized ball. Some of the most outstanding Cuban players of the first two decades of the twentieth century participated in the Negro leagues. Names like Antonio Garcia, Julian Castillo, Silvio Garcia, Strike Gonzalez, Jose Mendez, Luis Bustamente, Regino Garcia, and Eustaquio Pedroso dotted the rosters of teams like the All Cubans, and the Cuban Stars, beginning in 1904. Cuban teams continued to perform in the Negro leagues until 1950, when the New York Cubans with Sandy Amoros and Ray Noble played in the Negro American League East.

The quality of play in the Cuban league down through the years was of the highest caliber. It is possible to gain some insight into the capabilities of the league, since many of the players played in both the Negro leagues and the Cuban Winter League during the 1930s and '40s. A handful had even played in the major leagues, as far back as 1911. Many of the later players joined the high minor leagues and the major leagues once Jackie Robinson broke the color barrier in 1945.

This book has several tables showing these comparisons. In general, the Cuban Winter League appears to have been about on par with the AAA minor leagues. Obviously, many of the black Cubans who played prior to 1947 were of major league caliber and, not surprisingly, more than a few of them were superstars.

It is perhaps impossible to select a Cuban Winter League all-star team, but the primary purpose of this exercise is to obtain some recognition, however slight, for the many great baseball players who played out their careers in relative obscurity. They played for their love of the game. They received very little money, and no recognition outside their homeland. It is time their memories were honored.

Several Cuban baseball historians offered assistance with this project. Jorge S. Figueredo, Angel Torres, and Ralph Maya provided the author with their thoughts, suggestions and, in some cases, with their selections for Cuban League all-star teams. Jorge S. Figueredo, in fact, selected three separate all-star teams, by era. He selected one team for the period 1878–1909, a second all-star team for the period 1910–1939, and a third all-star team for the period 1940–1961.

The author has selected only one team. Figueredo is correct, in that it is difficult to compare players from different eras; however, major league all-star teams are selected in that manner, and the teams presented in this book will follow the same format.

CATCHER:

Cuba has been fortunate in having had many outstanding catchers in their history. Some of the more notable ones are Antonio Garcia, Gervasio "Strike" Gonzalez, Mike Gonzalez, Jose Fernandez, Ray Noble, and Regino Garcia.

Antonio Garcia and Mike Gonzalez were selected for the first team, while Jose Fernandez and Ray Noble were selected for the second team. Strike Gonzalez was not selected even though he was a superior defensive catcher, with a cannon for a throwing arm. The right handed hitter had a mediocre bat, compiling a .247 batting average in 17 years.

• Antonio Garcia, the #1 backstop on the Cuban League team, was arguably the greatest Cuban League player of the nineteenth century. In addition to his defensive capabilities, Garcia was a powerful hitter who won four batting titles, with averages of .448 in 1888, .364 in 1889-90, .362 in 1892, and .385 in 1892-93. He led the league in home runs twice, doubles once, and triples once.

Garcia's .316 career batting average is more impressive when you realize it was compiled during a time when pitching dominated. Very few batters hit more than .250 during the first 30 years of Cuban Winter League baseball due to the fact that games were played only on weekends, and each team carried only one or two pitchers. Great pitchers like Adolfo Lujan and Jose Pastoriza pitched in almost 90 percent of their team's games. There were no soft touches on the mound when Garcia played. But he hit them all with authority. In fact, he is

Antonio Garcia. (Refocus Productions.)

the only nineteenth century hitter with a career batting average over .300. The #2 hitter, Alfredo Arcano, hit .276 over a 19-year period.

In addition to his high percentage, Garcia was also the league's premier power hitter. His three home runs a year, in the dead ball era, and in the wide open parks of early Cuba, might well translate into 20 or more home runs a year in the major leagues, in the era of the lively ball.

Antonio Garcia also played in the American Negro leagues for seven years, from 1905 to 1912, as a member of the All Cubans and Cuban Stars teams. He usually batted in the cleanup position.

Garcia was elected to the Cuban Baseball Hall of Fame in the first year of its existence, 1939.

• Miguel "Mike" Gonzalez, a white Cuban, played baseball year round for 28 years. He played in the Cuban League for 23 years, in the Negro leagues for six years, and in the major leagues for 17 years. Gonzalez continued to coach in the major leagues for many years after his retirement as a player. He even managed 22 games for the St. Louis Cardinals, on an interim basis, in 1938 and 1940. His managerial record was 9–13.

Gonzalez was born in Havana, Cuba, on September 24, 1890. He began his professional baseball career with Fe in the Cuban Winter League in 1910 at the age of 19. One year later, he joined the Cuban Stars of the Negro league, and in 1912, he was a member of the Boston Red Sox of the American League.

Gonzalez was a superior defensive catcher, who was more than adequate at the plate. In Cuba, he had a career batting average of .290, with 29 extra base hits a year. He rapped the ball at a .324 pace for Havana in 1915-16. In the major leagues he hit the ball at a .253 clip, with 31 extra base hits. His most productive year was 1924, when he hit .296 with 53 RBIs.

PITCHER:

The Cuban Winter League (CWL) has seen an array of great pitchers. The pitchers selected for the all-star team include Jose Mendez, Luis Padron, Adolfo

Luque, Eustaquio Pedroso, Jose Munoz, Carlos Royer, and Manuel Garcia. The second team is just as formidable, with Jose Acosta, Rodolfo Fernandez, Adolfo Lujan, Agapito Mayor, Jose Pastoriza, and Ray Brown.

• The greatest pitcher in Cuban League history is Jose Mendez. Known as "The Black Diamond," Mendez demonstrated his skills in 18 contests against touring major league teams between 1908 and 1911, compiling an 8–7 record against the likes of Christy Mathewson, Eddie Plank, and Howie Camnitz. He outdueled Plank, the great Philadelphia southpaw, twice in 1910, by scores of 5–2 and 7–5. He was 1–1 against Math-

Jose Mendez. (Yuyo Ruiz.)

ewson, beating John McGraw's ace 7–4 with four shutout innings of relief.

Mendez, who stood only 5'8" tall and weighed 160 pounds soaking wet, was blazing fast, with a sharp breaking curveball, a change of pace, and good control. His smooth delivery and constant speed changes kept batters off balance and destroyed their timing. His Cuban League career statistics show a 72–26 record, for a winning percentage of .735.

In six years, as player/manager of the Kansas City Monarchs of the Negro National League, Mendez compiled a pitching record of 20–4, while leading the Monarchs to three league championships. He is a member of the 1900–1925 Negro league all-star team.

He was elected to the Cuban Baseball Hall of Fame in 1939.

• Luis Padron was the exact opposite of Jose Mendez. Where Mendez was right handed, Padron was a southpaw. Where Mendez was blazing fast, Padron's best pitch was his changeup. Where Mendez was an all-American out, Padron was a long ball hitter who could help himself with the lumber. His average of six home runs a year in the dead ball era might have skyrocketed to 25 or more had he played after 1920. When not pitching, Padron played second base, third base, and outfield. He was an exceptionally fast baserunner, who once stole 21 bases in just 43 games.

"The Mule," as he was called, compiled a record (still incomplete) of 39–23 in Cuba from 1900 to 1919, while hitting .251. His first year in the Cuban Winter League was his best. He racked up a league leading record of 13–4 on the mound, and pounded the ball at a .313 clip, only 20 points behind the league leader. The big left handed slugger was such a threat at the plate that he played most of his career in the outfield rather than on the mound. He led the league in hitting in 1902, with an average of .463, the highest season average in Cuban Winter League history. He also led the league in triples and home runs that year. In all, Padron led the league in home runs three times, in triples four times, and in doubles three times. His career extra base hit average of 28 extra base hits for every 550 at-bats is #2 on the all time list, for the period from 1881 to 1910, trailing only the powerful Julian Castillo. His average of six home runs a year is #1 in Cuba during the dead ball era.

Padron also pitched in the Negro leagues for 18 years, where his incomplete records show 26 wins against 18 losses. He is considered to be one of the three greatest pitchers in Cuban history, along with Mendez and Pedroso. He joined the other Cuban immortals in the Baseball Hall of Fame in 1943.

• Eustaquio "Bombin" Pedroso, the third member of the Cuban pitching triumvirate, was a big, rugged, right handed pitcher with an outstanding fast ball and good control. Although his Cuban League career statistics have not yet been compiled, he led the league in victories twice, with 11 wins in 1913 and 10 wins in 1914-15. He also led the league in batting one year, slamming the ball for a .413 average in 1915-16.

In 1909, he made headlines all over the little island when he tossed an 11-inning no-hitter against the American League Champion Detroit Tigers, winning 1–0. Overall, Pedroso won four of six decisions against major league barnstorming teams, from 1909 through 1911.

Pedroso, in addition to a 20-year career in the Cuban League, also pitched in the Negro leagues for 21 years, primarily with the Cuban Stars. He played first base, outfield, and catcher, when not pitching, to take advantage of his potent bat. He was elected to the Cuban HOF in 1962.

• Adolfo Luque, known as "The Pride of Havana," had a long, distinguished baseball career, both in Cuba and in the United States. A tough, hot tempered pitcher of superior talent, Luque, a white Cuban, pitched year round for more than 20 years. His 22-year Cuban League career resulted in 93 victories against 62 losses. He led the league in victories, with nine in 1928–29. In the American major leagues, the 5'10", 170 pound curveball artist, racked up 194 wins against 179 losses, from 1914 to 1935. In 1923, pitching for the Cincinnati Reds, Luque led the National League in victories (27), winning percentage (.771), shutouts (six), and earned run average (1.93).

Not only was Luque a world class pitcher, he was also a terror with the bat. He still leads all Hispanic major league pitchers in career batting average, runs, hits, RBIs, and triples. His .227 batting average included 46 extra base hits in

1043 at-bats, with 90 runs batted in. In Cuba, he hit .252, with 29 extra base hits in 671 at-bats. He won the Cuban League batting championship in 1917, with an average of .355.

Adolfo Luque managed in the Cuban League for many years. He once pulled a gun on a Negro league player who didn't want to take the mound on his scheduled day. The player quickly changed his mind. Luque joined other Cuban immortals in the HOF in 1958.

• Jose Munoz was another Cuban right hander with a smoking fastball and immaculate control. In addition, he possessed a crackling screwball that drove left handers off the plate in fear of their lives. Munoz was considered to be the premier pitcher in Cuba during the first decade of the twentieth century. He led the league in winning percentage in 1906, with an 8–1 record. He went 13–1 in 1908, losing the title to Jose Mendez who was 9–0. According to James A. Riley, Munoz beat Eddie Plank and the Philadelphia A's 2–1 in an exhibition game in Havana in 1910.

Jose Munoz pitched in the Cuban Winter League for 15 years, from 1900 through 1914, finishing with a total of 81 victories against 57 defeats. He also pitched in the Negro leagues from 1904 until 1916, but his statistics have not yet been tabulated. When not pitching, Munoz played the outfield, and reportedly had a good bat.

He was elected to the Cuban Baseball Hall of Fame in 1940.

• Carlos "Bebe" Royer, according to Ralph Maya, is the best kept secret in Cuban baseball. The right handed finesse pitcher was the most dominant pitcher in Cuba at the turn of the century, but his achievements have long since been forgotten. Martin Dihigo, Jose Mendez, and others seem to have had better press agents.

Bebe Royer led the league in winning percentage twice, with a perfect 17–0 in 1902, and 13–3 in 1904. He also compiled a 12–3 record in 1901. His three-year total of 42–6 has never been equaled. From 1901 through 1904 he was almost unbeatable, winning 60 of 76 decisions and throwing 74 complete games in 76 starts.

Royer was also a proficient hitter, with a career average of .228. Early in his career, he was a position

Bebe Royer

player, compiling a .256 batting average from 1890 to 1899. He batted .391 in 1894-95, losing the title to Alfredo Arcano, who hit .430. He pitched in only 15 games during his first ten years in the league, winning six and losing seven, but by 1901, approaching 30 years of age, he had established himself as a premier pitcher. He retired in 1911 with a career record of 87 victories against 40 losses, a .685 winning percentage. He was in the first group of players elected to Cuba's Hall of Fame in 1939.

• Manuel "Cocaina" Garcia was so nicknamed because his fastball made batters look like they were in a cocaine stupor and unable to focus on the ball. The 5'8", 185 pound southpaw also had a sharp breaking curveball and a spectacular drop. He was an outstanding pitcher in Mexico, Cuba, the Dominican Republic, Venezuela, and the American Negro leagues, from 1926 through 1949.

During his career, the little left hander won between 200 and 300 games. His exact victory total is not known because many of the statistics are still incomplete. In his homeland, he finished with a 91–60 record. He led the league in winning percentage three times: in 1942-43 with 10–3, the following year with 12–4, and in 1946-47 with 10–3. His Mexican statistics show 96 victories and 68 losses, from 1941 to 1949. In 1942, with Puebla, he went 19–14. Three years later, with Tampico, he was 18–11.

Garcia was also a good hitter, compiling an career average of .260 in Cuba and .281 in Mexico, with two .316 seasons. When he wasn't pitching, he often played the outfield or first base. In 1937-38, playing primarily in the outfield for Santa Clara in the Cuban Winter League, Garcia smoked the ball at a .314 clip in 172 at-bats.

Cocaina Garcia was elected to the Cuban Baseball Hall of Fame in 1969. He is also a member of the Venezuelan Hall of Fame.

FIRST BASE:

Julian Castillo and Jud Wilson hold down first base on the all-time Cuban Winter League team. Their backups are Lorenzo Cabrera and Jose Rodriguez.

• Julian Castillo, a big raw boned right handed hitter, a product of Cuba's sugar cane fields, was the premier power hitter of the first decade of the twentieth century. He was built like Lou Gehrig, except he was about two inches taller and 40 pounds heavier than the Iron Horse. He had the same broad shoulders as Gehrig, a massive chest, large forearms, and legs like tree trunks. The 6'2" first baseman routinely hit between .294 and .408, in an era when pitching dominated and batting averages of .220 to .250 were the norm.

During the Castillo era, baseball games were played only on the weekends, after the field work was completed for the week. Teams carried only one or two pitchers, so there were no soft touches anywhere in the league, as mentioned earlier. The batters faced outstanding pitching game after game.

Julian Castillo. (Yuyo Ruiz.)

Yet, Julian Castillo hit them all. He won four batting titles in his 13-year career, hitting .454 in his rookie year of 1901, .330 in 1903, .315 in 1908-9, and .408 in 1910. His .454 average is the second highest season average of all time. He also corralled two home run titles, and led the league in hits three times, doubles six times, and triples four times. His career average of 44 extra base hits a year included 25 doubles, 15 triples, and four home runs. Luis Padron, the #2 man, had only 28 extra base hits a year.

According to Riley, Castillo was not a good fielder or a good baserunner. He relied solely on his bat to carry the day and, by all accounts, that was good enough. His .310 career batting average is the highest average of the time. Castillo played in the dead ball era and in a park where the outfield fences were 400–500 feet distant. His 44 extra base hits a year compare favorably with those of his American contemporaries, Harry Stovey, Dan Brouthers, and Sam Thompson. Under today's conditions, he would probably slug 20–30 home runs a year, on average, with 40–50 homers in specific years not unlikely.

Julian Castillo also played in the Negro league from 1904 to 1912, but his statistics have not yet been amassed. He was elected to the Cuban Hall of Fame in 1943.

• Jud "Boojum" Wilson was an awesome hitter who compiled the highest career batting average in Cuban Winter League history —.372, over a six-year career. He led the CWL in batting twice, with averages of .430 in 1925 and .424

in 1927. He also led the league in homers (three) and stolen bases (10), in 1925, and triples (seven) in 1927.

Boojum's CWL home run average of 13 homers for every 550 at-bats would translate into 25 homers a year in the major leagues. To show he was not partial only to Cuban pitchers, the left handed slugger also pounded the ball to the tune of .347 in the Negro leagues over a period of 24 years. Against major league competition, he hit a robust .360, with 12 extra base hits in 25 exhibition games. His big league victims included Lefty Grove (three hits in five at-bats), Dizzy Dean (2 for 6), Ed Rommell (4 for 8), Dazzy Vance (1 for 3), and Fred Frankhouse (3 for 6 with two home runs).

Boojum Wilson was completely fearless at the plate. He felt he could hit any pitcher alive, and his statistics support that attitude. He was a hardnosed player, who played all out in every game. Built like an inverted triangle, he had broad shoulders, a massive chest that tapered down to a tiny waist, and spindly legs. He was an aggressive hitter, fielder, and base runner, whose well earned reputation as a brawler intimidated both opposing players and umpires. John Holway, in his outstanding book on Negro league baseball, *Blackball Stars*, said, "Jud was as famous for his fighting as for his hitting. He hated umpires." Wilson's friend Jake Stephens confirmed that observation, noting, "The minute he saw an umpire, he became a maniac." Teammate Clint Thomas, in the same book, added, "He'd kill you. He was dangerous. He was like a goddam gorilla. He was never out, the pitcher never throwed a strike. All ball players were scared of him."

Defensively, the stocky, bowlegged infielder usually played either third base or first base. Although not a Fancy Dan with the glove, he somehow got the job done in a creditable manner. At third base, he often surrounded the ball, knocked it down, then picked it up and threw the runner out. He had a cannon for an arm.

Jud Wilson is also a member of the 1926–50 Negro league all-star team.

Second Base:

• The premier second baseman in Cuban Winter League baseball was Manuel Cueto. His backup is Bienvenido Jiminez. Cueto, known as "Hombre Diablo" (Devil Man), was born in Havana on February 8, 1892. He played in the CWL from 1912 to 1933, batting a hefty .298. The 5'5", 157 pound infielder also played briefly with the Washington Senators from 1914 to 1919, batting .227 in 379 at-bats.

Cueto was a dependable defensive player with a good glove. But he was better known as an offensive threat. The little right handed hitter was an outstanding bat handler who could hit, hit and run, bunt, or coax a walk, depending on the situation. He was a contact hitter who rarely struck out, and who packed surprising power in his small frame, averaging 22 doubles, six triples, and three home runs, for every 550 at-bats. He combined 164 base hits a year with 75 bases on balls to score 89 runs and drive in another 46. He also stole 22 bases a year.

The Devil Man won three batting titles during his career, with .344 in 1918-19, .364 in 1924-25, and .404 in 1926-27. He also hit .406 in 1915-16, and .331 in 1923-24. He won the home run title in 1921.

Cueto was elected to the Hall of Fame in 1950.

• Bienvenido Jimenez was recognized as an outstanding second baseman in Cuba from 1913 to 1929. Jimenez, called "Hooks" because of his bowed legs, could do it all. He had exceptional range in the field, a reliable glove, and a strong throwing arm. At the plate, he was a better than average hitter, with some power. On the bases, he was a dangerous runner, who averaged almost 50 stolen bases a year. He often batted in the leadoff position to take advantage of his exceptional bat handling skills.

The big infielder also played in the Negro leagues during the same period. According to James A. Riley, Jimenez was a hardnosed player, and one of the top second basemen in the league, second only to Bingo DeMoss.

His 12-year career in the Cuban Winter League included one batting title and one home run crown. He had several .300 seasons, finishing with a career average of .266. In 1918-19, he enjoyed his finest season, batting .321, with 28 runs scored and 30 stolen bases in 36 games. He also batted .300 in 1922-23 and .291 in 1920-21. He was elected to the Cuban Hall of Fame in 1951.

SHORTSTOP:

• John Henry Lloyd was one of the world's greatest shortstops, not only in Cuba, but anywhere. He is generally considered to be on par with Honus Wagner as the #1 shortstop of all time. Lloyd, who stood 5'11" tall and weighed 180 pounds, was a true superstar. He had no weakness in the field on the bases, or at bat.

The Florida native was called "El Cuchara" (The Shovel) in Cuba because his big hands scooped the ball out of the dirt like a large shovel. As noted in the section on Negro league baseball, Lloyd had a career batting average of .353 in the States. His average in Cuba was almost as good, .331. He put together season averages of .400, .388, .341, .393, .344, .372, .373, and .365 during his winter sojourns to the island nation. He won the batting title in 1915 and led the league in hits once, doubles once, triples twice, and home runs once.

Lloyd was a member of the Cuban all-star team that played against the Detroit Tigers in 1910. Although the Cuban team lost the series seven games to five, Lloyd banged the ball at a .500 clip to win batting honors. Ty Cobb, the American League batting champion that year, with an average of .383, hit Mendez and company for an average of .369, fourth highest behind Lloyd and two other Negro leaguers.

• Silvio Garcia, a tall, stocky infielder, was born in Limonar, Cuba, on October 11, 1914. His career covered the years from 1937 to 1954, and included careers in Cuba, the United States, Mexico, Venezuela, the Dominican Republic, Canada, and Puerto Rico. Wherever baseball was played, there you could find Silvio.

The 6' tall, 195 pound shortstop batted right and threw right. He was a sensational defensive shortstop, a noted base stealer, and a powerful hitter. His Cuban Winter League career batting average of .284, was dotted with a number of .300+ seasons. He led the league in batting in 1941-42 when he hit .351 for Cienfuegos.

He compiled career averages of .332 in the Dominican Republic, .298 in Puerto Rico, .322 in the Negro leagues, .339 in Mexico, and .340 in the lower minor leagues at the end of his career.

Silvio Garcia entered Cuba's Baseball Hall of Fame in 1975.

THIRD BASE:

• Rafael Almeida, a white Cuban, played major league baseball for the Cincinnati Reds from 1911 to 1913, batting .270 in 102 games. He also played with the All Cubans team in the Negro leagues in 1904 and 1905. Most of his playing career, however, was spent in his native Cuba, where he played from 1904 to 1925. He broke into professional baseball as a 16-year-old third baseman with Habana in 1904. He held his own in the field, but was overmatched at the plate, batting only .136 in six games.

By the age of 20, he had developed into a respectable hitter, stinging the ball at a .297 clip for Almendares. He batted over .300 twice, hitting .388 in 1913, and .321 in 1914-15.

The graceful third baseman was one of the first players selected for the Cuban Baseball Hall of Fame when it opened in 1939.

• Ray Dandridge was one of the game's all-time greats. He is a member of the Hall of Fame in both the United States and Mexico. Ray batted .322 in the Negro leagues, .347 in Mexico, .316 in AAA minor league ball, and .282 in Cuba. He is also a member of the all-time Negro league all-star team.

Dandy played ball in the little island nation during the winter from 1937 to 1952. In addition to a dependable bat, he gave the Cienfuegos' fans some of the slickest defensive third base they had seen in decades. He also captured the stolen base crown in 1937, with 11 stolen bases in 211 at-bats.

The 5'7", 170 pound infielder was a true baseball vagabond, playing the game year round in the United States, Cuba, Mexico, Puerto Rico, and the Dominican Republic over a 23-year period. In the United States, Dandridge played in the Negro leagues during the summer, then played exhibition games against major league all-star teams in the fall. He tattooed pitchers like Sal Maglie, Vic Raschi, Dizzy Dean, and Allie Reynolds to the tune of .347 in 13 games.

Too old to play in the major leagues after Jackie Robinson opened the door, Dandridge played ball at AAA Minneapolis, a New York Giant farm club, stroking the ball at a .318 clip over a four-year period.

OUTFIELD:

The Cuban Winter League all star outfield could match bats with any outfield anywhere. The starting six includes Cristobal Torriente, Oscar Charleston, Bernardo Baro, Jacinto Calvo, Valentin Dreke, and Alejandro Oms. All six were world class hitters, with a good balance of power and speed. They were also gold glove caliber outfielders. Torriente, Charleston, and Oms were true superstars, possessing the five qualities necessary for that exalted station — to hit, hit with power, run, field, and throw.

• Cristobal Torriente was known as the Babe Ruth of Cuba. He starred in both the Negro leagues and the Cuban Winter League for 22 years, from 1913 to 1934. He won two batting championships in Cuba, hitting .387 in 1914-15 and .360 in 1919-20. He also hit .402 in 1915-16. In 13 years in Cuba, Torriente batted .350 or better, eight times. His career batting average of .352 is #3 all-time, behind Wilson and Charleston.

Cristobal Torriente also captured two home run crowns in 1920-21 and 1922-23. His eight home runs a year in the spacious Cuban ballparks, hitting against a dead ball, would translate to about 17 homers a year in the major leagues. The stocky left handed slugger concentrated on triples early in his career, leading the CWL in three base hits five times. He also led in doubles once.

In 1920, the Cuban strongman met his American counterpart, Babe Ruth, in an exhibition series in Havana. The New York Giants, with the great Bambino in the lineup, took the series six games to three, as noted earlier, but Torriente outhit the American home run champion .400 to .345, and outhomered him three to two.

He was elected to the Cuban Hall of Fame in 1939.

• Oscar Charleston could do it all. He had no weakness. Like Torriente, the tall, graceful center fielder was a genuine franchise player. Many baseball experts consider him to be the greatest player in Negro league history. His counterpart in the major leagues would be Willie Mays.

Charleston played in the Cuban Winter League for nine years, starting in 1920 and ending in 1931. He won the batting championship in 1930-31 with an average of .373. In all, he batted over .350, seven times, and four times exceeded the magic .400 mark. He also won a home run title, hitting five dingers in 1927-28.

The 6', 190 pound gazelle, not to be considered a one dimensional player, led the league in stolen bases in 1923, with 31 in 62 games, and 1927 with 11 in 33 games.

His .365 batting average trails only Jud Wilson in Cuban Winter League history. The handsome outfielder is a member of the Hall of Fame in two countries — the United States and Cuba. He is also on the all-time Negro league all-star team.

• Bernardo Baro was another all-around outfielder, who starred in both the Cuban Winter League and the Negro leagues during the second and third decades of the twentieth century. Baro hit .302 with five home runs a year in the Negro leagues from 1915 to 1929. Over the same period, he whacked the ball at a .313 pace for Almendares in the CWL. He led the league in batting in 1922-23 with an average of .401. He also had averages of .364 in 1918-19 and .352 in 1919-20.

Baro was a small player who relied on speed rather than power, although he could hit the ball for distance on occasion. In the field, he was a blur running down balls that most outfielders wouldn't even come close to.

The left handed hitter played in the ten-game exhibition series against Babe Ruth and the New York Giants in 1920, and led all hitters with an average of .405.

According to Riley, Baro was a hypersensitive, quick-tempered individual, who was involved in a number of on-field fights during his career. He suffered a mental breakdown in 1929 while playing for the Cuban Stars in the Negro leagues. He didn't play ball in Cuba that winter, but did return to the United States again in the spring of 1930. He returned home in June, and died shortly thereafter, at the young age of 37. Fifteen years later, he was voted into the Cuban Hall of Fame.

• Jacinto Calvo was a white Cuban who played in the Cuban Winter League from 1913 to 1927. He also played in the Negro leagues for three years, and with the Washington Senators of the American League for two years. In the majors, the 5'10", 160 pound left handed batter hit only .161 in 31 games, with one home run.

Calvo was born in Havana on June 11, 1894, and began his CWL career with Almendares in 1913. The 18-year-old outfielder hit the ball at a blazing .356 pace in his rookie year, with five doubles and seven stolen bases. He suffered a sophomore slump the next year, hitting only .235, but bounced back to hit a solid .331 in 1914-15.

Over the course of his career, he enjoyed nine .300+ seasons, including averages of .356, .331, .300, .341, .336, .300, .375, .317, and .342. His .310 career batting average is one of the highest in the annals of the Cuban Winter League.

Jacinto Calvo was a speedy outfielder, with good range and an accurate throwing arm. He also took advantage of his speed on the bases and was among the leaders in stolen bases year after year. In recognition of his superior skills, he was elected to the Hall of Fame in 1948.

• Valentin Dreke was a small, fleet-footed outfielder with excellent range and a strong throwing arm. The 5'8", 160 pound left hander was born in Union de Reyes, Cuba, on September 25, 1898. He began his Cuban league career as a 21-year-old center fielder in 1919, batting a respectable .270 for the America team.

He played a total of eight years in the CWL, seven of them with the Almendares club, finishing with a career average of .307. His best years were 1924-25, when he hit .354 and 1925-26 when he legged out a .385 average. He was an ideal leadoff man, with a good batting eye and blinding speed. Several years he played in the same outfield with Bernardo Baro and Armando Marsans, giving Almedares one of the finest outfields in CWL history.

Dreke played with the Cuban Stars in the Negro leagues for nine years, compiling a batting average of .334. He retired from the game in 1928 when he was only 30 years old.

He was elected to Cuba's Baseball Hall of Fame in 1945.

• Alejandro Oms, another all-around outfielder, often dazzled the fans with acrobatic catches in the outfield. He was another superstar, with no apparent weakness. The native of Santa Clara, Cuba, began his professional career at the age of 22, and played in both the United States and Cuba for 19 years.

The sleepy-eyed Oms had a compact build, packing 190 pounds of muscle in a 5'9" frame. In addition to his ballhawking abilities, the man known as "El Caballero" (The Gentleman) hit the ball with authority wherever he played. He hit his peak in Cuba between 1928 and 1930, when he won two successive batting championships, hitting .432 in 1928-29 and .380 the next season. He also captured the home run title in 1931-32. The right handed slugger finished his career with the third highest career batting average in CWL history, .351. He also hit .306 in the Negro leagues.

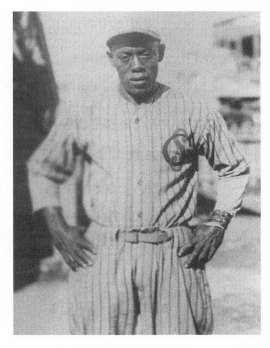

In 1923, Oms teamed up with Oscar Charleston and Pablo "Champion" Mesa to give the Santa Clara ballclub the greatest outfield in Cuban Winter League history. That team has been called one of the greatest baseball teams in history, comparable to the

Alejandro Oms. (Yuyo Ruiz.)

1927 New York Yankees. Other team members included Jose Mendez, Eustaquio Pedroso, Dobie Moore, Oliver Marcelle, and Oscar "Heavy" Johnson.

Oms entered Cuba's Baseball Hall of Fame in 1944.

UTILITY:

• Martin Dihigo and Lazaro Salazar were the most versatile players ever to set foot on a baseball diamond. Dihigo was a 6'3", 190 pound bundle of grace and skill. He was equally at home on the mound, at second base, or in the outfield. Wherever he played, he was considered to be the best at the position.

He was called "El Maestro" (the Master) in Cuba, where he became a national treasure. As a pitcher, Dihigo won more than 256 games in his career, against 136 losses, for a brilliant .653 winning percentage. The record includes games pitched in Cuba, the Negro leagues, Venezuela, the Dominican Republic, and Mexico. In the CWL, he ran up a record of 106–59 from 1922 through 1947. He led the league in games won four times, with records of 2–0, 11–2, 14–2, and 8–1.

With a bat in his hand, El Maestro was a consistent hitter, and a serious long ball threat. His CWL statistics showed a .293 career batting average (.330 for his first 17 years in the league), with nine home runs a year (the equivalent of about 29 homers in the major leagues). In the Negro leagues, he hit .303 with 20 home runs a year, and in Mexico he batted .317, with 16 home runs. He won batting championships in every league he played in —.358 in 1935-36 in Cuba, .391 in 1936 in the Negro National League, and .387 in 1938 in the Mexican League. He also won two home run titles in the Negro leagues.

In 1938, Martin Dihigo had a

Martin Dihigo

career season. In Mexico, he captured the batting championship, as noted above. He also led the league in several pitching categories, including winning percentage (.900 with an 18–2 record), earned run average (0.90), and strikeouts (184 in 167 innings). His 14–2 record in Cuba gave him an overall pitching record for the year of 32–4.

He is a member of the Hall of Fame in four countries — the United States, Mexico, Venezuela, and Cuba.

• Lazaro Salazar, a native of Havana, Cuba, played professional baseball in Cuba, the United States, and Mexico from 1931 to 1952. The chunky left hander hitter and pitcher was the poor man's Martin Dihigo. He could do everything Dihigo could do, but not quite as well. He was a triple threat wherever he played, however, starring on the mound and holding down either first base or one of the outfield spots on his off days. He was a consistent winning pitcher throughout his career, compiling a career record of 154–109, including 37–24 in the CWL.

He hit for a high average in all the leagues, although he was not the long ball threat Dihigo was. Salazar had a career average of .292 in Cuba, .322 in the Negro leagues, and .334 in Mexico. He averaged about 45–50 extra base hits a year, including nine home runs. Lazaro Salazar is a member of the Hall of Fame in both Mexico and Cuba.

Cuban Winter League All-Star Team, 1882–1960

Catcher	Antonio Garcia*
	Mike Gonzalez
Pitcher	Jose Mendez*
	Luis Padron
	Adolfo Luque
	Eustaquio Pedroso
	Jose Munoz
	Carlos Royer
	Manuel Garcia
First Base	Julian Castillo*
	Jud Wilson
Second Base	Manuel Cueto*
	Bienvenido Jimenez
Shortstop	John Henry Lloyd*
	Silvio Garcia
Third Base	Raphael Almeida*
	Ray Dandridge

Outfield	Cristobal Torriente*
	Oscar Charleston*
	Bernardo Baro
	Jacinto Calvo
	Valentin Dreke
	Alejandro Oms*
Utility	Martin Dihigo
	Lazaro Salazar

Note: An asterisk (*) denotes one of the starting nine players.

A second team, consisting of such players as Jose Fernandez, Lorenzo Cabrera, Willie Wells, Luis Bustamente, Carlos Moran, Estaban Montalvo, Pedro Formenthal, Adolfo Lujan, and Jose Pastoriza was also selected. The career batting and pitching statistics for these players can be found in the back of the book.

Two other tables of interest: a comparison of the American AAA minor leagues to the Cuban Winter League, based on the performances of players who played in both leagues, primarily during the 1940s, and a comparison of the major leagues to the CWL, based on the performances of nine players who played in both leagues during the 1910s, 1920s, and 1940s.

This study is concerned only with the Cuban Winter League that ceased operations in 1960. Baseball, however, did not end in Cuba after 1960. It continued to be played under the Castro regime, but on an amateur basis. Over the ensuing 39 years, many great Cuban baseball players have showcased their skills in International competition, such as the Olympic Games and the Pan American Games. In fact, the Cuban National Team has dominated the amateur sport for decades and is presently enjoying an unsurpassed run in International competition. They have won more than 140 consecutive games, going back to the 1988 World Championships.

Unfortunately, it is not possible to fairly evaluate the caliber of the Cuban players after 1960 because their opposition has been primarily of college level or amateur quality. Also, in recent years the Cuban players have gone to the aluminum bat, which provides a substantial increase in a player's power and overall batting average. This is reflected in the batting averages of the 1980s and 1990s. Prior to 1985, there had been no .400 hitters in Cuban League baseball. Since 1985, six batting champions have hit over .400, a total of ten times in 13 years, including Omar Linares, who has broken the magic barrier five times. Over the same period, home runs have increased by an estimated 10 percent. Over a 162 game schedule, the Cuban home run leader, since 1985, would have hit approximately 52 home runs a year.

There are a few outstanding players who should be recognized, however, although they will not be rated or compared to any players on national all-star

Wilfredo Sanchez. (Yuyo Ruiz.)

teams. Some of the following facts have been gleaned from Peter C. Bjarkman's fine article on Cuban baseball in *The National Pastime*.

- Omar Linares — A 6' tall, 198 pound, right handed hitting, power hitting third baseman, who has a 13-year career batting average of .373, with 38 home runs for every 550 at-bats.
- Wilfredo Sanchez — Known as "El Hombre Hit" (The Hit Man), the left handed hitting Sanchez won five batting titles, including a mark of .385 in 1984. His career batting average is a hefty .332.
- Alexander Ramos — A career .337 hitter, an outstanding second baseman, and a brilliant double play maker.
- Lazaro Junco — The Cuban League's all-time home run leader, with 405 (an average of 39 home runs a year), and more than 1000 RBIs. Junco is a right handed hitting outfielder who stands 6' tall and weighs 189 pounds.
- Orestes Kindelan — A 6', 187 pound right handed hitting first baseman with 402 career homers (45 home runs a year) and a .310 career batting average. Kindelan can also catch or play the outfield.
- Antonio Munoz — He is the all-time leader in games played (1945), runs scored (1281), doubles (355), total bases (3569), and runs batted in (1407). The first baseman played for more than 15 years.
- Braudilio Vinent — He is Castro Cuba's top pitcher, with 221 career victories against 167 losses. He is the all-time career leader in games pitched (447), complete games (265), shutouts (63), and innings pitched (3260). Vinent is a right handed pitcher with a blazing fastball.

• Rogelio Garcia — He is the all time strikeout leader, with 2499 strikeouts.

• Victor Mesa — Mesa was a slugging outfielder and a lifetime .313 hitter. An outstanding all around player, the 6'2", 196 pound right handed hitter was a brilliant base stealer, who averaged more than 50 stolen bases a year while hitting 20 home runs a year.

• German Mesa — He is considered by many to be Cuba's all-time greatest shortstop. The small, 5'7" infielder has above average power (15 homers a year). He is a .284 hitter, with 110 runs scored, and 50 stolen bases.

• Lazaro Valle — The 6'1", 202 pound right handed pitcher has a 90+ mph fastball and a devastating slider. He is the all-time Cuban League percentage leader, with a mark of .784. He was still active in 1994, when he had a won/loss record of 102–36.

Braudilio Vinent (Yuyo Ruiz.)

• Jorge Luis Valdes — This 6'3", 169 pound stringbean right hander throws a full assortment of pitches, including a fastball, a slider, a curve, and a sinker. Valdes, with 217 victories against 151 losses through 1994, is the #2 all-time winning pitcher in Cuban League baseball.

Japanese Professional All-Star Team

The Japanese professional baseball leagues offer the highest quality baseball outside the major leagues. This fact is indelibly documented in the experiences of more than 400 former major league players who have made the trek across the Pacific Ocean, to play for a professional team in the Japanese Central League or Pacific League. The names of the players who have chosen this route make up a veritable who's who of major league baseball: Clete Boyer, Cecil Fielder, Orestes Destrade, Willie Davis, Dick Stuart, Matty Alou, Don Blasingame, Davey Johnson, Felix Millan, and Roy White.

Many of the players, who had baseball experience on both sides of the big pond, of course, played only a few games in the major leagues, or a few games in the Japanese leagues. There were, however, more than 60 players, including those mentioned above, who accumulated a total of more than 90,000 at-bats in Japan and more than 170,000 at-bats in the major leagues. The statistics of those players were used to compare the quality of play in the two organizations.

According to the statistics, a player moving from the major leagues to the Japanese leagues could generally expect to hit approximately 18 points higher, and slug more than twice as many home runs. The complete player list, including batting averages and home runs, can be found later in the book.

Although the overall quality of baseball in Japan at the present time appears to be between the major league level and the AAA minor league level, there are many Japanese players who could play in the major leagues immediately. This has already been demonstrated most impressively by pitcher Hideo Nomo, who moved effortlessly from the Kintetsu Buffalos of the Japanese Pacific League to the Los Angeles Dodgers of the National League. Nomo, in four full years in Japan, averaged 18 victories a year against 10 losses, with a 3.15 earned run average, and 270 strikeouts in 234 innings, an average of 10.4 strikeouts a game.

Ichiro Suzuki. (James R. Madden, Jr.)

His five-year major league record shows an average of 12 wins a year against 10 losses, with an earned run average of 3.81, and 1031 strikeouts in 960 innings, an average of 9.7 strikeouts a game. Several other Japanese pitchers are also working their way onto major league rosters successfully, including Hideki Irabu, who went 29–20 for the New York Yankees in 1997–99.

At the present time, there are no position players who are attempting to make the adjustment from Japan to the United States, although there are a number of Japanese League players who could probably do so very easily. The greatest player in Japan today is 25 year old Orix Blue Wave outfielder Ichiro Suzuki. Ichiro, who uses only his first name, has a six-year career batting average of .350 through 1999 — with six batting championships. The slim southpaw swinger, who appears to be a carbon copy of Rod Carew, is 6' tall, and weighs a wispy 165 pounds. He hits the ball to all fields, is a good base runner, and is a talented outfielder with a strong, accurate, throwing arm. If his statistics were adjusted to a major league base point using the comparative data found in the appendix, the stats for the two ballplayers would look like this:

	Ichiro Suzuki	Rod Carew
Doubles	31	26
Triples	4	7
Home Runs	8 (adjusted)	5
Stolen Bases	37	21
Batting Avg.	.331 (adjusted)	.328

The level of play in Japan has been increasing at a steady rate over the past 40 years. Back in the 1920s and '30s, Negro league all-star teams ran roughshod through the Japanese teams, going 23–0–1 in 1927 and 23–1 in 1932. In 1931, Lefty O'Doul brought a major league all-star team to Japan for a 17-game exhibition tour. The Americans, with Lou Gehrig in the lineup, won every game, usually by lopsided scores like 22–4 and 19–1. The Ruth-Gehrig all-stars visited the island nation three years later and racked up 17 wins without a loss. Babe Ruth banged out 13 home runs during the tour, much to the delight of the Japanese fans. The highlight of the series, from the Japanese perspective, was the pitching of 18-year-old Eiji Sawamura, who shackled the major leaguers without a hit for five innings, at one point fanning Charlie Gehringer, Babe Ruth, Lou Gehrig, and Jimmie Foxx in succession. A seventh inning home run by Gehrig defeated the young fireballer, 1–0, but could not dim his brilliant accomplishment. Sadly, ten years later, after compiling a dazzling 63–22 record in the Japanese League, Eiji Sawamura, in the service of his country during World War II, was lost at sea when his troop ship was sunk.

By 1955, when the New York Yankees embarrassed their hosts with a 15–0–1 record, the unofficial won-loss record stood at 67 victories for the Americans and three victories for the Japanese.

Then things began to change. Although the major leaguers still won the majority of the games, the individual scores were much closer, and the Americans began to take a beating now and again. In 1966, Walter Alston's Los Angeles Dodgers barely got out of the country with their skins, winning nine games against eight losses. Four years later, the San Francisco Giants were beaten by the Japanese all-stars, six games to three. The Japanese have kept the pressure on ever since. In 1990, Japan defeated the major league all-stars, with Barry Bonds, Randy Johnson, Roberto Alomar, and Cecil Fielder, four games to three, and in 1992 they took the Los Angeles Dodgers to task, two games to none. In 1998, Sammy Sosa and his cohorts won six games in nine meetings. Over the past 12 years, Japan has won two of seven series, winning a total of 15 games against 29 losses.

Japanese professional baseball is getting closer in quality to the major

Tadashi Wakabayashi. (Gary Engel.)

leagues each year, but certain weak areas will have to be strengthened before they can compete on an equal basis. One of the problems in Japan at the present time appears to be the lack of an extensive minor league farm system. Japanese League teams have only one farm team each, limiting them to a player base of roughly 60 players, less than 10 percent of the major league player base. By necessity, players are often rushed into action with the big clubs immediately after graduation from high school or college, without being given the necessary time to develop their natural talents. Young players are force-fed the game at the highest professional level, subjecting them to intense pressures to perform. Many promising careers may have been destroyed as a result of this practice. Many players who were destined for greatness may have struggled through mediocre careers with their confidence shattered. In the United States, major league teams have as many as nine farm teams, with individual players receiving an average of five or six years of minor league training in successively higher levels of competition before they are added to a major league roster.

In general, Japanese League talent is a mixed bag. Many batters are good contact hitters with exceptional bat control, but they lack power. Also, batting averages tend to be lower than in the major leagues. This may be due, in part, to the regimented Japanese baseball system, which promotes strenuous exercise programs, severe personal sacrifice, and unquestioning obedience to team dictates. Long, exhausting workouts, which are conducted for several hours each day, even prior to league games, may sap a player's strength during a game, causing him to perform at less than optimal efficiency. Taking time off because of an injury is unacceptable. Players are encouraged to "play through" their injuries. Individuality is discouraged. Batting stances are often dictated by the manager, thereby stifling a player's natural ability. Ichiro Suzuki, forced by his manager to use an unnatural batting stance one year, hit a measly .188. After his new manager permitted him to return to his unique "pendulum" style swing, Ichiro responded with a whopping .385 average.

American players, even those with mediocre batting averages in the U.S. major leagues, frequently challenge Japanese batters for the batting championship. For instance, Alonzo Powell, a .211 hitter in short trials with Montreal and Seattle, won three successive Central League batting championships: 1994 (.324), 1995 (.355), and 1996 (.340). Tom O'Malley, a .256 hitter in the majors, won the 1993 Central League batting championship with a .329 average for the Hanshin Tigers. Jack Howell, a .236 hitter in 737 major league games, batted a cool .331 to take the 1992 Central League title. And Boomer Wells, a .228 hitter in two brief major league trials, won the Pacific League triple crown in 1989 with a .322 batting average, 40 home runs, and 124 runs batted in. Other former major leaguers who have captured Japanese League batting titles over the years include Felix Millan, Randy Bass, Warren Cromartie, Jim Paciorek, Larry Raines, and LeRon Lee.

The high quality of Japanese baseball is reinforced one more time by the experiences of O'Malley and Howell. Although both men won batting titles in Japan after producing poor major league statistics, it should be noted that they both terrorized high minor league pitching in the United States. Playing at the AAA level in the International League, the American Association, and the Pacific Coast League, Tom O'Malley pounded the ball at a .324 clip with 14 home runs a year over a five-year period, while Jack Howell whaled AAA pitching for a stratospheric .368 average, with 20 home runs, over two years.

American players, who are generally bigger and stronger than their Japanese counterparts, captured 22 of 48 home run titles between 1974 and 1997, even though they represented less than 10 percent of the active players. Orestes Destrade, who averaged 19 home runs a year in the major leagues, averaged 46 homers a year in Japan, winning three successive home run crowns: 1990 (42), 1991 (39), and 1992 (41). Ralph Bryant, who hit eight home runs in 150 at-bats with the Dodgers in the late '80s, captured three home run crowns in Japan between 1989 and 1994. His career home run average in Japan was 49 home runs for every 550 at-bats.

Today, the American players in Japan generally out-homer their Japanese counterparts by a wide margin, simply because they are bigger, and they utilize more weight training. As the Japanese players develop physically, this gap should continue to narrow. Although there are some weaknesses in Japanese batting techniques, that is not to say that American pitchers would overpower their eastern adversaries. In fact, Japanese batters have not been easy pickings for American pitchers over the years. Of all the Americans who have pitched in Japan, only three of them have compiled impressive records. Leo Kiely, a seven-year veteran of the major league wars, with a 26–27 lifetime record, sparkled during a one-year stint in Japan, winning six games in six starts with a 1.80 earned run average. Joe Stanka, who went 1–0 in an abbreviated trial with the Chicago White Sox in 1959, pitched in Japan for seven years, winning 100 games against only 72 losses with a fine 3.08 earned run average. Gene Bacque, a right hander from Louisiana with no major league experience ran up a 100–80 record in Japan, with an outstanding 2.34 ERA from 1962 through 1969. Guy Hoffman, 17–17 in the majors, went 20–19 in Japan. Don Schulze, who won 15 games against 25 losses in the majors, won 12 games against 11 losses with the Orix Blue Wave. Clyde Wright, who ran up a career record of 100–111 with California, Milwaukee, and Texas, compiled a 22–18 record with the Yomiuri Giants.

Japanese pitching is probably closer to major league standards than the other skills. There appear to be a number of Japanese pitchers, in addition to Nomo and Irabu, who could step on a major league mound today and pitch effectively. Many Japanese moundsmen have a full repertoire of pitches, with good movement and good control. They have a reputation, however, of working the count by nibbling at the corners rather than trying to put a batter away quickly. Most Japanese pitchers have slight builds, and therefore rely on finesse and control to win games. They usually possess a more-than-adequate fastball, and they supplement it with exceptional breaking balls and above average change-of-pace pitches. They pitch to spots extremely well, and are proficient at setting up a batter. Contrary to popular belief, however, there are also many power pitchers in Japan, who stand over 6' tall, weigh more than 200 pounds, and bring the ball to the plate at speeds in excess of 90 miles per hour.

Defensively Japanese infielders are the equal of their major league counterparts, with superior quickness and play making ability. There have been dozens of infielders over the years who would have excelled in the major leagues, if given the opportunity. Gold Glove caliber infielders like Shigeo Nagashima, Yoshio Yoshida, and superstar Sadaharu Oh would have been welcomed into the Hall of Fame in Cooperstown, New York, with open arms. Recent all-star infielders include shortstops Takehiro Ikeyama and Yoshihiko Takehashi, second baseman Kazunori Shinozuka, and third baseman Masayuki Kakefu.

Catchers in the Japanese leagues seem to be good handlers of pitchers and good glovemen. They are quick afoot, and they are excellent at blocking the plate. In general, however, they have weak throwing arms. And many of them are poor hitters.

Japanese outfielders are reported to be weak defensively. They have limited range and weak throwing arms. According the Brian Maitland in his excellent book, *Japanese Baseball*, outfielders do not appreciate the art of throwing out base runners or of holding runners to singles after hits into the gap.

Maitland feels that two keys to the success of Japanese baseball are the development of a better minor league system and improved coaching, all the way from the high school and college level, up to the Japanese League itself. Until those things happen, Japan will not be able to challenge the major leagues for world baseball supremacy.

Japanese baseball has been a national sport since 1873, when Horace Wilson, an American professor living in Tokyo, first taught the fundamentals of the game to his students. Over the following decades, the game quietly spread through the high schools and colleges around the Tokyo area. In 1905, the Waseda Imperial University of Tokyo baseball team toured the West Coast of the United States, compiling a 7–19 record against a variety of college, high school, and amateur teams.

Three years later, the Reach All-Americans, a combination of major league subs and minor league players from the Pacific Coast League, toured the Land of the Rising Sun. The team, the first U.S. professional baseball team to visit the island, won 17 consecutive games against Japanese college teams.

In 1909, the Wisconsin Badgers visited Japan as guests of the Athletic Association of Keio University. The Badgers lost three straight games to Keio University, but whipped a Tokyo all-star team by scores of 10–0 and 8–7. In 1913, the New York Giants and Chicago White Sox played two games against each other in Tokyo on the first leg of a world tour. Then they combined to defeat Keio University 12–3. Major league all-star teams continued to visit Japan on a regular basis over the next 20 years. For the record, the first Japanese victory over a major league team occurred in 1922, when a Japanese southpaw named Ono, of the Mita Club of Shibaura, defeated New York Yankee ace Waite Hoyt, 9–3.

Shortly after the turn of the century, baseball, or *beisu boro* as it was called, had grown into a major high school sport. By 1915, organized high school leagues were underway and by 1924 the annual national high school baseball tournament was in full swing. Today, it is the most popular sporting event in the country, far exceeding the lure of professional baseball — even more popular than the age-old sumo wrestling. Over 4000 teams from the country's 47 prefectures participate in the single elimination tournament, with the 47 regional champions advancing to the finals in Koshien Stadium near Osaka. It is estimated that more than 1,000,000 people now attend the tournament to root for their high school heros, while millions more watch the excitement on television.

College baseball also gained in popularity during the first quarter century. In 1925, the Tokyo Six University League was formed, consisting of Waseda, Keio, Meiji, Hosei, Rikkyo, and Tokyo Universities. The Tokyo Six now has its own annual tournament, although it is nowhere near as popular as the high school tournament.

Professional baseball made its debut in Japan in 1934 when the Yomiuri (Tokyo) Giants were organized by Matsutaro Shoriki, the owner of the Yomiuri Newspaper group. As a result of Yomiuri's sponsorship of the Giants (called Kyojin in Japanese), it became the practice for all Japanese professional baseball teams to be sponsored by corporations. Hence, names like Hanshin Tigers and Chunichi Dragons do not refer to a team's home city, but to their corporate owner, like the Hanshin railway company or the Chunichi newspaper chain. In 1936, the first Japanese professional baseball league enjoyed its inaugural season. Other teams in the league, in addition to the Tokyo Kyojin, were the Osaka Tigers, Nagoya, Hankyu, Dai Tokyo, and the Tokyo Senetars.

The first season was actually broken up into two spring tournaments, followed by a fall season consisting of 21 games. The first batting champion was Yuki Nakane of Nagoya, who hit a resounding .376. The first pitching leader was 20-year-old Eiji Sawamura, who won 13 games against only three losses. The league has operated continuously since 1936, with the exception of the last year of World War II—1945—when the schedule was cancelled.

Initially, pitchers dominated the game. Three-hundred hitters were few and far between, the legendary Tetsuharu Kawakami, a lifetime .313 hitter being the lone exception. During several seasons, there were only one or two .300 hitters in the league. In 1942, Ha Go Kyojin won the batting championship with an average of .286. Pitching leaders routinely had earned run averages of less than 1.00.

By 1948, things began to change. New, smaller ballparks, the introduction of a livelier baseball, and expansion shifted the emphasis of the game from pitching to hitting. Home runs increased significantly, and the number of .300 hitters went up accordingly. Pitching leaders still had earned run averages in the low to mid 2.00s but, because of the establishment of a 130-game season and the increased pitching rotation, the overall load on individual pitchers was reduced, causing big winners to all but disappear from the scene over the last half of the century.

In the early years of the Japanese League, it was normal for a pitcher to throw more than 300 innings a year. In fact, pitching legend Masaichi Kaneda hurled more than 300 innings a year for 14 consecutive years. Yasuo Hayasi holds the all-time record, pitching 541 innings in 1942 over a 105-game schedule. Hayasi pitched in 71 games that year, winning 32 and losing 22. No one has reached the 400 inning mark since 1961, when Hiroshi Gondo of the Chunichi Dragons pitched 429 innings. Osamu Higashio was the last pitcher to break the 300 inning barrier when he tossed 303 innings for the Crown Lighter Lions in 1978. Yoshinori Sato of the Hankyu Braves was the last pitcher to go over the 250 inning mark, in 1985. The last 40-game winner was Kazuhisa Inao in 1961. The last 30-game winner was Mutsuo Minagawa of the Nankai Hawks in 1968. There hasn't been a 20-game winner since Masaiki Saito went 20–5 in 1990.

In 1950, the league was expanded into two leagues, the Central League and the Pacific League. The total number of teams fluctuated from 13 to 15 for several years, finally stabilizing at 12, six in each league, in 1958. The length of the season also fluctuated during the '50s and '60s, ranging from a low of 96 games to a high of 154 games. It has been 130 games long since 1969.

The Japanese Baseball League has produced some great players over its 62 year history. Tetsuharu Kawakami was Japan's first great professional baseball player, setting the standard for batting with a career average of .313. Slugger Sadaharu Oh holds both the Japanese single season home run record (55), as well as the world career home run record (868). Catcher Katsuya Nomura holds the world record for most games played by a catcher, an amazing 2918 games. Shigeo Nagashima, Japan's most popular player, walked off with six batting crowns while leading the Tokyo Giants to an unprecedented 11 Japan Series championships. Yutaka Fukumoto is the Japanese stolen base king with 1065 career stolen bases. His world record was broken by Ricky Henderson in 1993. Sachio Kinugasa holds the Japanese record for the most consecutive games played—2215. His total was the world record until Cal Ripken broke it in 1996.

Victor Starffin, a Russian immigrant, and Kazuhisa Inao both won 42 victories in a single season, another world record. Randy Bass, an American import, is the single season batting average record holder with a mark of .389 in 1986.

Selecting a Japanese League all-star team is not easy because there are so many deserving players. In addition to the 25-man all-star roster, a second all-star team has been selected to supplement the first.

CATCHER:

Some of Japan's most noteworthy catchers include Katsuya Nomura, Koichi Tabuchi, Masaaki Mori, and Takeshi Doigaki. Nomura and Tabuchi were chosen as the catchers on the #1 all-star team.

• Katsuya Nomura is the greatest catcher in the history of Japanese professional baseball. He is a legend around the world. His 657 home runs are the most home runs hit by a catcher in professional baseball history: #2 all-time in Japan, behind Sadaharu Oh. But, more importantly, Nomura was the most durable catcher in the annals of professional baseball. The chunky backstop played in the Japanese League for 27 years, during which time he set the all-time record for most games played by a catcher—2918. Major league receiver Carlton Fisk is second with 2499.

Nomura once caught every inning of a 150-game season, including 16 double headers. He played in every game during six seasons.

Katsuya Nomura. (Gary Engel.)

In spite of his durability records, the right handed slugger is best remembered for his offensive fireworks. He won nine home run championships during his career, including eight in a row. He is tied for the most home runs in a season in the Pacific League, with 52. Nomura also captured six consecutive RBI titles and one batting championship. He won the triple crown in 1965 with a batting average of .320, 42 home runs, and 110 runs batted in. He was a five time recipient of the Pacific League Most Valuable Player award.

When he retired in 1980, the 5'9", 187 pound backstop held the Japanese record for most total games played (3017), and most career at-bats (10,472). He accumulated 2901 base hits, 1988 runs batted in, and 1509 runs scored, while batting .277. His average season batting statistics are mirror images of those of Roy Campanella, the Hall of Fame catcher of the Brooklyn Dodgers.

Name	AB	R	H	D	T	HR	RBI	BB	SO	BA
K. Nomura	550	79	152	21	1	35	104	66	78	.277
R. Campanella	550	82	152	23	2	32	112	70	65	.276

Katsuya Nomura is a member of the Japanese Baseball Hall of Fame. He is also the recipient of Japan's most prestigious honor, membership in the MEIKYUKAI, an organization that honors professional baseball players with 2000 career base hits or 200 career pitching victories.

• Koichi Tabuchi, of the Hanshin Tigers, was a Hall of Fame caliber catcher in his own right. Many experts consider Tabuchi to be the greatest catcher ever. As Johnson noted, "At 6'3", 210 pounds, Tabuchi was unusually large for a Japanese player, and he utilized his frame's power and strength both as a hitter and fielder. He was an excellent defensive catcher, and was a Central League Best-Nine selection for five straight seasons."

Tabuchi was a devastating hitter. Although he played in the country's largest park, he still launched 474 career homers. Over the course of a distinguished 16-year career, the handsome backstop averaged 44 round trippers and 106 runs batted in for every 550 at-bats. He is the second most prolific home run hitter in Japan, on a frequency basis, behind Sadaharu Oh.

In 1975, Tabuchi ended Sadaharu Oh's 13 year grip on the home run title by smashing 43 homers to Oh's 33. He also hit .303 and drove in 90 runs that year. His best year was 1974, when he hit .278, with 45 homers and 95 RBIs in 407 at-bats. When he retired in 1984, Tabuchi left behind, in addition to his 474 home runs, a total of 1135 RBIs and a batting average of .260.

PITCHER:

Japan has had literally dozens of Hall of Fame quality pitchers over the past 60 years, pitchers who have demonstrated superior ability over an extended period of time. There have been six pitchers who have won 300 or more games, and another 16 pitchers who exceeded the 200 mark. Seven pitchers were chosen for the all-star team. Seven more were selected for the alternate team.

• Masaichi Kaneda is the ace of the staff. The handsome Japanese-born Korean pitcher averaged 20 victories a season over a 20-year career, en route to a 400 win, 298 loss record. He is the only Japan League pitcher to win 400 games, and only the third pitcher in the world to win that many, the others being Cy Young and Walter Johnson.

According to Dan Johnson, Kaneda "had a fiery temper and was a relentless competitor." The 6' tall, 161 pound southpaw had a blazing fastball that helped him lead the league in strikeouts ten times. He was the first pitcher to break Walter Johnson's "untouchable" strikeout record, and he still holds the Japan League record, with 4490 strikeouts. He was the only pitcher to fan Shigeo Nagashima four times in one game. He also holds the career records for most innings pitched (5526) and most complete games (365) and is #2 in shutouts, with 82. He has the world record for most consecutive shutout innings, with 64.

Known as "The Golden Arm," the rangy fireballer led the Central League in victories three times and in earned run average three times. He also won the coveted Sawamura Award as the best pitcher in the league three times. After playing for the weak Kokutetsu Swallows for 15 years, he joined the powerful Yomiuri Giants, and he helped them win five Central League pennants and five Japan Series championships in five years. After his retirement, he was elected to the MEIKYUKAI and the Baseball Hall of Fame.

• Tetsuya Yoneda was the right handed counterpart of Masaichi Kaneda. He pitched for 22 years, most of them with the Hankyu Braves, winning 350 games against 285 losses. During that time, the Braves won five Pacific League pennants and one World Championship.

The 5'11", 192 pound fastball pitcher holds the Japan League record for most games pitched in a career, with 949. He is #2 in career victories, #2 in strikeouts, #7 in shutouts, and #8 in complete games. During one 12-year period, from 1957 through 1968, the hard working Yoneda pitched in an amazing 40 percent of his team's games, pitching 25 percent of all the team's innings. That would be equivalent to a major league pitcher averaging 365 innings pitched every year for 12 consecutive years.

Yoneda led the Pacific League in victories in 1966 with 25, and in earned run average in 1973 with 2.47. He was voted the league's Most Valuable Player in 1968. He is a member of MEIKYUKAI.

• Keishi Suzuki was another fiery, hard throwing southpaw, who hurled for the Kintetsu Buffalos from 1966 through 1985. Although he pitched for a weak team most of the time, he still won 317 games against 238 losses. In 1967, he racked up a 21–13 record, playing for a last place team that managed to win only 59 games of their 130-game schedule, and that finished a distant 16 games behind the pennant winning Hankyu Braves.

The big lefty led the Pacific League in victories three times, in earned run average once, and in strikeouts six times. He won more than 20 games eight times, including five years in a row. When he retired, he was in the top four in several career categories, including victories (#4), shutouts (#4), strikeouts (#4), complete games (#3), and innings pitched (#4).

• Victor Starffin was a 6'4", 230 pound white Russian, whose parents fled to Japan during the Bolshevik Revolution. The big flamethrower went on to become one of Japan's leading pitchers in the early days of professional baseball. He joined the Tokyo Kyojin when they were first formed in 1936, and played for them for nine years before being sent to a detention camp near the end of World War II. After the war, he returned to the league, but was never quite the same pitcher. He toiled for four different teams over his final ten years.

Starffin was the league's first big winner, piling up a dazzling record of 141 victories against just 42 losses from 1937 through 1940. His 42 victories in 1939, although tied by Kazuhisa Inao in 1961, is still the mark to shoot for. Starffin's four-year record included an incredible 1563 innings pitched. In 1941, he understandably suffered from arm problems, but still managed to win 15 games against only three losses.

Victor Starffin won a total of 303 victories over a 19-year career against 175 losses. He was Japan's first 300-game winner. He also holds the record for most career shutouts with 84. In recognition of his achievements, he is a member of both the MEIKYUKAI and the Baseball Hall of Fame.

• Kazuhisa "Iron Man" Inao was one of Japan's most amazing pitchers. The muscular right hander was a tireless worker who averaged 29 victories and 346 innings pitched a year during his first eight years in the Pacific League. Over his 14-year career, he led the league in victories four times, in strikeouts three times, and in earned run average five times. He also captured two MVP awards, and five Sawamura awards. In 1956, he was voted the league's Rookie of the Year after finishing the season with a 21–6 record.

Inao acquired his nickname during the hectic 1958 pennant chase. With his team, the Nishitetsu Lions, engaged in a knock-down fight with the Nankai Hawks, the 5'11", 176 pound Hercules pitched in *all* of the Lions last nine games, leading them to the pennant by the slim margin of one game. He continued his superhuman feats in the Japan Series, pitching in six of the seven games, and winning the last four, as the Lions overcame a 3–0 deficit in games, in the biggest comeback in baseball history. In the crucial fourth game, Inao pitched six innings in relief, and hit a home run in the tenth inning to save the game.

Inao holds the record for most games pitched in a season, with 78 (56 percent of his team's games), and most victories in a season, with 42 (tied with Victor Starffin). He led the Nishitetsu Lions to four Pacific League pennants and three consecutive Japan Series championships. When he retired he had won 276 games against 137 losses, a spectacular .668 winning percentage. His 1.98 career ERA is the third best in Japan baseball history. He is a member of MEIKYUKAI.

• Takehiko Bessho pitched for the Yomiuri Giants for 12 years of his 17-year career. He was a major contributor to eight Central League pennants and four Japan Series titles with the Giants, as well as to two other Japan League titles with the Nankai Hawks and the Yomiuri Giants, in 1948 and '49 respectively, prior to the formation of the two league concept.

During his career, Bessho captured the Most Valuable Player trophy twice, and the Sawamura award twice. He led the league in ERA once, and in victories three times. He won 30 or more games twice in his career, and won more than 20 games six times. He retired with an outstanding winning percentage of .635 on 310 victories and only 178 losses.

Bessho stands #5 all-time in career victories. He is #7 in earned run average, at 2.18, and #4 in shutouts, with 72. He is a member of both the MEIKYUKAI and the Hall of Fame.

• Yutaka Enatsu is the most extraordinary pitcher in the history of Japanese baseball, the Dennis Eckersley of the Far East. He exploded on the baseball scene as a 20 year old in 1968, after having compiled a 12–13 record as a rookie the year before. The big, strapping 198 pounder won 25 games in '68 and struck out a record 401 batters in 329 innings, an average of 11 strikeouts a game.

The flamethrowing southpaw continued to bedevil batters for the next seven years. In the 1971 All-Star game, he fanned all nine men he faced. In 1973, he tossed an 11-inning no-hitter at the Yomiuri Giants, winning his own game, 1–0, with a home run. The following month, he pitched a 14-inning one-hitter, in which he retired 33 consecutive batters. The next year, after seven years as a starting pitcher, with a record of 135–87, arm problems sent him to the bullpen, where he became the greatest relief pitcher in Japan. Over his last 11 years in professional baseball, the free wheeling sidearmer racked up 193 saves to go along with 71 victories and 71 losses.

Enatsu was a four-time 20-game winner who led the league in victories twice, in ERA once, in strikeouts five times, and in saves five times. He was the Most Valuable Player in the Central League in 1979, and the Most Valuable Player in the Pacific League in 1981. He won the Sawamura award in 1968. He still holds the record for most strikeouts in a season, and the record for most career saves. His team won two league pennants and one Japan Series championship. He is a member of the MEIKYUKAI.

Takehiko Bessho. (Gary Engel.)

FIRST BASE:

Notable Japanese League first basemen include Sadaharu Oh, Tetsuharu Kawakami, Katsuo Osugi, Kihachi Enomoto, Michio Nishizawa, and Tokuji Iide.

• Sadaharu Oh is arguably the greatest player in the annals of Japanese baseball. Over a 22-year period, from 1959 to 1980, Oh completely dominated the sport. The 5'10", 174 pound left handed slugger set home run records that may never be broken. He is the all-time world leader in career home runs with an astounding 868 round-trippers to his credit. He hit 30 or more homers 19 times, three times exceeding the magic 50 mark. His American counterpart, Hank Aaron, exceeded 30 homers 15 times, with a high of 47 in 1971. Oh has a commanding lead in home run frequency, smashing 52 homers for every 550 at-bats, compared to Aaron's 34.

The first baseman for the Yomiuri Giants won 15 home run titles during his career, including a record 13 in a row. His 55 homers in 1964 is still the Japanese league single season record. Oh was not just a slugger. He was a consistent .300 hitter with a good batting eye. His 2504 career bases on balls is 448 more than the major league leader, Babe Ruth. He is one of the few home run hitters in the world who had more home runs than strikeouts: he accomplished that feat five times in his career. Other world class sluggers who achieved that distinction included Joe DiMaggio, Ted Williams, and Josh Gibson.

Oh won five batting crowns, including back-to-back triple crowns in 1973 (.355 batting average, 51 homers and 114 runs batted in) and 1974 (.332, 49, 107). He is a nine-time Central League MVP.

Over his 22-year career, the Yomiuri Giants won 14 Central League championships and 11 Japan Series titles, including nine in a row.

Sadaharu Oh is a member of the Japan Baseball Hall of Fame and the MEIKYUKAI.

• Tetsuharu Kawakami was the first world class batter in Japanese professional baseball. Known as "The God of Batting," he played during a time when pitching dominated the game. Yet, he still compiled a .313 career batting average, using his famous red bat. Kawakami, a practitioner of Zen, claimed he could stop the ball in flight just before it reached his bat. In 1941, when he captured the batting championship with an average of .310, he was the league's only .300 hitter. The #2 man was a distant 43 points in arrears, at .267.

The 5'9", 165 pound, left handed swinger hit over .300 thirteen times, with a high of .377 in 1951. He won five batting titles, two home run crowns, and three RBI titles during his 21-year career. He was a three time Most Valuable Player. In an 18-game exhibition series against the National League Champion Los Angeles Dodgers in 1966, Kawakami slugged the ball at a .364 clip with two home runs.

Following his playing career, Kawakami had an even more distinguished managing career, leading the Yomiuri Giants to 11 Japan Series championships in 14 years. According to Dan Johnson, "Kawakami refrained from using any foreign players. He wanted to prove that he could win with only Japanese athletes." He apparently proved his point.

Tetsuharu Kawakami is a member of both the Hall of Fame and the MEIKYUKAI.

SECOND BASE:

• Morimichi Takagi is the all-star second baseman, backed up by Shigeru Chiba. The second team keystoners are Yutaka Takagi and Toshio Shinozuka. Morimichi Takagi played with the Chunichi Dragons from 1960 to 1980, a period of 21 years. Takagi was a firebrand who as Johnson noted, "displayed extraordinary speed, intensity, and dedication. He was the sparkplug of the Dragon teams of the '60s and '70s."

Sadaharu Oh. (Gary Engel.)

In addition to being a fabulous fielder, Takagi was also a good hitter with surprising power for a little man. The 5'9", 159 pound right handed hitter smashed 236 home runs during his career, an average of 16 homers a year. His high mark was 1965 when he put 24 balls into orbit.

The fleet-footed infielder also sparkled on the bases, swiping 369 sacks in 21 years, an average of 24 stolen bases a year. He won three stolen base crowns, stealing 50 bases in 1963, 44 bases in '65, and 28 bases in '73.

Morimichi Takagi compiled a career batting average of .272, with 2274 base hits. He is a member of MEIKYUKAI.

Shigeru Chiba. (Gary Engel.)

• Shigeru Chiba sparked the Yomiuri Giants to five Japan League pennants during the 1930s and '40s, and five Central League championships, with four Japan Series titles during the '50s.

Chiba was a defensive standout for 15 years, teaming with Tetsuharu Kawakami to give Yomiuri a tight inner defense on the right side of the diamond.

The tiny 5'6", 141 pound right hander was not a one dimensional player, however. He usually hit in the leadoff spot in the lineup, setting the table for the powerful run producers on the team. He was a constant thorn in the side of the opposing team, punching out base hits, coaxing bases on balls, stealing bases, and bringing home important runs. He hit .284 over 15 years, with an average 15 stolen bases, and 96 runs scored. He also showed some occasional pop in his bat, as witnessed by his 33 extra base hits a year, nine of which were home runs.

Shigeru Chiba was elected into the Japan Baseball Hall of Fame in 1980.

SHORTSTOP:

• Yoshio Yoshida was known as Mr. Shortstop in Japan, with good reason. The 5'6", 123 pound infielder was the best fielding shortstop Japan has ever produced. He was built like Freddie Patek, but fielded like Ozzie Smith. He was a defensive genius, with outstanding speed, great range, a sure glove, and a strong accurate throwing arm.

In addition to his fielding prowess, he was a pesky hitter, with a career average of .267. As the leadoff hitter for the Hanshin Tigers, Yoshida exhibited exceptional bat control, striking out only 26 times a year. He was a contact hitter and a bad ball hitter, who could hit away, sacrifice, or execute the hit-and-run to perfection. He led the league in sacrifice hits four times in his career, averaging 13 sacrifices a year. Once on base, he was a constant threat to run. He led the league in stolen bases twice, with 51 stolen bases in 1954 and 50 stolen bases in 1956.

His 17-year career spanned the years from 1953 to 1969. He was elected to the Hall of Fame in 1992.

• Yasumitsu Toyoda, Yoshida's backup, played for the explosive Nishitetsu Lions during the 1950s. He was a member of the famed Lions' "H-Bomb Row," which included himself, Futoshi Nakanishi, Hiroshi Oshita, and Seiji Sekiguchi. The Lions defeated their hated rivals, the Yomiuri Giants, three straight times in the Japan Series, capturing titles in 1956, '57 and '58.

As Johnson noted, "Toyoda was a solid, all around performer who often saved his heroics for dramatic situations. He had a .362 career batting average in the Japan Series, including .458 in 1956, when he was the Series MVP, and .500 (with four home runs) in 1958."

Toyoda, standing 5'9" tall and weighing a rugged 181 pounds, was the hardest hitting shortstop in Japanese baseball history. The right handed slugger, usually hitting second or third in the H-Bomb lineup, pounded out a tough .277 batting average, with 24 doubles and 24 homers a year. In addition to knocking in 80 runs a year, he also displayed good speed with 19 stolen bases. He was voted Rookie of the Year in 1953 and captured the Pacific League batting championship in 1956, with an average of .325.

THIRD BASE:

• Shigeo Nagashima is Japan's all-time third baseman.

Yasumitsu Toyoda. (Gary Engel.)

He is unquestionably the most popular player ever to play baseball in the island nation. He is credited with hitting the most dramatic home run in the history of the country. In 1959, in the first Emperor's Game, with the Emperor and Empress in attendance, Nagashima hit a ninth-inning, game-winning home run.

Teaming with Sadaharu Oh to form the Yomiuri Giants terrifying "O-N Cannons," the handsome third sacker led the Giants to 13 Central League pennants and 11 Japan Series titles in 18 years. During that time, he walked off with five Most Valuable Player awards, six batting titles, two home run titles, and five RBI titles.

Nagashima was noted as a great clutch hitter, who got the big hit at the right time. His timely heroics over the years earned him the title "Mr. Giant."

Shigeo Nagashima. (Gary Engel.)

When he retired, after 17 years with Yomiuri, he had accumulated 2471 base hits, 444 home runs, and 1522 runs batted in, to go along with a .305 batting average.

He has managed the Yomiuri Giants since 1975, winning nine Central League titles and three Japan Series championships. He is a member of the MEIKYUKAI and the Hall of Fame.

• Futoshi Nakanishi, a stubby, 5'8", 205 pound third baseman, was called the Japanese Hack Wilson. He was a powerful slugger who led the Pacific League in home runs five times in six years, from 1953 to 1958. He averaged 33 home runs a year and batted .312 during a time when pitching still dominated the league. Earned run averages under 2.00 were common.

Nakanishi was voted Rookie of the Year in 1952. He went on to win two batting titles, with .332 in 1955 and .314 in 1958, and helped the Nishitetsu Lions H-Bomb Row win five Pacific League championships and three successive Japan Series.

The right handed hitter had his promising career cut short in the spring of 1959 when he injured his wrist while batting. He hung on for another 11 years as a part-time player but was never the same. He batted only 949 times in the ensuing 11 years, with 54 home runs.

Following his retirement, he managed for 13 years.

OUTFIELD:

The all-star outfield consists of Isao Harimoto, Koji Yamamoto, Hiromitsu Ochiai, Hiroshi Oshita, Yutaka Fukumoto, and Hiromitsu Kadota. Many other deserving outfielders were considered for the team, and six of them were selected for the #2 squad, which is listed in Table XVI.

• Isao Harimoto was the most proficient hitter in Japan from 1959 to 1981, capturing an unprecedented seven batting championships. When he retired, he had the highest season batting average (.383), and the highest career batting average (.319) in league history. Both records have since been surpassed.

Harimoto, a Japanese-born Korean, was a veritable hitting machine. Over the course of a 23-year career, he rapped out a record 3085 base hits, with 1523 runs scored, 504 home runs, and 1676 runs batted in. He is the all-time leader in hits, and is in the top six for runs scored (#3), doubles (#4), triples (#5), home runs (#6), extra base hits (#3), and runs batted in (#4). He also swiped 319 bases (#20).

The left fielder for the Toei Flyers had the misfortune of playing for mediocre teams during most of his career. He did, however, win one Japan Series title, with Toei in 1962, and two Central League championships with the Yomiuri Giants in 1976 and '77. He is a member of both the MEIKYUKAI and the Hall of Fame.

• Koji Yamamoto, the fourth most productive home run hitter in Japanese history, with 536 circuit clouts to his credit, was the spark that carried the Hiroshima Carp to five Central League titles and three Japan Series championships between 1969 and 1976. He won four home run titles during that time, as well as one batting title and three RBI crowns. He was voted the Most Valuable Player in the Central League on two occasions.

The 6' tall, 181 pound Yamamoto was not only a powerful hitter, he was also a gifted fielder, who won 10 consecutive Gold Glove awards. A career .290 hitter, he hit over .300 seven times, with a high of .336 in 1980. He drove in over 100 runs six times, and blasted more than 40 home runs five straight years.

Yamamoto is a member of the MEIKYUKAI.

• Hiromitsu Ochiai was still active in 1998. The big slugger, at 5'10", 181 pounds was not a very good fielder, either in the outfield or at first base. He was slow footed and nonchalant on defense. He also hit into an average of 16 double plays a year. But his offensive numbers were awesome. Through 1998, he accumulated 2371 base hits, 510 home runs, and 1564 runs batted in, to go along with a .311 batting average.

Playing primarily with the Lotte Orions and the Chunichi Dragons, the outspoken Ochiai was on three pennant winners and one Japan Series champion. He won an unparalleled three triple crowns in 1982 (.325, 32 home runs, 99 RBIs), 1985 (.367, 52, 146), and 1986 (.360, 50, 116). His 52 home runs in 1985 ties him with Katsuya Nomura for the most single season home runs in Pacific League history. In all, Ochiai won five batting titles, five home run crowns, and five RBI titles.

He is already a member of MEIKYUKAI, and should be a shoo-in for the Hall of Fame when he becomes eligible.

• Hiroshi Oshita was one of the idols of Japanese baseball in the years following World War II. From 1946 through 1959, the 5'8" slugger bombarded Japanese pitchers to the tune of .313, with 201 home runs and 861 runs batted in. His average of 20 home runs a year is especially impressive, since it was achieved during the dead ball era. He was the only batter to hit more than 12 home runs in a season during that time, and he did it twice, with the awesome total of 20 home runs in 1946 and 17 more in 1947.

Oshita was a natural opponent of the Yomiuri Giants' Tetsuharu Kawakami in post-war Japan, and the media gave considerable press time to the duels between Oshita's blue bat and Kawakami's red bat. According to *Total Baseball,* the lefty Oshita had a smooth, graceful swing that sent balls on high arcs into the Japanese sky.

During his first six years in the league, with the Senetars and the Tokyu Fliers, Oshita played with mediocre teams, but after 1951, he became the cleanup hitter for the famed H-Bomb Row of the Nishitetsu Lions. He helped the Lions to four Pacific League titles, and to three consecutive Japan Series championships over Kawakami and the Tokyo Giants, from 1956 to 1958. He was elected to the Hall of Fame in 1980.

• Yutaka Fukumoto came out of Fujiyama in 1969 to set the Japan League on its ear with his blazing speed. Beginning in his rookie year of 1970, the 5'6", 150 pound greyhound ran away with 13 consecutive stolen base crowns, an unprecedented record in any league. His .781 stolen base percentage is higher than such renowned major league base thieves as Ty Cobb, Maury Wills, and Lou Brock.

He also stole six bases in seven attempts against major league catchers like Johnny Bench in exhibition games.

Fukumoto set Japanese records for most stolen bases in one year (106), and most stolen bases in a career (1065). His career record, which was also the world record, was subsequently broken by Ricky Henderson in 1993.

In addition to his basepath adventures, the leadoff hitter for the Hankyu Braves had other weapons as well. On defense, he was a sensational center fielder, with 12 consecutive Gold Gloves to his credit. At the plate, he compiled a career batting average of .291, with 1656 runs scored, 449 doubles, 115 triples, and 208 home runs. He batted over .300 seven times. He is the career leader in doubles and triples, #6 in base hits and #2 in runs scored. Over his celebrated 20-year career, he led the league in runs scored 10 times, doubles three times, triples eight times, and bases on balls six times. He was the Most Valuable Player in the Pacific League in 1972.

Yutaka Fukumoto is a member of the prestigious MEIKYUKAI.

• Hiromitsu Kadota was a powerful hitter who blasted 567 home runs, primarily for the Nankai Hawks, during his 23-year career. He trails only Sadaharu Oh and Katsuya Nomura in that category. The husky 5'7", 178 pound left handed slugger was a nine-time all-star, based solely on his offensive pyrotechnics. He was slow afoot, and only so-so on defense.

With a bat in his hand, however, Kadota was a destructive force. His 1678 runs batted in is the fourth highest total in Japanese league history. He was a career .289 hitter who batted over .300 nine times. The muscular outfielder won three home run crowns, with totals of 44 in 1981, 40 in 1983, and 44 in 1988. He also walked off with two RBI titles, and was voted the Most Valuable player in the Pacific League in 1978 when he hit .311 with 44 homers and 125 RBIs. His average of 110 RBIs a year is #3 all-time behind Sadaharu Oh and Hiromitsu Ochiai.

Hiromitsu Kadota is a member of the MEIKYUKAI, based on his 2566 career base hits.

UTILITY:

• Tsutomu Wakamatsu was a hitting machine for the Yakult Swallows from 1971 to 1989. During his career he compiled a scintillating .319 batting average, just .00084 behind LeRon Lee's career leading .320. The little 5'6", 165 pound left handed hitter generally batted in the third slot in the batting order, driving in an average of 71 runs per year. Unfortunately, his statistics were adversely affected by weak hitting teams. The Swallows won only one Central League crown in 19 years, while finishing last six times and fifth three times.

Wakamatsu was a solid, all-around player. He won two batting titles, with an average of .329 in 1972 and .358 in 1977. In 1978, he captured the Central League's Most Valuable Player award, as he led the Swallows to their only Central League pennant and Japan Series championship. He hit .341 that year, with 17 homers, 71 RBIs and 12 stolen bases.

He also was a Gold Glove outfielder twice, and was voted to the Central League Best Nine team nine times. He is a member of MEIKYUKAI.

• Sachio Kinugasa was a dedicated, hard working third baseman–outfielder for the Hiroshima Toyo Carp for 23 years, from 1965 to 1987. He helped his team to five Central League pennants and three Japan Series championships during that time. In 1984, he won the RBI title with 102, and also carried home the Most Valuable Player trophy.

Kinugasa's main claim to fame, however, was his durability and his tremendous dedication. From the time he broke into the starting lineup, on October 18, 1970, until the day he retired in 1987, he never missed a game. He played in 2215 consecutive games, breaking Lou Gehrig's record of 2130 games, on June 13, 1987. He subsequently lost his world record to Cal Ripken in 1996.

Kinugasa played through five broken bones, numerous illnesses, and occasional family problems to establish one of the most admired and enduring records in Japan baseball history. His achievement is all the more remarkable because it was accomplished over a 130 game schedule, compared to the 154 and 162 game schedules of Gehrig and Ripken respectively. Kinugasa's record was set over a period of 17 years. Cal Ripken would have had to play into 1999 to match it.

Sachio Kinugasa was a fun loving individual who loved fancy cars, expensive clothes, and the night club scene. Still, he never missed his daily routine of swinging a bat 100 or more times. Although small in stature, at 5'9", 161 pounds, he swung from the heels on every pitch, establishing a Japan record of 1587 career strikeouts along the way. He also punched out a career .270 batting average, with 2643 base hits (#5 all-time) and 504 home runs (#6). He drove in 1448 teammates (#6) and scored 1372 runs (#5) himself. He is a member of the MEIKYUKAI.

Ichiro Suzuki was not selected for the all-star team although he may be the greatest hitter in Japanese baseball history. The Orix Blue Wave outfielder, at 26 years of age, has played just six full seasons in Japan's Pacific League, not long enough to be considered for all-star status. Although he has captured the league batting championship all six years, he is just now entering his peak years as an athlete, and could conceivably establish batting records that will never be broken.

Japanese Professional All Star Team

Catcher	Katsuya Nomura*
	Koichi Tabuchi
Pitcher	Masaichi Kaneda*
	Tetsuya Yoneda
	Keishi Suzuki
	Victor Starffin
	Kazuhisa Inao
	Takehiko Bessho
	Yutaka Enatsu
First Base	Sadaharu Oh*
	Tetsuharu Kawakami
Second Base	Morimichi Takagi*
	Shigeru Chiba
Shortstop	Yoshio Yoshida*
	Yasumitsu Toyoda
Third Base	Shigeo Nagashima*
	Futoshi Nakanishi
Outfield	Isao Harimoto*
	Koji Yamamoto*
	Yutaka Fukumoto*
	Hiromitsu Ochiai

Hiroshi Oshita
Hiromitsu Kadota

Utility   Tsutomu Wakamatsu
Sachio Kinugasa

Note: An asterisk (*) denotes one of the starting nine players.

Puerto Rican Winter League All-Star Team

Puerto Rico was first discovered by Christopher Columbus on November 19, 1498, and was subsequently conquered by Juan Ponce de Leon in 1509. It became part of the Spanish Empire and remained such until the Spanish-American War in 1898. The American general, Nelson Appleton Miles, freed the island from Spanish rule in July 1898. It was ceded to the United States by Spain after the Spanish-American War as part of the treaty of Paris, December 19, 1898. Puerto Rico is now an autonomous Commonwealth of the United States, free to govern itself as it sees fit.

By the time the Spanish-American War began, baseball was already being played on the island. It had been brought to Puerto Rico in 1890 by a Spanish diplomat who was introduced to the game in Cuba. It was subsequently popularized by sugar plantation owners, who felt it would keep their workers out of trouble and would be good for morale. Soon "sugar league" teams were springing up all over the tiny island. Government agencies, schools, and other industrial groups organized baseball teams as well.

The first recorded baseball game in Puerto Rico, according to Michael M. and Mary Adams Oleksak in *Beisbol*, took place at the San Juan bicycle course on January 9, 1898, between the Almendares and Borinquen teams. Tickets cost 40 cents for seats in the shade, and 20 cents for seats in the sun. It was a strange game, in that it took three weeks to complete. On January 9, the game was called after three innings, due to rain. The rematch was rained out after four innings. Finally, on the 30th of the month, the game was completed, with Borinquen winning 9–3.

Shortly after the turn of the century, professional teams were organized on the island. The first teams included Almendares, Havana, and San Cristobal. As reported by the Oleksaks, games were often played on the parade grounds of El

Morro Castle, the old Spanish fort at the west end of San Juan islet. There were no organized leagues, but there were frequent tournaments, and annual championships, staged.

According to Eduardo Valero in *Puerto Rico's Winter League*, baseball began to explode after World War I. Many American and Cuban teams were invited to the island during the off-season, and a number of players took advantage of the opportunity to travel and to earn extra money. Major leaguers like Leon Cadore and Heinie Zimmerman were among the first Americans to play baseball in Puerto Rico. Cuban greats Jose Mendez, Alejandro Oms, Cristobal Torriente, and Adolfo Luque made the trek south from their homeland. And Puerto Rican legends Pedro Miguel Caratini, Jacinto "Jayase" Hernandez, and Jose "Pepe" Santana began their baseball careers during this period.

Caratini spent some time in the Dominican Republic, where he taught school — and baseball. Later, he brought Dominican teams to Puerto Rico to play against the locals. According to Valero, "During the 1920s and 1930s, local promoters brought teams from Cuba, Mexico, Venezuela, and the Dominican Republic, and from the minor leagues and the Negro leagues in the United States." It was a veritable potpourri of international baseball.

By 1936, the major league color barrier was showing some signs of cracking. The Cincinnati Reds held their spring training in Puerto Rico, and played exhibition games against local integrated clubs, as well as against integrated and black teams from the U.S. Negro Leagues, Mexico, and Cuba. Some of the greatest baseball players in Puerto Rican history strutted their stuff during this period. Although there were no formal leagues, and no records were kept, their exploits were carefully guarded in the hearts of those who watched them perform their magic on the field.

In 1938, the Puerto Rican Winter League opened its inaugural season with teams from Guayama, Humacao, San Juan, Ponce, Caguas, and Mayaguez. The league was an immediate success, and the Guayama Witches, sparked by the league's Most Valuable Player, shortstop Perucho Cepeda, captured the title by 5½ games. Cepeda also walked away with most of the offensive honors, leading the league in batting average (.465), runs batted in (48 in 39 games), and hits (79). Negro leaguer Eddie Stone took the home run title, with nine. "The Dominican Deer," Tetelo Vargas, batted .414 and led the league in runs scored and triples, while Cuban legend Alejandro Oms contributed to the Witches' potent attack, whacking out six straight hits in one game.

The next year, 1939, saw the greatest pitching exhibition in Puerto Rican Winter League history. The inimitable Satchel Paige brought his pitching magic to the island, and left six months later, a legend. The league at that time ran from October 1 through April 7, with 28 Sunday doubleheaders. Paige started 24 games, won 19 of them, against only three losses, and posted an all-time record of 208 strikeouts in 205 innings pitched. He also tossed six shutouts. On December 3, 1939, the 33-year-old Satchel man fanned seven batters in a row, on his way to a 17 strikeout performance against the Mayaguez Indians, winning 1–0. Naturally, Paige won the Most Valuable Player award for the season.

In the 1941–42 season, it was Josh Gibson's turn to dazzle the fans. Josh pounded the ball at a league leading .480 clip, the highest single season batting average in Puerto Rican history. He also slammed 13 home runs in just 123 at-bats, on his way to carrying off the Most Valuable Player trophy.

Puerto Rican baseball historian Luis Alvelo called the '40s "The Golden Age" of baseball in Puerto Rico. Perhaps from a fan-player relationship standpoint, Alvelo is correct. Certainly the Negro League players endeared themselves to the people of the island. As Alvelo noted, "They filled the park with music and unforgettable moments." They played major league quality baseball, and they took time to instruct the youngsters in the finer points of the game, visited fans in their homes, and brought toys and good cheer to the children in the hospitals. Just as in Japan, the Negro League players were some of America's most effective good will ambassadors.

Other Negro League players who played in the Winter League during the '40s, in addition to Paige and Gibson, were Billy Byrd, Roy Campanella, Bus Clarkson, Leon Day, Buck Leonard, Monte Irvin, Willard Brown, and Bill Wright.

With the collapse of the color barrier in the major leagues in 1946, the Negro Leagues soon disappeared, cutting off that source of talent to the Puerto Rican Winter Leagues. But that didn't destroy the PRWL. In fact, it might have strengthened it over the long haul. Major League owners quickly saw the value of having a winter league, where rookies and minor league prospects could sharpen their baseball skills between seasons.

The owners also recognized the vast pool of talent that was waiting to be tapped in the young black players in Puerto Rico and neighboring countries. During the 1950s and '60s, black Puerto Rican baseball phenoms like Vic Power, Orlando Cepeda, Roberto Clemente, Ruben Gomez, and Juan Pizzaro honed their talents in their homeland from November to February. They were reinforced by young stateside players like Willie Mays, Dixie Howell, Bob Thurman, Mickey Stanley, and Jim Northrup.

Over the past 40 years, PRWL rosters have read like a who's who of

Roberto Clemente. (Yuyo Ruiz.)

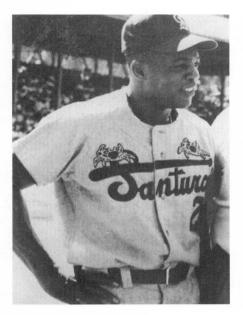

Willie Mays. (Yuyo Ruiz.)

baseball. Some of the more famous names to play on the island include Sandy Koufax, Mike Schmidt, Cal Ripken, Ron Cey, Johnny Bench, Roberto Alomar, Carlos Baerga, Bobby Bonilla, Frank Howard, and Edgar Martinez. The quality of play in the Puerto Rican Winter League has improved significantly since its beginning over 60 years ago.

Luis Alvelo misses the good old days of the late '30s and early '40s when Josh Gibson, Satchel Paige, and company instructed Puerto Rican youngsters in the fundamentals of the game and socialized with the fans in the taverns and in their homes. Those long ago days were surely the golden age of baseball in Puerto Rico, but for factors off the field, rather than on it.

It appears as if the quality of play in the PRWL is higher today than it has ever been. From 1938 to about 1958, the level of play, based on player comparisons in different leagues, was slightly better than a class AA league. There were many players in the league during that period who were of major league caliber, players like Francisco Coimbre, Perucho Cepeda, Josh Gibson, Roy Campanella, Junior Gilliam, and Monte Irvin, but the majority of the players were not as talented.

The AA+ level estimate is supported by Puerto Rico's performance in the Caribbean Series from 1949 to 1960. The Series, billed as the Caribbean World Series, brought together the best teams from Puerto Rico, Cuba, Panama, and Venezuela. The Cuban Winter League was estimated to be a AAA level league, while Panama appeared to be slightly below a AA league, and the quality of play in Venezuela was unknown. Over the 12 year period, Cuba won seven championships, Puerto Rico captured four, and Panama one. Venezuela was shut out.

Since 1959, the PRWL has improved to a point where it now appears to be at a AAA level or higher. After a nine-year interruption, the Caribbean Series was renewed in 1970, with Puerto Rico, the Dominican Republic, Venezuela, and Mexico, competing for the championship. Through 1998, Puerto Rico (class AAA+) won nine titles, the Dominican Republic (class AAA) won 11, Venezuela won six, and Mexico (class AA) won three.

In 1995, a powerful Dominican Republic squad, with major league stars Raul Mondesi, Jose Offerman, Jose Rijo, Pedro Martinez, and Pedro Astacio trounced Mexico and Venezuela in the preliminary rounds before running into the Puerto Rican champions in the finals. The San Juan juggernaut, with Roberto Alomar, Edgar Martinez, Bernie Williams, Juan Gonzalez, Carlos Baerga, and Ricky Bones, buried the Dominican team under a barrage of extra base hits. It was a major league exhibition all the way.

The testimony of major league players who received valuable training in the Puerto Rican Winter League, as reported by Tom Van Hyning, bears testimony to the quality of play in that league over the last 40 years.

Vic Power was quoted in *Puerto Rico's Winter League* as saying, "Puerto Rico ball was better than AAA in the 1950s." Frank Howard, in 1960-61, said the PRWL was "better than AAA." Tony Perez, in 1964-65, said, "Puerto Rico was almost major league caliber in the 1960s." Cal Ripken thought the winter league was "between AAA and the big leagues." The testimony of major league players like David Nied, Sid Bream, Jon Matlack, Tom Candiotti, Roberto Kelly, Rafael Palmero, and Wade Boggs was unanimous in the belief that the PRWL was AAA caliber or better.

The Puerto Rican Winter League has been divided into two periods for the purpose of this study: the "organized baseball segregation period," which was in effect in 1938, and which effectively carried through to 1958, and the period from 1959 to the present, with integration in full force. In the beginning, there were many great players who were barred from participating in major league ball because of the color of their skin. More than a few of these men would also have been candidates for election to Baseball's Hall of Fame.

Two separate all-star teams have been selected for the Puerto Rican Winter League (see Table XXI). The first all-star team covers the Pioneer period, from the early days through 1958, and includes many players whose achievements are only imprinted in the hearts of their countrymen. Players like Pedro Miguel Caratini, Jayase Hernandez, and Pepe Santana are indistinct shadows from the misty past, legendary figures whose great exploits have been passed on by word of mouth. Their records, in most cases, have been lost forever. At best, a few fragmentary statistics exist.

The second all-star team is an all-time all-star team of the Puerto Rican Winter League, based on the recorded history of the league from 1938 to the present. The early all-star team is of the most interest for this study, since we are primarily concerned with the great players who performed outside the umbrella of organized baseball, and who, as a result, have never been recognized for their outstanding skills by the American baseball community. Such Puerto Rican legends as Francisco Coimbre and Perucho Cepeda fall into this category.

The Pioneer All-Star team consists of the following players.

CATCHER:

• Josh Gibson played in the Puerto Rican Winter League for three years. In 1941, his second year, the 29-year-old bomber, at the peak of his fantastic career, literally destroyed PRWL pitching, with a record-setting .480 batting average. He also led the league in home runs (13 in 123 at-bats), on his way to the Most Valuable Player award. He is a member of the Puerto Rican Baseball Hall of Fame, having been elected to that elite forum in 1996. He is also a member of the Hall of Fame in both Mexico and the United States.

• Luis Villodas, a native of Ponce, starred in the PRWL for 13 years, primarily with the Mayaguez Indians. The 6'2" 210 pound catcher was called "King Kong" because of his imposing size. He also played in the Negro Leagues, with the Baltimore Elite Giants and the New York Cubans. He was elected to the Puerto Rican Baseball Hall of Fame in 1993.

PITCHER:

• Cefo Conde was one of Puerto Rico's great pitchers during the pioneer period. Although his record is incomplete, he had records of 12–8 in '39-'40, 10–10 in '42-'43, and 10–6 in '48-'49, in the twilight of his career. He was elected to the Hall of Fame in 1992.

• Juan Guilbe, a big strapping right handed pitcher, pitched for Ponce from the early '30s until the late '40s. He also pitched in the Negro Leagues, as well as in the Dominican Republic, Canada, Venezuela, and Colombia. The 6'1", 207 pound fireballer had a full repertoire of pitches and was a good control pitcher. Leon Day called him one of the best pitchers he had ever seen, as reported by Todd Bolton.

The big power pitcher led the Ponce Lions to four consecutive league championships from 1941 through 1944. He led the league in pitching in '41-'42, with an 11–2 record. He went 8–4 in '47. The husky Guilbe was also a dangerous hitter who played first base when not pitching. He led the league in home runs in '43-'44, with two in 103 at-bats. He entered the Hall of Fame in 1992.

• Jose Antonio Figueroa was born in Mayaguez on June 19, 1914. He developed into an all-around athlete who excelled in track as well as baseball. In 1935, Figueroa won a gold medal in the javelin competition in the Caribbean Olympic Games. Three years later, according to Todd Bolton, "he made history in two sports. In baseball, he pitched the Puerto Rican team to victory over Cuba. This win had special significance since it was the first time Cuba had ever lost in the Caribbean Games. Following that performance, he proceeded to set the all-time javelin record in Caribbean Olympic competition."

Figueroa pitched during the formative years of the PRWL. He was 14–13 in '39-'40, with a team that finished with only 20 wins in 55 games. That year, he hurled 26 complete games, with 242 innings pitched. He was also a formidable hitter who compiled a lifetime batting average of over .300, according to Bolton. He was elected to the Hall of Fame in 1992.

• Luis Raul Cabrera pitched in the PRWL for 18 years, from 1939 to 1955.

His 105–99 career record included a 10–8 record in '40-'41, 13–8 in '41-'42, 13–7 in '43-'44, and 13–10 in '44-'45. "Cabrerita" was the league's MVP, with Santurce in 1940-41, as he led the team to the second half championship. The 5'10", 175 pound right handed pitcher was primarily a breaking ball pitcher, with an occasional fastball thrown in. Cabrera also pitched in the Negro Leagues, in Mexico, and in organized ball from 1949 to 1951.

• Roberto Vargas was credited with a 51–24 record in the PRWL over a 13-year career. He led the league in winning percentage in '50-'51 with an 11–1 record. The tall, lanky southpaw pitched in the Negro Leagues one year (compiling a 6–8 record), as well as in Mexico, where he went 39–32 over a four year period. He pitched in organized baseball from 1952 to 1959, including a stop-over with the Milwaukee Braves in 1955 (he pitched in 25 games with no record).

• Rafaelito Ortiz was selected to the early all-star team by both Alvelo and Ruiz. "The Magician of Magas" as he was called, pitched in the PRWL from its inception in 1938 until 1950. He won 11 games against only three losses in his rookie season, helping the Guayama Witches win the pennant by 5½ games. According to Van Hyning, Ortiz "pitched brilliantly in Guayama's 1939 Semi-Pro World Series victory over the Duncan Cementers with two shutouts, one a six inning no-hitter called because of rain."

The right handed pitcher made history when he went 15–0 for the Ponce Lions in '43-'44. He also captured the earned run average title on two occasions. Ortiz pitched on five pennant winners with four different teams during his career. He was elected to the Hall of Fame in 1992.

• Tomas "Planchardon" Quinones ran up an 82–38 career record over a colorful 13-year career. The hard throwing right hander, after a commendable 13–5 record in '43-'44, went 16–3 in '44-'45, including the league's first no-hitter. He was voted the league's Most Valuable Player both years. The "Iron Man" won a league leading 10 games against six losses in '45-'46, as Ponce won their third straight championship. Two years later, he pitched Ponce to their fourth title, defeating the Caguas Criollos. In 1993, he was elected to the Hall of Fame.

• Raymond Brown was a great pitcher in four countries, winning over 250 games during his much traveled 23-year career. He pitched in Puerto Rico six years, winning 40 games against 20 losses. His record included a 7–0 season in '38-'39, another 7–0 season in '39-'40, and a 12–4 season in '41-'42.

• Satchel Paige only pitched in Puerto Rico two years, but one of those years may never be equaled. In 1939-40, Paige pitched Guayama to the pennant by one game, with a superhuman effort. Pitching in 24 of his team's 56 games, the lanky flame thrower went 19–3, with 208 strikeouts in 205 innings.

• Leon Day, another Negro League legend, pitched in the PRWL four years, running up a 35–28 record. The 5'10", 180 pound fastball pitcher was 12–11 in '39-'40, 10–6 in '40-'41, and 12–9 in '41-'42.

FIRST BASE:

• Jacinto "Jayase" Hernandez was a big, strong slugger with the Humacao Stars and the All-Borinquen team from the mid–'20s until 1938–39, according to Alvelo. The 6'2", black first baseman-outfielder hit some memorable homers against the Cuban Stars and the New York Lincoln Giants.

• Jose "Pepe" Santana was another early home run hitter. Known as "El Bambino," the tall, rugged, first baseman-outfielder played professional baseball for about twenty years, beginning in the mid–'20s. He batted a respectable .302 during the first PRWL season. He finished his career with the San Juan Senators in the early '40s.

SECOND BASE:

• Fernando Diaz Pedroso, a native of Marianao, Cuba, enjoyed a 14-year career in Cuba, Mexico, the Dominican Republic, Nicaragua, and the Negro Leagues, as well as in Puerto Rico. He had his greatest successes in Mexico and Puerto Rico. The 5'11", 175 pound second baseman played in the PRWL for seven years, compiling a .325 batting average with good power, averaging 21 home runs for every 550 at-bats over his career. He led the league in batting in '45–'46, with an average of .368. He also led the league in home runs one year, and in stolen bases one year. In addition to his skill with the bat, he was a fancy fielding second baseman, with quick reflexes and an accurate arm.

• Emilio "Millito" Navarro was born in Patillas, on September 26, 1905. He began his baseball career in 1922, at the age of 17 as a right handed hitting second baseman. The 5'5", 160 pound infielder was an excellent fielder, as well as an outstanding hitter. In 1928, he became Puerto Rico's first player in the Negro leagues, playing two years with the Cuban Stars. The little leadoff hitter batted .337 in 1928, according to James A. Riley. When the Puerto Rican Winter League began operations in 1938, the 33-year-old Navarro was one of its star performers. He played in the PRWL for five years, retiring from active play in 1943 after suffering a knee injury. He was elected to the Hall of Fame in 1992.

• Menchin Pesante played in the PRWL during the formative years of the league. He was selected as an all-star by Puerto Rican baseball historian Yuyo Ruiz.

• Jose "Pepe" Seda was an all-around athlete. In addition to playing a sizzling second base, he also excelled in volleyball, track, and basketball. In the first year of the Winter League's operation, 1938-39, Seda hit the ball at a .304 pace. He was still playing baseball in 1940-41 as a member of the Caguas Criollos. According to Van Hyning, he also wrote a baseball rule book, managed the San Juan Senators for a number of years, and scouted for the New York Yankees.

• Pito Alvarez de la Vega was a second baseman of the 1930s and early '40s. He was the player-manager for the Caguas Criollos in 1938-39, and was still active in 1940-41, platooning with Seda at the keystone sack. The '40-'41 team, with 19-year-old Roy Campanella behind the plate and 15-game winner Billy Byrd on the mound, beat Guayama by three games for the title. Alvarez was elected to the Hall of Fame in 1993.

SHORTSTOP:

• Pedro Miguel Caratini is a legend in Puerto Rico. He was born in Coamo around the turn of the century, and gained a reputation as a great shortstop and a powerful home run hitter in the early days of professional baseball. According to baseball historian Luis Alvelo, Caratini was active on the diamond from the early 1900s through the 1930s, first as a player, then as a manager. He helped popularize baseball in the Dominican Republic as an instructor and a manager. His contributions to baseball in both countries was recognized when he was elected to the Hall of Fame in both Puerto Rico and the Dominican Republic.

• Pedro Anibal "Perucho" Cepeda was a bona fide Cooperstown Hall of Fame candidate who missed his chance at major league glory because of the "color problem." Cepeda, who was born in San Juan in 1906, was the greatest shortstop in Puerto Rican history. In addition to dazzling defensive play, Cepeda was a powerful offensive threat who averaged over 100 runs batted in a year. Although he was 32 years old when the Puerto Rican Winter League kicked off its inaugural season, he quickly demonstrated his superior baseball skills by capturing the batting title with an average of .465. He won it again in '39-'40, with an average of .383. He also walked off with the Most Valuable Player award both years. Cepeda led the league in RBIs three times, hits three times, and triples once. In 1939-40, the 5'11", 200 pound slugger whacked out six hits in seven at-bats, in one game.

The slugging shortstop had numerous opportunities to play baseball in the United States in the Negro Leagues during the '20s and '30s, but he turned down all offers. He was aware of the racial atmosphere that existed in the United States at the time and, with his quick temper, he decided it would be too dangerous for him to make the trip.

When he retired in 1950, he left behind a career batting average of .325, the

Pedro Caratini. (Yuyo Riuz.)

Left to right: **Perucho Cepeda and Jose De La Vega. (Luis Alvelo.)**

third highest average in PRWL history. He died just five years later, at the young age of 49. Perucho Cepeda was one of Puerto Rico's greatest players. He was in the first group of players elected to Puerto Rico's Baseball Hall of Fame.

• James Buster Clarkson, better known as "Bus," was a rugged shortstop who had a celebrated 11-year career in the PRWL between 1940 and 1955. The 5'11", 200 pound right handed slugger was not only a powerful hitter, he also had exceptional speed. Over his career, he averaged 27 home runs a year, to go along with a .301 batting average. Some of his more notable accomplishments:

– He led the PRWL in stolen bases in '41-'42, with 18.
– He led the league in runs scored in '40-'41, with 48 in just 140 at-bats.
– He hit for the cycle on May 1, 1941, while playing for Mayaguez.
– He hit two home runs in the same inning on May 2, 1941.
– He had 62 RBIs in 261 at-bats in 1950-51.
– He led the league in home runs with 18 in 261 at-bats during the 1950-51 season.
– He hit two grand slam home runs during the 1951-52 season.
– He led the league in RBIs in '54-'55, with 60 in 240 at-bats.

• Coco Ferrer was selected as an early all-star by both Ruiz and Alvelo. He led the league in stolen bases in '46-'47. His career statistics are not available.

THIRD BASE:

• One of the great third baseman in Puerto Rican history, in any era, was Luis "Canena" Marquez. He was a sensational hitter who put together a record .361 season as a rookie in 1944-45, then went on to compile a .300 batting average with 15 home runs for every 550 at-bats over a colorful 20-year career. He led the league with 14 home runs in '46-'47, edging Larry Doby by two. In 1953-54, he won the batting championship, with an average of .333, beating out Hank Aaron by 11 points.

The good natured Marquez could do it all, defensively as well as offensively. He led the league in stolen bases four times, while averaging almost 50 stolen bases a year. He is the all-time season record holder (tie) in doubles with 27 and triples with 10 in seasons that did not exceed 60 games. He entered the Puerto Rican Baseball Hall of Fame in 1991.

Marquez played four years in the Negro leagues during the late '40s, leading the league with an astronomical .417 average in 1946. He also led in stolen bases that year, with 29. His Negro League career average was .389, with 11 home runs a year.

• Augustin "Tingo" Daviu, a native of Ponce, played baseball during the 1920s and '30s. He was a third baseman who played minor league ball in the United States for a time, signing with Allentown in the Class A Eastern

Luis Marquez. (Yuyo Ruiz.)

League. He was the first Puerto Rican native to play organized ball in the United States, according to Thomas E. Van Hyning in his book *Puerto Rico's Winter League*.

• Nenene Aniceto Rivera played third base and pitched during the 1920s and '30s. He was a right handed pitcher who played one year for the Cuban Stars in the Negro League.

OUTFIELD:

Outfielders on the all-star team include Pancho Coimbre, Willard Brown, Bob Thurman, Tetelo Vargas, Nino Escalera, Carlos Bernier, Juan "Chico" Sanchez, Manuel "Manolo" Garcia, and Monchile Concepcion.

• Francisco "Pancho" Coimbre was arguably Puerto Rico's greatest baseball player. The 5'11", 180 pound outfielder could have been a clone of Roberto Clemente, although Clemente always claimed that Coimbre was the better player. Coimbre was a five pointer: he could hit, hit with power, run, field, and throw. On defense he showed outstanding speed, great range, and a strong throwing arm. On the bases, he was a fast, aggressive, and intelligent runner. With a bat in his hand, he was a dangerous clutch hitter. He was a true superstar.

Coimbre was born in Coamo on January 29, 1909. By the time the Puerto Rican Winter League began, he was a well traveled 29-year-old veteran, having played baseball in the United States, Mexico, Cuba, Venezuela, and the Dominican Republic, as well as in Puerto Rico. Still, he put together some outstanding years for Ponce, from 1938 to 1951, when he finally retired at the age of 42.

The powerful right handed hitter was a line drive hitter who sprayed extra base hits to all sections of the ballpark. During his 13-year PRWL career, Coimbre led the league in batting twice (.342 in '42-'43, and .425 in '44-'45), in runs scored once, base hits once, RBIs once, doubles twice, and stolen bases once. He averaged 51 extra base hits, 106 runs scored, and 85 runs batted in during his career. He retired with a career batting average of .337, #2 all-time. Coimbre also played in the Negro League four years, pounding the ball at a torrid .361 pace, including a .423 average in 1943. In Mexico, in 1945, he batted .346 for Puebla, driving in 85 runs in 89 games.

One of Coimbre's greatest assets was his amazing eyesight. Throughout his career, the bat wizard struck out only eight times for every 550 at-bats. Joe Sewell of the Cleveland Indians is the major league record holder, with nine. Coimbre has the best home run to strikeout ratio of any player in the history of professional baseball (0.875). He went two years, '41-'42 and '42-'43, a total of 278 at-bats, without a strike-out. In 1948-49 he struck out only one

Francisco Coimbre. (Luis Alvelo.)

time in 239 at-bats. Ichiro Suzuki set the Japan League record in 1997, with 216 at-bats without a strikeout. Coimbre could probably have been a consistent .300 hitter in the major leagues if he had been given the chance. In 1991, he was elected to the Hall of Fame.

• Willard Brown, the Negro League legend, was also a legend in Puerto Rico. Over the course of a 10-year career, the solidly built 200 pounder set a season home run record with 27 round trippers in just 234 at-bats on his way to career total of 101 homers. His average of 29 home runs a year is the highest in the annals of the PRWL, for players with more than 500 at-bats.

Brown was known as "Ese Hombre" (That Man) in Puerto Rico, in deference to his enormous baseball talents. He captured two triple crowns in the PRWL, with a .432 average, 27 home runs, 86 runs batted in, in 234 at-bats, in 1947-48, and a .353 average, 16 home runs, 97 runs batted in, in 1949-50. He added

Willard Brown. (Yuyo Ruiz.)

Bob Thurman. (Yuyo Ruiz.)

another batting championship in '46–'47, with an average of .390, and won another home run title and two more RBI titles during his career. He joined the Hall of Fame family in 1991.

• Bob Thurman was another big banger from the Negro Leagues who became a hero in Puerto Rico. Thurman, over the course of a 12-year PRWL career, accumulated the most career home runs, with 120, an average of 21 for every 550 at-bats. He also holds the PRWL record for most career RBIs, with 565. "El Mucaro," or The Owl, as he was called, was a consistent hitter who never led the league in batting but was always near the top, compiling a .323 career average. He led the league in runs scored once, hits twice, doubles once, triples twice, and home runs twice. In 1991, Thurman was elected to the Hall of Fame.

• Tetelo Vargas, "The Dominican Deer," starred in the Puerto Rican Winter League for 16 years, from the late '30s through the mid–'50s. Vargas was an outstanding all-around player, who excelled at the plate, on the bases, and in the field. He covered acres of ground in the outfield, had a good glove and a strong throwing arm.

He was a consistent contact hitter who rarely struck out. Although not a power hitter, the 5'10", 160 pound right hander was a consistent .300 hitter, whose speed helped him leg out many extra base hits. He led the PRWL in triples twice, in runs four times, and in stolen bases twice. He whacked the ball at a torrid .410 pace in 1943-44.

When Tetelo Vargas retired, he left behind a .320 career batting average, the sixth highest batting average in Puerto Rican history. He is a member of the Hall of Fame in both Puerto Rico and the Dominican Republic.

• Nino Escalera was a 16-year veteran of the PRWL, starring for San Juan from 1947 through 1963 before finishing his career with Caguas in the '63-'64 season. The hard hitting outfielder is #3 on the all-time PRWL hit list. He batted .337 in 1947-48, en route to a career average of .275. He helped San Juan win five league championships and Caguas one. He was elected to the Hall of Fame in 1992.

• Carlos Bernier, a native of Juana Diaz, appeared in 105 games for Pittsburgh in 1953, batting .213. He played much longer and much better in Puerto Rico, compiling a .268 batting average over 19 seasons and stealing a career record 285 bases. The 5'9", 180 pound speedster was an aggressive baserunner, who won five stolen base crowns over his career. He was a 1992 inductee into the Hall of Fame.

• Juan "Chico" Sanchez was a slugging outfielder for the Santurce Crabbers and the Aguadilla Sharks during the 1940s. He led the league in RBIs four times, in hits twice, stolen bases once, and home runs once. He was elected to the Baseball Hall of Fame in 1996.

• Manuel "Manolo" Garcia was an outstanding all-around player during the 1920s and '30s. By the time the Winter League began, Garcia was in the twilight of his career. Still, the 36-year-old outfielder contributed to Caguas' stirring pennant in 1940-41. He hit three triples in one game during the season, and slugged a clutch three bagger against Santurce in the playoffs. More surprising, one year later, the aging veteran was selected for the Northeast All Star team. He entered the Hall of Fame in 1993.

• Ramon "Monchile" Concepcion, an infielder and outfielder, was at his peak during the 1930s. He was an excellent hitter according to Alvelo. He later became a scout for the Los Angeles Dodgers.

UTILITY:

• Luis Olmo played in the Puerto Rican Winter League for 16 years, beginning in 1938 and continuing into the '50s. He hit a solid .338 in the league's inaugural season. He hit three triples in one game in 1940-41. Over his career, he compiled a .290 batting average, with 10 home runs a year. The 5'11", 190 pound outfielder captured two home run titles and one RBI crown. He also led the league in doubles once and triples once. He was the league's MVP in '46-'47.

The right handed hitter was the second Puerto Rican national (after Hiram Bithorn) to play baseball in the major leagues. He starred for the Brooklyn Dodgers for four years, from 1943 to 1945, and 1949. He played baseball in Mexico in 1946 and '47, batting .297 with 21 home runs a year. He became the first Puerto Rican to hit a home run in the World Series when he connected against Joe Page of the New York Yankees in the ninth inning of game three of the 1949 fall classic. Olmo played for the Boston Braves in 1950 and 1951, retiring with a six-year career major league batting average of .281. He was elected to the Puerto Rican Baseball Hall of Fame in 1992.

• Monte Irvin starred in the PRWL, the Negro Leagues, and the major leagues over a storied 21-year career. The fleet footed outfielder slugged the ball wherever he played, leaving behind career averages of .345 with 25 home runs in the Negro Leagues, .359 with 18 homers in the Puerto Rican Winter League, and .293 with 22 homers in the major leagues. It should be noted that Irvin's major league statistics were produced at the end of his career, from age 30 to 37. Based on his achievements in the Negro Leagues and the Puerto Rican Winter League, Irvin could have been expected to hit about .312 in the major leagues during a normal career.

The powerful right handed hitter enjoyed five exciting years with San Juan Senators, winning the Most Valuable Player award in 1945-46 when he led the league in hitting with a .368 average. He also showed the way in hits, doubles and home runs.

As might be expected, the Puerto Rican Winter League all-time all-star team, for the period from 1938 to 1997, is dominated by major league players. Once the color barrier was broken in 1947, and opportunities for black players opened up in organized baseball, a veritable flood of talented players made their way to the States to pursue their dream. During the 1950s, 14 native-born Puerto Ricans, led by Luis "Canena" Marquez, made their major league debuts. Twenty-four more entered the majors during the '60s, 41 during the '70s, and 46 during the '80s. In all, more than 160 native-born Puerto Ricans have entered the major leagues since 1951, compared to only two (Bithorn and Olmo) prior to that time.

The all-time, Puerto Rican Winter League all-star team for the period from 1938 to 1997 is listed below. Of the 32 players on the roster, 23 are native Puerto Ricans, two are from the Virgin Islands, one from Cuba, one from the Dominican Republic, and five from the United States (three Negro Leaguers, and two of Puerto Rican extraction). Twenty-six of them had major league experience. Three are still active in the majors (Alomar, Baerga, and Edgar Martinez). The statistics for these players (major league, Puerto Rican Winter league, and in some cases, Negro League), can be found in the respective tables later in the book.

Puerto Rican Winter League All Star Team — All-Time

Catcher	Jose Morales
	Elrod Hendricks
Pitcher	Ruben Gomez
	Juan Pizzaro
	Luis Arroyo

	Jose G. Santiago
	Jose R. Santiago
	Luis Cabrera
	Tomas Quinones
	Julio Navarro
First Base	Orlando Cepeda
	Vic Power
	Tony Perez
	Willie Montanez
Second Base	Roberto Alomar
	Carlos Baerga
Shortstop	Perucho Cepeda
	Bus Clarkson
	Dickie Thon
Third Base	Canena Marquez
	Edgar Martinez
Outfield	Roberto Clemente
	Pancho Coimbre
	Willard Brown
	Bob Thurman
	Jose Cruz
	Tetelo Vargas
	Juan Beniquez
	Carlos Bernier
	Nino Escalera
	Gil Flores
	Carmelo Martinez

Before leaving the Puerto Rican Winter League review, it is fitting to recognize the top career batters in the circuit. The players listed below all had eight or more years of service in the league.

Name	Years	PRWL Avg.	ML Avg.	Est. ML Avg.
Willard Brown	10	.350	insig.	.317
Pancho Coimbre	13	.337	DNP	.304
Perucho Cepeda	11	.325	DNP	.292
Orlando Cepeda	13	.323	.297	.307
Roberto Clemente	15	.323	.317	.307
Tetelo Vargas	16	.320	DNP	.287
Bob Thurman	12	.313	.246	.280

Name	Years	PRWL Avg.	ML Avg.	Est. ML Avg.
Tony Perez	10	.308	.279	.292
Jose Morales	19	.302	.287	.286
Bus Clarkson	11	.301	insig.	.268
Canena Marquez	20	.300	insig.	.267
Jose Cruz	21	.296	.284	.280
Carlos Baerga	9*	.294	.293	.277
Vic Power	16	.296	.284	.280
Dickie Thon	13	.292	.264	.276
Roberto Alomar	10*	.301	.302	.285
Edgar Martinez	9*	.286	.318	.269

Key:

* . . . . .Still active. The data is through 1995.

Insig. . . . . . . .Insignificant times at bat in the major leagues.
                  Willard Brown batted .179 in 67 at-bats.
                  Bus Clarkson batted .200 in 25 at-bats.
                  Canena Marquez batted .182 in 143 at-bats.

DNP . . . . .Did not play in the major leagues.

Est. ML Avg. . .Estimated major league average based on the comparison of major
                  league statistics to PRWL statistics, as found in the appendix.

Note: Bob Thurman's major league average was compiled when he was between the ages of 38 and 42 years old.

The Mexican League All-Stars

Baseball was brought to Mexico by American railroad workers in the 1870s, according to Michael M. and Mary Adams Oleksak, in *Beisbol*. They also noted that the first baseball game played on Mexican soil took place in Nuevo Laredo during the late 1870s.

In 1906, the Chicago White Sox visited the country, sparking more interest in the American game. One of Mexico's early baseball pioneers was Lucas Juarez, who played from about 1900 to 1918. "El Indio," or The Indian, as he was known, was both a pitcher and a catcher. He was Mexico's greatest pitching star during the early days, but he also carried a powerful bat, so he played catcher when not pitching. He was Mexico's answer to Cuba's Martin Dihigo and America's Babe Ruth.

Julio Molina was considered to be the greatest right handed pitcher of his time. Known as "El Diamante Blanco" or The White Diamond, his career spanned from 1910 to 1925. In the greatest pitching exhibition in Mexican history, Molina dueled Cuba's ace Camilo Pujadas in Merida in 1910. The game was called after 16 innings, with both pitchers still on the mound and the game still scoreless.

By the 1920s, baseball had reached a semi-pro status with the formation of the Mexican League. Leonardo "Najo" Alanis was an outstanding center fielder in the league from 1924 to 1941. Alanis' great speed enabled him to cover acres of ground on defense and circle the bases in record time. Alanis played organized baseball in the United States during the 1920s primarily in the Texas area. He played with San Antonio of the Texas League in 1924. He also played with Okmulgee in the Western Association in 1925, where he was the league's home run king, with 34. He missed his chance at major league stardom when he broke his leg shortly after the Chicago White Sox purchased his contract. He returned to Mexico, where he finished his career with Mexico City of the Mexican League in 1941.

Mel Almada, a 6', 170 pound speedster from Sonora, became Mexico's first major league player when he was added to the Boston Red Sox roster in 1933. Almada enjoyed a seven-year career in the majors, batting .284 with four different teams. He hit a resounding .342 in 102 games for the St. Louis Browns in 1938.

During the 1930s, according to the Oleksaks in *Beisbol*, Mexican League teams often played exhibition games against American Negro league teams, as well as major league all-star teams. As a result, the Mexican fans became familiar with the extraordinary baseball skills of Martin Dihigo, Josh Gibson, "Cool Papa" Bell, Jimmie Foxx, and Rogers Hornsby. John Holway, in *Josh and Satch*, reported that a three-game exhibition series between the major leaguers and the Negro leaguers ended up in a 2–0–1 victory for the big leaguers. Foxx and Hornsby both homered in the series.

The Mexican League became a professional baseball league in 1940, with seven teams playing a 90-game schedule. The league has operated continuously since that time, although it has fluctuated between being an independent league and being a member of organized baseball. It was an independent league from 1940 until 1954. From 1955 until 1967, it was a class AA league, and from 1968 until 1992 it was a class AAA league. It is now, once again, an independent league.

When the league became a professional league, the owners recruited the best baseball players money could buy from Cuba, the United States, the Dominican Republic, Puerto Rico, and elsewhere. Some of the early recruits included Martin Dihigo, Silvio Garcia, Ramon Bragana, and Cocaina Garcia from Cuba, Francisco Coimbre from Puerto Rico, and Satchel Paige, Cool Papa Bell, Josh Gibson, Willie Wells, and Ray Dandridge from the Negro leagues.

The 1941 pennant-winning Vera Cruz Blues were unarguably the greatest team ever assembled in Mexico. The Blues, whose 67–35 record led the league by 13½ games, had a major league quality lineup which included Josh Gibson (.374, with 33 home runs and 124 runs batted in, in 102 games), Ray Dandridge (.367), Willie Wells (.347), Lazaro Salazar (.336 and a 7–3 record pitching), Augustin Bejerano (.366 and 7–5 won-loss), Barney Brown (.323, 16–5), Ramon Bragana (13–8), John Taylor (13–10), and Roberto Cabal (9–1).

Cocaina Garcia. (Yuyo Ruiz.)

Josh Gibson played only two years in Mexico, 1940 and 1941, but he literally destroyed the league's pitching while he was there. The rugged backstop hit a sizzling .393, with 44 home runs and 162 RBIs in just 116 games, numbers that would average out to 54 homers and 198 RBIs over a full 550 at-bat season. Gibson's numbers also showed an average of 38 strikeouts and 111 bases on balls, per 550 at-bats.

In general, the Negro league players thrived on Mexican cooking. In addition to Gibson's statistics, other career averages included Cool Papa Bell (.367), Monte Irvin (.397), Alonzo Perry (.355), Willie Wells (.323), Ray Dandridge (.347), Wild Bill Wright (.335), and Buck Leonard (.326). On the pitching side, significant won-loss records belonged to Theolic Smith (121–90), Martin Dihigo (119–57), Lazaro Salazar (112–78), Barney Brown (84–53), and Ray Brown (51–36).

Willie Wells. (John B. Holway.)

During World War II, the United States government made an agreement with the government of Mexico, which allowed American Negro league players to play baseball in Mexico, in exchange for Mexican laborers to help the war effort in the United States.

In 1946, another crisis arose between the major leagues and the Mexican League, when Mexican tycoon, Jorge Pasquel, lured a number of major league stars to Mexico with enormous salaries. The most prominent of the major leaguers were Sal "The Barber" Maglie, Max Lanier, Freddie Martin, Mickey Owens, Luis Olmo, and George Haussman. The major leagues stalled the Mexican attack by threatening a lifetime ban on anyone who jumped to the Mexican League. Those players who did make the jump in 1946 were reinstated in 1949. Sal Maglie was the only one of the jumpers who returned to a productive major league career. After going 20–12 and 20–13 for Puebla in the Mexican League in '46 and '47, he sparked the New York Giants to the National League pennant in 1951, with a record of 23–6. Five years later, he won 13 games in half a season to help the Brooklyn Dodgers nail down the flag. Included in Maglie's 13 wins was a no-hitter thrown at the Philadelphia Phillies in the heat of the stretch run.

Once peace was restored to the baseball scene, the United States and Mexico embarked on a path of peaceful coexistence. One of the major points that sets Mexico apart from the other western hemisphere countries outside the States is their relationship with Mexican-born baseball players. All Mexican players are the property of the Mexican teams they play for. As a result, if an American major league team is interested in a Mexican player, they must purchase the player from the Mexican team at fair market value. This policy discourages most major league teams from purchasing Mexican players because they can normally obtain equally promising youngsters elsewhere, and with a lower investment.

This situation, as well as the spector of racism in the United States, has prevented American baseball fans from enjoying the exploits of such Mexican stars as Ramon Arano, Mario Ariosa, Matias Carrillo, and Hector Espino. Espino, particularly, decided to play out his career in his homeland, after experiencing discrimination while playing minor league ball in Florida. He was, after all, a larger-than-life hero in Mexico, who was treated royally throughout the width and breadth of the land, even after his career was over. He remains an icon in Mexico.

As a result of this unique state of affairs, it is possible to select a Mexican League All-Star team, for the period from 1937 through 1997, without running into a significant conflict with the major leagues.

The Mexican League All-Star team follows:

CATCHER:

• Francisco "Paquin" Estrada starred behind the plate in Mexico and the United States for 28 long years, the world record for catching longevity. His 2747 games caught is #2 all time, behind the Japanese legend, Katsuya Nomura. During his storied career, the native of Navojoa accumulated 2378 base hits, one of only seven catchers in the entire world to compile more than 2000 hits. The others were Katsuya Nomura of Japan, and Gary Carter, Ted Simmons, Yogi Berra, Johnny Bench, and Carlton Fisk, of the U.S. major leagues.

Estrada, a 5'8", 182 pound right handed hitter, tried his hand at organized ball for three years during the early '70s. He managed to get into one game with the New York Mets in 1971, going one for two, but returned home three years later, after spending the year in the Texas League.

When Estrada retired in 1991, he had posted a career .275 average, including seven .300 seasons.

• Orlando Sanchez was a catcher for several teams from 1985 to 1993. The left handed batter was a prolific hitter, who twice exceeded .400, batting .402 for Puebla in 1986 and .415 for the same team the following year. Over his eight-year career, Sanchez batted .344, with 24 home runs and 110 runs batted in per year.

• Carlos Soto was a slugging catcher for Nuevo Laredo, and several other teams, from 1973 to 1991. He pounded the ball at a .301 clip for 19 years, averaging 25 homers and 99 RBIs per year. Soto put together ten .300 seasons, including .348 in 1985, .336 in '86, and .324 in '84. He whacked the ball to the tune of .366 in 1980, but was limited to 34 games because of injuries. He led the league with 22 home runs in 1983.

When he retired, Soto had accumulated 1743 base hits, with 264 home runs.

• Roberto Herrera played in the Mexican League for ten years, from 1965 to 1975. Over that period he hit a solid .301, averaging 18 homers and 100 runs batted in per year. The native of Havana, Cuba, batted over .300 his first seven years in the league, with a high of .353 as a 26-year-old rookie.

PITCHER:

• Ramon Arano is generally regarded as the greatest pitcher ever to
play in the Mexican League. The
5'8", 160 pound hurler is the all-time
Mexican League record holder for
years pitched (30), games (809), victories (334), innings pitched (5092),
shutouts (57), and strikeouts (2377).
His won-loss record increases to 421–
350 when his winter league stats are
included, making him the second
winningest pitcher in baseball history, behind the immortal Cy Young.

The little right hander spent his
entire career in Mexico, except for
three games with Oklahoma City of
the American Association in 1962.
His career is unique in that he accomplished everything without ever
experiencing a 20-win season. He

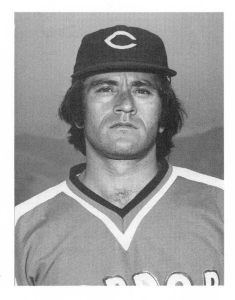

Ramon Arano. (Salon de la Fama, Mexico.)

even outdid Don Sutton, who won 324 major league games with just one 20-
win season.

Arano retired in 1986, but returned nine years later to pitch five games for
Aguila, at the age of 56. His 2–2 record included a complete game shutout, making him the oldest pitcher in Mexican League history to toss a shutout. He was
elected to Mexico's Baseball Hall of Fame in 1993.

• Alfredo Ortiz, a pint-sized southpaw, won 255 games against 210 losses
over a 28-year career. He spent 25 of those years with the Mexico City Reds,
helping them to seven league titles. The 5'8", 150 pounder, from Medellin de
Bravo, led the league in victories in 1969, going 23–9 for a team that finished
with a record of 74–80, 17 games out of first place.

Ortiz won ten or more games 14 times, en route to his 255 career win total,
second highest in Mexican League history. He is a member of the Baseball Hall
of Fame.

• Antonio Pollorena was born in Los Mochis on April 17, 1947. He debuted
in the Mexican League in 1965 at the age of 18, winning two games for Jalisco.
Twenty-two years later, the little right hander retired, with 233 victories under
his belt. He lost just 170 times.

Pollorena was noted for his excellent control, wide variety of pitches, and
coolness under pressure. He averaged five strikeouts and two bases on balls for
every nine innings pitched. The stocky 5'8", 180 pound hurler strung together

four consecutive 20-victory seasons, from 1974 to 1977, winning 85 times against 38 losses. He was elected to the Hall of Fame in 1991.

• Jose Pena, a 6'2", 190 pound fireballer from Ciudad Juarez, starred in the Mexican League for 19 summers, as well as in the Mexican Pacific League for 22 winters. His won-loss totals were 390–270, including 214–154 in the summer league and 176–116 in the winter league.

In addition to his Mexican exploits, the big right hander played in organized ball in the United States for six years, including four years of major league ball. Pitching mostly in relief for the Cincinnati Reds and Los Angeles Dodgers, Pena appeared in 61 major league games with a 7–4 record and five saves. He was elected to the Hall of Fame in 1992.

• Ramon Bragana, a native of Havana, Cuba, pitched in Mexico from 1938 through 1955, winning 211 games against 162 losses. According to James A. Riley, Bragana "had a 90-mph fastball, a devastating curve, a tremendous drop, and an effective slider, and he used good control to keep them down." He pitched in the Negro leagues, as well as the Cuban Winter League and in Venezuela, in the late '20s and '30s, but his major effort was in Mexico.

"The Professor," as he was called, holds the single season record for most victories in the Mexican League, going 30–8 for Vera Cruz in 1944. He remains the only 30-game winner in Mexican League history. Like many pitchers of his era, the 5'10", 170 pound right hander was a punishing hitter. He hit .243 with an average of 12 home runs and 87 RBIs over 18 years. He entered the Hall of Fame in 1964.

• Cesar Diaz pitched in the Mexican League for 21 years, winning 208 games and losing 184. He won ten or more games during his first 13 years in the league, with a high of 17 in 1973. The right handed pitcher tossed 42 shutouts during his career, #6 all-time, while compiling a strong 3.28 earned run average.

Diaz went 17–7 in 1973, with a 1.86 ERA. Seven years later, he won 10 games against four losses, with a 1.96 ERA.

• Vincente Romo was born in Santa Rosalia on April 12, 1943. He enjoyed a 16-year career in the Mexican League, as well as an eight-year career in the major leagues. Romo, a 6'1", 190 pound right hander, holds the Mexican League record for the lowest career earned run average, with 2.49, one of only five pitchers with career ERAs under 3.00 (for pitchers with over 2000 innings pitched). He is tied for the most shutouts in a season, with 10, and is #3 in career shutouts, with 52.

He won 182 games against 106 losses in Mexico, for a winning percentage of .632 (#5 all-time). In the major leagues, he was used primarily as a relief pitcher. He appeared in 335 games between 1968 and 1982, with 32 victories, 33 losses, 52 saves, and a fine 3.36 ERA. In his first year in the majors, with the Cleveland Indians, Romo went 5–3 with 12 saves and an outstanding 1.62 ERA, in 40 games. The next year, he was 8–10 with 11 saves and a 3.13 ERA in 55 games. He was elected to the Mexican Baseball Hall of Fame in 1992.

• Salome Barojas was another Dennis Eckersley clone, much like Yutaka Enatsu of Japan. Barojas both started and relieved during his first nine years in the Mexican League, then was used exclusively as a reliever during his last seven years. His career records include 115 wins against 58 losses, for a winning percentage of .665 (#2 all-time). He is #13 in earned run average, at 2.88 (for pitchers with over 1000 innings pitched), and #3 in saves, with 152.

The chunky right hander pitched in the major leagues for five years, between 1982 and 1988. He was used primarily in relief, pitching in 179 games with a 18–21 won-loss record and a 3.95 ERA.

Ramon Bragana. (Yuyo Ruiz.)

• Miguel Solis was a right handed pitcher who was active in Mexico from 1972 to 1989. Pitching mostly for Saltillo, the native of Arriaga ran up a career record of 202 victories against 140 losses. His greatest year was 1979 when he went 25–5, with a sparkling 1.84 earned run average.

• Angel Moreno was a hard throwing southpaw who enjoyed a 16-year career in the Mexican League from 1975 to 1995. He won ten or more games 13 times, with a high of 18 (against 7 losses) in 1992. He fanned an average of six batters a game, while walking only three. Moreno's winning percentage of .639 (182–103) is #3 all-time for pitchers with more than 2000 innings pitched.

• Andres Ayon, from Havana, Cuba, won 169 games with just 98 losses over a 14-year career in Mexico. His .633 winning percentage is #4 all-time. The little right hander was a control pitcher who walked less than three men a game. Ayon compiled a fine 16–5 record in his rookie season. He went on to lead the AAA Mexican League in pitching in 1967, with a record of 25–6, and in 1972 when he went 22–3. He also won 20 games in 1970, losing 12.

• Ernesto Escarrega, a native of Los Mochis, pitched in the Mexican League for 20 years, compiling a 192–141 record. His greatest successes were with Puebla, from 1974 to 1980, when he won 116 games against only 59 losses. He was 20–9 in 1979.

• Francisco "Panchillo" Ramirez had an excellent 17-year career in Mexico, racking up 184 victories against 161 losses. In 1956, he dominated the league's pitching statistics, leading in victories (20), winning percentage (20–3, .870), strikeouts (148), and earned run average (2.25).

FIRST BASE:

• The #1 first baseman in the Mexican League and the greatest player in Mexican baseball history was Hector Espino, a right handed power hitter, who launched hundreds of monstrous home runs into the rarefied Mexican atmosphere. His 24-year career consisted of 2420 games, all but 32 of them in the Mexican League. He played 32 games with Jacksonville in the International League in 1964 (where he batted .300), but he preferred playing in his own country.

The 5'11", 185 pound slugger terrorized Mexican League pitchers, smashing a record 453 home runs during his career. He was a model of consistency,

Hector Espino. (Leo W. Banks Collection.)

winning four home run titles and hitting 20 or more home runs 11 times.

Proving he was not just a home run hitter, the big right hander also won five batting championships, with marks of .371, .369, .379, .365, and .377. When he retired in 1984, Espino left behind numerous records. He is #1 in career batting average, .335 (for players with more than 4600 at-bats), runs scored (1505), runs batted in (1573), home runs (453), and total bases (4574). He is #2 in base hits (2752), games played (2388), at-bats (8205), doubles (373), and bases on balls (1330).

Hector Espino also played in the Pacific Winter League for 24 years, where he accounted for another 310 home runs. His career total of 763 home runs is exceeded only by Japan's Sadaharu Oh. Espino captured another seven home run titles in the Pacific League, giving him 11 total. He pounded out a career total of more than 4500 base hits, winter and summer, making him the all-time professional baseball base hit champion.

He was elected to the Mexican Baseball Hall of Fame in 1988.

• Another outstanding first baseman was Jesus Sommers, the son of Negro league star Lonnie Summers. Jesus was a big, rugged, right handed hitter who starred in the Mexican League for 27 years, retiring in 1996, after establishing a new summer league record for career base hits, with 3004.

The 5'11", 175 pound Sommers holds career records in games played (2890), at-bats (10326), and doubles (488), as well as years played and base hits. He was a consistent hitter, who batted over .300 nine times, and who hit ten or more home runs 11 times. His career batting average was .291, with 13 home runs and 80 runs batted in.

• Angel Castro was a long ball hitter from the pioneer days, who played during the first professional season in 1938, and who retired in 1957, after a colorful 20-year career. He was the most powerful left handed hitter ever to play baseball in Mexico in the early days. Over his long career, he averaged 20 home runs and 107 runs batted in for every 550 at-bats.

Castro enjoyed twelve .300 seasons, which included winning the triple crown in 1951, with an average of .354, 22 home runs and 79 RBIs in 84 games. He also captured three more home run titles and three more RBI titles. His career statistics include a .306 batting average, 230 home runs, and 1219 runs batted in.

Angel Castro was also an outstanding defensive first baseman. He was elected to the Hall of Fame in 1964.

• Alonzo Perry was an all-star first baseman in four countries, the United States (Negro league), Cuba, Mexico, and the Dominican Republic. He is a member of the Dominican Republic Sports Hall of Fame. He was a career .300 hitter wherever he played.

Perry spent seven years in Mexico, compiling a .355 career batting average, the second highest average in Mexican League history. He led the league in RBIs four times, in runs twice, hits twice, doubles twice, triples twice, and home runs once. In 1956, he walked off with almost every offensive record, winning the triple crown (.392, 28, 118), while also leading in runs scored, hits, doubles, and triples.

Perry's average statistics are eye popping. Based on a 550 at-bat season, the 6'3", 200 pound left handed slugger hit .355, with 36 doubles, 10 triples, 24 home runs, and 127 runs batted in.

SECOND BASE:

Second base on the all-star team is crowded with qualified candidates. Rather than trying to select the two premier all-stars, on a minimum of information, seven players will be reviewed, in alphabetical order.

• Mario Ariosa, a native of Remidios, Cuba, played in the Mexican League for 20 years, from 1947 to 1972. He didn't play in the league in 1948, or from 1967 to 1971. Ariosa was an all-around player, whose play was referred to as "stupendous" by the Hall of Fame committee. His average yearly statistics showed a .308 batting average, with 89 runs scored, 25 doubles, four triples, 10 home runs, and 77 runs-batted-in. He compiled 1836 base hits during his career. He is a member of the Mexican Baseball Hall of Fame.

• Moises "Moi" Camacho had the longest playing career of any second baseman — 21 years. He had also the most pop in his bat of any second baseman, cracking 185 career homers. According to his Baseball Hall of Fame plaque, Camacho was a respected player in the Mexican League, both offensively and defensively.

His career batting statistics include a .291 batting average, 2110 base hits, 1046 runs scored, and 1169 runs batted in. He averaged 14 homers and 88 RBI's a year, for 21 years.

• Arnoldo "Kiko" Castro was a sensational player who played baseball 12 months a year for 20 years. He played in the Mexican League in the summer, and the Mexican Pacific League in the winter. He was an outstanding fielder, as well as a dangerous hitter. The right handed batter compiled a .293 career average in the Mexican League, which included six .300+ seasons, with a high of .340 in 1965. He accumulated 2224 base hits in 20 years, 494 of them for extra bases.

Castro was a very outgoing person, who related well to fans all over the country. He was elected to the Baseball Hall of Fame in 1995.

• Vinicio "Chico" Garcia enjoyed a 26-year career in professional baseball, 15 years in the Mexican League and 11 years in organized baseball in the United States, including 39 games with the Baltimore Orioles in 1954. In his first year in the American minor leagues, with Juarez in the Class C Arizona-Texas League in 1949, the 24-year-old infielder led the league in batting (.377), runs (170), hits (227), and triples (20).

After his return to Mexico in 1960, Garcia was an offensive terror over the next five years, with batting averages of .351, .346, .341, .368 (to lead the league), and .335. When he finally retired in 1970, he had accumulated 2229 hits in the Mexican League (3116 hits in all), and a solid .323 batting average. He was elected to the Mexican Hall of Fame in 1981.

• Roberto Mendez played 20 years in the Mexican League, the first 11 of them with Jalisco. Like his compatriots, he was a good fielder and a reliable hitter. He hit over .300 five times during his career, en route to a .290 batting average. The 5'8", 160 pound right hander was primarily a punch hitter, who averaged only 27 extra base hits a year, but those hits, coupled with 133 singles and 69 bases on balls, produced 86 runs scored a year.

When Mendez retired, he had banged out 2091 hits, scored 1131 runs, and knocked in 615 teammates.

• Juan Navarette was the top hitting second basemen in the Mexican League, with a career batting average of .327. Not a slugger like Moises Camacho, Navarette was a contact hitter who struck out only 23 times a year. The slim, 6'1" left handed hitter was primarily a singles hitter, but he could bunt, hit and run, or sacrifice, as required. He also stole an average of 21 bases a year.

The native of Gomez Palacio accumulated 1979 base hits during his career, with 1005 runs scored and 668 RBIs. He averaged 91 runs scored and 61 runs batted in. He also played in the minor leagues in the United States for six years, acquitting himself commendably in the International League and the American Association.

• Juan Rodriguez, a native of Monterrey, played in the Mexican League for 20 years, batting .293 with six .300+ seasons. He rapped the ball at a .362 clip for Leon in 1987. During his career, he piled up 1948 base hits, scored 1130 runs, and batted in 666.

The right handed hitter had little power, but was a good contact hitter who struck out only 28 times a year while coaxing 69 walks from opposing pitchers. Attesting to his speed and good base running instincts, he stole 16 bases and scored 93 runs a year, crossing the plate 40 percent of the time he reached base.

SHORTSTOP:

• The top two shortstops in Mexican League history are both imports, Silvio Garcia from Cuba and Ray Dandridge for the U.S. Negro Leagues. Garcia played all over the western hemisphere, including the United States, Puerto Rico, the Dominican Republic, Cuba, and Venezuela, as well as Mexico. He starred in all of them.

The 6' tall, 190 pound infielder was a five point player who could hit, hit with power, run, field, and throw. According to Tommy Lasorda, in James A. Riley's fine book, *The Biographical Encyclopedia of the Negro Leagues*, Garcia was one of the best hitters who never played in the major leagues. Riley also said that "Leo Durocher raved about him being a great fielder."

The big right handed hitter averaged .335 in Mexico over a seven year period, with 12 home runs and 103 RBIs for every 550 at-bats. He was an aggressive hitter who rarely struck out and rarely walked. He was also an aggressive base runner who averaged 31 stolen bases a year.

• Ray Dandridge, a member of the Baseball Hall of Fame in Cooperstown, New York, is also a member of the Mexican Baseball Hall of Fame. Interestingly, Dandridge was honored as a third baseman in the United States, and as a shortstop in Mexico. In fact, the bowlegged infielder could play any infield position with equal skill and dexterity. He had quick reflexes, great hands and a rifle arm.

At the plate, he was a talented contact hitter who struck out only 17 times a year, while drawing 37 bases on balls. His .347 career batting average in the Mexican League included 35 doubles, five triples, and seven home runs for every 550 at-bats. The 5'7", 175 pound speedster stole 25 bases a year, crossed the plate 104 times, and drove in 87 teammates.

Ray Dandridge could beat you many ways — at the plate, on the bases, or in the field. He was a winner.

Ray Dandridge. (James A. Riley.)

• Francisco "Chico" Rodriguez, a native of Cananea, was the brother of Aurelio Rodriguez, who played in the major leagues for 17 years, most of them with the Detroit Tigers. Where Aurelio was a third baseman, Chico was a short-stop. He was one of the top shortstops in the Mexican League for 20 years, from 1965 to 1985, except for 1966 when he was out of the league.

The right hander was a decent hitter, compiling a career .270 average, with 2186 base hits, 970 runs scored, and 808 runs batted in.

• Beltran Herrera was a switch hitting shortstop who stung the ball from both sides of the plate. He was a career .287 hitter who put together five .300+ seasons over a period of 15 years. He had his greatest year in 1986, when he hit .331 for Monterrey, and scored 109 runs. Herrera averaged 35 stolen bases and 96 runs scored a year. His career stolen base total of 337 is #4 all-time, in Mexico.

• Rigoberto "Rigo" Mena, a native of Managua, Nicaragua, played in the Mexican League for 13 years, beginning in 1964. The right handed hitter was a career .300 hitter, playing with Monterrey, Tampico, and Saltillo. His best year was 1973, when he pounded the ball at a .352 clip, leading his team, the Saltillo Sarape Makers, to the North West Division title by a whopping 20½ games over Union Laguna.

THIRD BASE:

• The top third basemen in the Mexican League are Enrique Aguilar, Luis Garcia, and Oscar Rodriguez. Aguilar was a dependable third baseman for 21 years, 18 of them with Aguascalientes. The native of Villa Azueta played in 2202 games, with 2389 hits (#4 all-time), 1328 runs scored (#3), 372 doubles (#3), 295 home runs (#7), and 1400 runs batted in (#5).

Aguilar was a hard hitting third baseman, who averaged 26 doubles, 21 home runs, 12 stolen bases, 99 RBIs, and 93 runs scored per year. His .306 career batting average included ten .300+ seasons. Six times he hit more than 20 home runs. Five times, he drove in more than 100 runs. His best year was 1988 when he hit a personal high of .343, with 35 home runs, 115 RBIs, and 104 runs scored.

• Oscar Rodriguez was another slugging third baseman whose .324 career batting average included 1808 base hits, 1011 runs scored, 195 home runs, and 995 runs batted in. His .324 average is the third highest batting average of all time for players with at least 4600 at-bats. The native of Cabo Rojo, Puerto Rico, was slow afoot, but he could drive the ball with authority, as witnessed by his 33 doubles, six triples, and 19 home runs per year. He also scored 100 runs and drove in 98.

The big right handed slugger also caught and played first base during his 13-year career.

• Luis "Camelion" Garcia, from Carupano, Sucre Venezuela, played in the

Mexican League for ten years, from 1956 to 1965, primarily with Poza Rica. Garcia was a right handed hitter who averaged 54 extra base hits a year, including 30 doubles and 22 home runs. He drove in 100 runs a year and scored 86 himself.

When he retired, he left behind a .322 career batting average, the 17th highest batting average in Mexican League history for players with at least 3000 at-bats.

OUTFIELD:

• There have been many great outfielders in Mexican League history, but probably the most interesting one of all was Alfred Pinkston, from Alabama. The 6'5", 215 pound black bomber was a late bloomer in organized baseball, but once he began to swing a bat, he created havoc whenever he stepped to the plate. He played briefly in the Negro league in the late forties, then appeared four years later in the Provincial League, where he terrorized pitchers to the tune of .301 and .360, winning the batting title his second year. He clouted Southern Association hurlers at a .369 pace, capturing another batting title.

After two seasons in the Western League (.372 and .337), Pinkston finally settled down in Mexico. He was 41 years old when he began his Mexican League career, but that didn't slow him down at all. He won the batting championship his first four years in the league, with averages of .369, .397, .374, and .381. He followed that up with averages of .368, .364, and .345, then retired, at the ripe old age of 47.

During his Mexican tenure, the big left handed batter also led the league in runs scored once, hits four times, doubles twice, and runs batted in three times. He left behind a career batting average of .372, the all-time Mexican League record. His nearest challenger is a full 17 points behind. Al Pinkston was elected to the Mexican Baseball Hall of Fame in 1976.

• Jimmie Collins, American import from Mississippi, also demolished Mexican League pitchers. The 6'2", 185 pound outfielder bounced around the American minor leagues for seven years, compiling a modest .279 batting average, before finding his niche in Mexico. His first year with Chihuahua, the sweet swinging southpaw rapped out 185 base hits, good enough for a .350 batting average. The following year, he won one of his two batting crowns, slamming 206 hits in 124 games, for a .438 average. He won his second batting title six years later, when he hit .412 with Mexico City and Cordoba.

Collins played in Mexico for 11 years, retiring in 1987 at the age of 38. His career batting average was a sizzling .354, #3 all-time.

• Andres Mora is the hardest hitting outfielder in Mexican League history. The 6' tall, 180 pound slugger played in the American minor leagues for four years, and spent parts of four other years with the major league entries in Baltimore and Cleveland. He hit International League pitching at a near .300 pace, with an average of 34 home runs for every 550 at-bats. His major league stats reveal a disappointing .223 batting average with 21 home runs.

The big right handed hitter returned to Mexico in 1980, and proceeded to carve out a legend for himself over the next 16 years. He hit over .300 ten times, winning four home run crowns and three RBI titles along the way. His best years were with Nuevo Laredo, from 1984 to 1987, when he put together four spectacular seasons. In '84, he hit .383 with 32 home runs and 95 RBIs. He followed that with season averages of .360-41-110, .355-33-117, and .368-38-123.

Andres Mora retired in 1995, with a batting average of .314. Over his career he banged out 2247 base hits (#6 all-time), scored 1138 runs (#6), drove in 1492 runs (#3), and hit 419 home runs (#2), an average of 32 home runs a year. He should be a shoo-in for the Hall of Fame as soon as he becomes eligible.

• Matias Carrillo is a stocky 5'11", 190 pound slugger, who has played in both the United States and Mexico. Carrillo played in the major leagues for three years (a total of 107 games), but was never able to break through. In Mexico, it has been a different story. He is one of the premier hitters in Mexican League history, with a batting average of .342 through 1996.

The left handed hitter has put together some impressive seasonal averages during his nine years in the league — 120 runs scored a year, 32 doubles, eight triples, 25 home runs, and 116 runs batted in. He has fanned an average of 89 times a year, but has also coaxed 75 walks out of opposing hurlers. His .418 on-base percentage is one of the highest in Mexican League history, as is his .562 slugging percentage.

• Miguel Suarez played in the Mexican League for 18 years, from 1971 to 1987. The native of Guasave started his career with a bang — a .372 batting average for the Mexico City Reds at just 18 years of age. He batted over .300 his first nine years in the league and exceeded the magic .300 mark 13 times in his career. His .323 career batting average included 2444 base hits, 1009 runs scored, and 749 runs batted in.

• Lazaro Acosta, from Maracaibo, Venezuela, was a nine-year veteran of the Mexican League. He was 30 years old when he made his debut in Mexico, yet he hit over .300 eight straight years, retiring in 1976 at the age of 38. The little left handed hitter didn't have much power, but he was a solid contact hitter who struck out only 26 times a year, pounded out a .345 batting average, stole 18 bases a year, scored 85 runs, and generally kept the opposition on its toes.

• Ramon "El Diablo" Montoya was an outstanding all-around player for the Mexico City Reds for 16 years, off and on, from 1965 to 1980. Over that period he covered center field like a blanket, stealing base hits from opposing hitters with monotonous regularity. At the same time, he compiled a career batting average of .316, with 1692 base hits, 340 of them for extra bases. He also scored 822 runs, drove in 680 runs, and stole 96 bases. The Devil, as he was called, was elected to the Mexican Baseball Hall of Fame in 1990.

• Daniel Fernandez, a native of Cardel, has played in the Mexican League for 14 years, 12 of them with the Mexico City Reds. The 31-year-old outfielder was still going strong in 1996, batting .313, with 86 runs scored in 402 at-bats. Over his career, Fernandez has averaged .323, with 125 runs scored a year, 61 runs batted in, 38 stolen bases, and 92 bases on balls. His on-base percentage of .421 is one of the highest ever recorded in Mexico. His runs-scored-per-game average of 0.84 may well be the highest RPG average in the annals of Mexican League baseball.

Other outstanding outfielders of note:

• Ossie Olivares of Venezuela compiled 1061 base hits over a nine-year career, with a .345 batting average.
• Augustin Bejerano, a 16-year veteran from Cuba, batted .312, with 1061 base hits.
• Santos Amaro, from Cuba, batted .314 over 17 years, with 1339 base hits.
• Bobby Rodriguez, from the United States, played nine years, with a .325 batting average and 1065 base hits.
• Dave Stockstill, from the United States, averaged .347, with 1187 base hits during an eight-year career.
• "Wild Bill" Wright, a veteran of the American Negro leagues, starred in Mexico for 10 years, during which time he batted .335, with 969 base hits.

UTILITY:

• The two most versatile players in the history of the Mexican League were Martin Dihigo and Lazaro Salazar, both natives of Cuba. Dihigo is a member of the Hall of Fame in four countries, the United States, Mexico, Venezuela, and Cuba. The well respected Dihigo, known as "El Maestro" (The Master), was a five point player who could hit, hit with power, run, field, and throw. He was also one of the greatest pitchers in the game.

In Mexico, Dihigo was primarily a pitcher, although he could also play center field or second base with equal skill. In fact, he was selected as the all-time Negro league second baseman by many baseball experts. The big 6'3", 190 pound slugger was a terror at the plate. His .317 batting average included 38 doubles a year, 10 triples, and 19 home runs. He scored 105 runs and drove in 129. He also stole 20 bases a year, just to show he was not a one-dimensional player.

On the mound, Dihigo was almost unbeatable, piling up a won-loss record of 119–57 over an 11-year period. His winning percentage of .676 is the highest ever recorded in the Mexican League for pitchers with more than 1000 innings pitched. His earned run average of 2.84 is #11 all-time. Dihigo was a power pitcher most of his career, averaging seven strikeouts against only three bases on balls per game.

• Lazaro Salazar is in the Baseball Hall of Fame in both Mexico and Cuba. Like Dihigo, the 5'9", 177 pounder could do it all. As a southpaw pitcher, Salazar won 112 games against 78 losses, for a winning percentage of .589. He was not the power pitcher that Dihigo was, averaging only four strikeouts a game. He had to rely on off-speed pitches, and deception, to record outs. He was also on the wild side, issuing five bases on balls per game.

Salazar was a terrific hitter who could drive the ball to all sections of the park with authority. Over a typical 154 game season, the rugged Cuban averaged 31 doubles, eight triples, and eight home runs, with 106 runs batted in and 112 runs scored. He had an outstanding batting eye, striking out only 27 times a year, while drawing 97 walks. He was also an excellent baserunner, stealing 24 bases a year. His .434 on base percentage is one of the highest in Mexican League history.

The lineup for the Mexican League all-star team follows. The Mexican League statistics for the all-star team can be found in Table XXV.

Mexican League All Star Team, 1938 to 1997

Catcher	Francisco Estrada
	Orlando Sanchez
	Carlos Soto
	Roberto Herrera
Pitcher	Ramon Arano
	Alfredo Ortiz
	Antonio Pollorena
	Jose Pena
	Ramon Bragana
	Cesar Diaz
	Vincente Romo
	Salome Barojas
	Miguel Solis
	Angel Moreno
	Andres Ayon
	Ernesto Escarrega
	Francisco Ramirez
First Base	Hector Espino
	Jesus Sommers
	Angel Castro
	Alonzo Perry
Second Base	Mario Ariosa
	Moises Camacho

	Arnoldo Castro
	Vinicio Garcia
	Roberto Mendez
	Juan Navarette
	Juan Rodriguez
Shortstop	Silvio Garcia
	Ray Dandridge
	Francisco Rodriguez
	Beltran Herrera
	Rigoberto Mena
Third Base	Enrique Aguilar
	Luis Garcia
	Oscar Rodriguez
Outfield	Alfred Pinkston
	Jimmie Collins
	Andres Mora
	Matias Carrillo
	Miguel Suarez
	Lazaro Acosta
	Ramon Montoya
	Daniel Fernandez
Utility	Martin Dihigo
	Lazaro Salazar

Other Leagues

This book is a study of the world's greatest baseball players, from all professional leagues around the world, outside of the American major and minor leagues. In previous chapters, the best players in the Negro Leagues, the Japanese Leagues, the Mexican League, the Cuban Winter League, and the Puerto Rican Winter League have been reviewed. It was possible to evaluate the players from these different leagues because their playing statistics, or at least some of them, were available, and there were many eyewitness accounts of their superior skills and extraordinary accomplishments.

Baseball, however, has also been played in many other countries over the past 140 years, including the Dominican Republic, Colombia, Venezuela, Nicaragua, and Panama. Unfortunately, only fragmentary records exist of most of the players in these countries. Their skills are harbored in the minds of a few older citizens, whose memory is fading with each passing year. This chapter will review the game as it developed in those countries, with a look at the country's greatest players but, for the most part, it will be difficult to compare the players in these countries to the players studied thus far, due to a paucity of statistics.

THE DOMINICAN REPUBLIC

The Dominican Republic has a long and glorious baseball history going back to the 1870s. The game was brought to the island by refugees from Cuba's Ten Years War, which decimated the Cuban countryside between 1868 and 1878. Over the last three decades of the nineteenth century, the game grew in popularity. It was promoted by the industrial interests in the country who felt it was a valuable outlet for their employees, keeping their workers out of trouble, and increasing their morale.

As in Cuba and Puerto Rico, the sugar plantation owners formed teams, as did the cacao and tobacco companies. By 1900, most towns and villages in the

Dominican Republic had their own teams, and regular tournaments and other competitions were being held around the island. The country's first professional team, Licey of Santo Domingo, was formed in 1907, according to Rob Ruck in *Total Baseball*. Three other professional teams soon followed suit: the Estrellas Orientales of San Pedro de Macoris, the Aguilas Cibaenas of Santiago, and Escogido of Santo Domingo.

During the first three decades of the twentieth century, professional baseball became an important part of life in the Dominican Republic. Professional championships were held on a regular basis, and the various teams competed for the best baseball talent available in the western hemisphere. In addition to the island's own talent, professional players were imported from the Negro leagues in the United States, as well as from Cuba, Puerto Rico, Mexico, and Central and South America. Jose Mendez and Alejandro Oms were two visitors who brought their baseball skills to the island. As mentioned previously, Pedro Miguel Caratini, a native of Puerto Rico, also spent several years in the Dominican Republic, teaching school and playing and managing baseball. He became a baseball legend by the time he hung up his spikes in the 1930s.

During the brutal regime of dictator Rafael Trujillo, the Dominican Republic supported professional baseball summer leagues in the '30s. In 1937, the league became a major political tool, with several presidential candidates sponsoring league teams. Trujillo was backing Los Dragones of Ciudad Trujillo. Other candidates were supporting the Estrelles Orientales of San Pedro de Macoris, or the Aguilas Cibaenas of Santiago. Trujillo left no stone unturned to guarantee victory for his team. He scoured the entire western hemisphere in search of the best players money could buy. When the championship tournament got underway, Los Dragones fielded a team that included Satchel Paige, Josh Gibson, "Cool Papa" Bell, and Sam Bankhead from the U.S. Negro leagues, Silvio Garcia and Rodolfo Fernandez from Cuba, and Perucho Cepeda from Puerto Rico. Dominican native Tetelo Vargas, along with Cubans Cocaina Garcia and Ramon Bragana, joined the Estrellas Orientales, while Cubans Martin Dihigo and Luis Tiant, Sr., joined Negro leaguers Chet Brewer, Spoony Palm, and Showboat Thomas, on the Aguilas Cibaenas team.

The league was a virtual life and death struggle as far as Trujillo was concerned. A baseball victory could have a major impact on the presidential election. After Los Dragones lost a late season series to Santiago, as reported by John Holway in *Josh and Satch*, the militia began firing their guns in the air, while shouting, "El Presidente doesn't lose." A nervous Cool Papa Bell asked a bystander, "They don't kill people over baseball, do they?" "Down here, they do," was the chilling reply.

The situation got more tense as the final game of the season arrived with Los Dragones in a tie with Aguilas Cibaenas for the league lead. Chet Brewer tried to visit his buddies, Satch and Josh, at their hotel, the night before the big game, but was unable to locate them. When he inquired about them, he was told they were in jail. Trujillo had them locked up for the night, to prevent them from going out on the town.

The final game lived up to its pre-game hype. Aguilas Cibaenas, with Chet Brewer doing the pitching, held a slim 3–2 lead into the bottom of the seventh inning. Then, with two out, Cool Papa Bell singled and Sam Bankhead sent a home run screaming over the left field fence. Satchel Paige retired the final six batters in succession, to nail down the 4–3 victory, and guarantee the National Championship for Los Dragones. Paige, Gibson, Bell, and the other Negro leaguers caught the first Pan American Clipper north the next day.

Satch and Josh earned their money that summer. The inimitable Paige was the leading pitcher in the league with an 8–2 record, while Gibson led all hitters with a .453 batting average. Dihigo finished second in both pitching and batting. He went 6–4 on the mound, and stung the ball at a .351 clip, with four home runs.

After the 1937 season, Dominican baseball disappeared from the front pages for 14 years. Then, in 1951, a summer league was revived. It lasted only four years, however, and the Winter League returned in 1955. It is still active today. When the color barrier finally came down in the United States, baseball players from the Dominican Republic began to filter north to try their hand in organized ball. From 1947 through 1991, a total of 148 players succeeded in breaking into the major leagues, almost one-third of them from San Pedro de Macoris. The port town of 80,000 has sent more players per capita to the majors over the past 50 years than any town in the world. At one time in the '80s, six of the 26 major league shortstops were from San Pedro.

Over the past 40 years, the Dominican Winter League has been a training ground for future major leaguers, both native born sons and American minor leaguers sent there by their major league owners. Many Dominican-born major leaguers also participate in the league to show their appreciation to the home fans and to give the fans a taste of what major league baseball is like. Some of the big league stars who have played winter ball in their homeland include the Alou brothers Felipe, Jesus, and Matty, Felipe's son Moises, Manny Mota, Rico Carty, Juan Marichal, Tony Pena, Pedro Guerrero, Ralph Garr, George Bell, and Sammy Sosa.

As with the Puerto Rican Winter League, it is not possible to select a Dominican League all-star team for the period from the early days to 1958 because organized leagues did not exist in the country prior to 1951, with the exception of the 1937 National Tournament. As a result, statistics are not available. A few of the country's celebrated players will be recognized, however, for their outstanding accomplishments, not only in their own country, but throughout the western hemisphere.

• Tetelo Vargas was probably the Dominican Republic's all-time greatest baseball player. "The Dominican Deer," as he was known, was a great all-around player. He excelled on defense, with outstanding range, and a formidable throwing arm. He was a consistent .300 hitter at the plate, with excellent bat control. He was a dangerous base runner, whose base stealing ability intimidated catchers, and whose blinding speed from first to third was legendary.

Most of Vargas' professional career in the Dominican Republic was played in relative obscurity on teams where no statistics were kept. He was still active when the Dominican Summer League began operations in 1951 and, in fact, he captured the batting championship in 1953, with an average of .355, at the advanced baseball age of 47. He

Tetelo Vargas. (Yuyo Ruiz.)

played in the Summer League for five years before retiring at the age of 50. When he did put his bat down for the last time, he left behind a career batting average of .322, with just 26 strikeouts a year, a tribute to his keen batting eye.

The Dominican Deer also played baseball in Puerto Rico, the Negro leagues, and Mexico, smacking the ball at a .300+ pace wherever he played. In Puerto Rico, over a 16-year career, he compiled a .320 batting average. He won the batting championship in 1943-44, scorching the ball at a torrid .410 pace. He was 37 years old. He also led the PRWL in runs scored four times, in triples twice, and in stolen bases twice.

His Negro league career spanned 18 years, from 1927 to 1944. Once again, he excelled, putting together a career average of .342. He had the fourth highest season batting average in Negro league history, batting .479 for the New York Cubans in 1943. He also hit about .326 in two years in Mexico, including .355 with Estraellas Orientals, in 1953.

Tetelo Vargas is a member of the Sports Hall of Fame in the Dominican Republic and the Professional Baseball Hall of Fame in Puerto Rico.

• Diomedes "Guayubin" Olivo was the Dominican Republic's greatest pitcher during the days prior to major league integration. Unlike Vargas, however, Olivo was still young enough to enjoy a brief taste of major league stardom before he retired.

Olivo began his professional career in his homeland in the late '30s. In 1947, he pitched the first recorded no-hitter in Dominican history, defeating Licey, for Escogido, according to Dominican baseball historian, Dr. Jose de Jesus Jiminez . He pitched a second no-hitter in the Summer League in 1954.

When the Summer League began in 1951, the 32-year-old southpaw was its premier pitcher. He led the league in wins that first year with 10, over a 55-game schedule. In '52, he won 10 more. When the Winter League started in

1955-56, Olivo supplemented his income by pitching in Mexico in the summer and the Dominican
Republic in the winter. Over his 11-year Dominican career, summer and winter, Olivo won 86
games against only 46 losses.

From 1955 through 1959, the talented left
hander won 55 games in Mexico, against 29
defeats, including a 21–8 season in 1959. His outstanding skills came to the attention of the Pittsburgh Pirates, who quickly signed him to a major
league contract. The 41-year-old hurler pitched in
four games down the stretch, as the Pirates captured the 1960 National League pennant. Two years
later, the 43 year old pitcher went 5–1 with the
Pirates, compiling a 2.79 earned run average in 62
games.

Diomedes Olivo. (Yuyo
Ruiz.)

Diomedes Olivo is a member of the Dominican Republic Sports Hall of
Fame.

• Horacio "Rabbit" Martinez may have been the Dominican Republic's
greatest defensive shortstop, although he would receive serious challenges from
the bevy of short fielders who poured out of San Pedro de Macoris during the
1970s, '80s, and '90s.

Martinez was a defensive wizard of the caliber of Ozzie Smith. He had
speed, grace, exceptional intuition, a sure glove, and a rocket for an arm. He
was generally recognized as the best shortstop in the Negro leagues during the
late '30s and early '40s. He was selected for the all-star team every year from
1940 to 1945, except 1942, according to James A. Riley.

The chink in Martinez's armor that kept him from becoming an all-time
great was his weak bat. During his Negro league career his average hovered
around the .230 mark. No records of his professional career in the Dominican
Republic are available.

Horacio Martinez is a member of the Dominican Republic Sports Hall of
Fame.

The floodgates to major league baseball were opened in 1947. Until that
time, only 54 Latin American players, all white (or mostly white), played major
league ball. Over the next 40 years, more than 600 Latin Americans reached the
baseball summit. Ossie Virgil was the first Dominican to play in the majors
when he joined the New York Giants in 1956. He was followed four years later
by Felipe Alou, Matty Alou, Julian Javier, Juan Marichal, Rudy Hernandez, and
Diomedes Olivo.

The Dominican Winter League all-star team for the period from 1951
through 1997 is dotted with major league players. In fact, all but two members
of the all-star squad presented below had major league experience. The major

league and Dominican Republic League statistics for the players on the all-star team can be found in Table XXII.

Dominican Winter League All-Star Team, 1951–1997

Catcher	Tony Pena
	Federico Velasquez
	Ramon Lora
	Gilbert Reyes
Pitcher	Juan Marichal
	Arturo Pena
	Joaquin Andujar
	Diomedes Olivo
	Federico Olivo
	Danilo Rivas
	Arnulfo Espinosa
	Pascual Perez
	Mickey Mahler
First Base	Alonzo Perry
	Rafael Batista
Second Base	Pedro Gonzalez
	Tito Fuentes
Shortstop	Felix Fermin
	Alfredo Griffin
Third Base	Winston Llenas
	Manuel Castillo
Outfield	Miguel Dilone
	Manny Mota
	Felipe Alou
	Jesus Alou
	Matty Alou
	Rico Carty
	Ralph Garr
	Tetelo Vargas
	Cesar Geronimo
	Cesar Cedeno
	Pedro Guerrero
Utility	Rafael Landestoy
	Rufino Linares
	Mario Guerrero
	Teodoro Martinez

Other Countries—Venezuela, Panama, Nicaragua, Colombia

Baseball was not restricted to the United States. Japan, Cuba, Mexico, Puerto Rico, and the Dominican Republic were actively involved in baseball during the first one hundred years of its existence as an American sport. It also developed and prospered in many other countries in the western hemisphere, including Venezuela, Colombia, Panama, and Nicaragua.

Unfortunately, from the perspective of this study, it will not be possible to present all-star teams from any of those countries, or even to recognize the great pioneers who helped to develop the game. There were no professional leagues established in those countries until midway through the twentieth century. And there were no records maintained of the great individual players who popularized the game in those countries in the late nineteenth century and early twentieth century.

Baseball was introduced into Venezuela by Cuban visitors. According to the Oleksaks, "Cuban ballplayer Emilio Cramer brought a traveling "All-Star" team south in 1895." The first game reportedly was played in Stand del Este, in Caracas. John Krich, in *El Beisbol*, states that the word baseball made its first appearance "in the Venezuelan press on August 5, 1895." That being the case, baseball was a late arrival in Venezuela, compared to the countries that have been reviewed thus far.

Alonzo Perry. (Yuyo Ruiz.)

In 1922, according to the Oleksaks, an oil discovery under Lake Maracaibo brought an influx of American business, American workers, and American money to Venezuela, accelerating the development of the grand old game. Soon Negro league players, as well as players from other western hemisphere countries, were being recruited to play baseball in Maracaibo, Caracas, and other cities that had organized baseball clubs.

Amateur leagues were in operation in Venezuela at least as early as 1930. They may even have been operating five or ten years earlier. A number of Cuban players made the trek south for an occasional taste of South American hospitality in the 1930s. The legendary Martin Dihigo pitched in Venezuela for three years, from 1932 to 1934. In '33, he went 6–0, with a sensational 0.15 earned run average. Silvio

Garcia played with La Guaira and Pastora in the Venezuelan League for at least three years between 1932 and 1937. Cocaina Garcia pitched in Venezuela from 1932 to 1937, with the exception of the 1935-36 season when he pitched in Cuba. Ramon Bragana pitched for Gavilanes in 1936-37. Although Bragana's pitching record is not available, his batting record shows a .318 batting average. Other Cubans active in Venezuela in the '30s included Alejandro Oms and Jose Fernandez.

Venezuela's amateur teams competed on an equal basis with Cuba and Puerto Rico during the 1940s. In fact, Venezuela won the Amateur World Championship in 1941, 1944, and 1945. Then, in 1946, the Venezuelan Winter League was formed to compete with similar leagues in Cuba and Puerto Rico. The Winter League is still in operation, remaining a popular training ground for young major league prospects.

As reported in Beisbol, the first professional winter league "included four teams: Cerveceria Caracas, Vargas, Magallanes, and Venezuela. The leadoff hitter in the inaugural game was Magallanes's star shortstop, Luis Aparicio Sr.... The Magallanes pitcher, major leaguer Alejandro "Paton" Carrasquel, pitched a complete game for a 5–2 victory over the team named Venezuela."

In 1949, the Caribbean World Series was organized to bring together the best teams in the Caribbean area in a season-ending championship tournament. The participants included Puerto Rico, Venezuela, Cuba, and Panama. During the first 12 years of tournament play, Cuba completely dominated the championship, winning seven of 12 crowns. Puerto Rico captured three crowns, with Panama winning one, and Venezuela coming away empty handed.

After the Cuban revolution, the Caribbean World Series was replaced with the Interamerican series, which lasted four years. Each of the participants — Venezuela, Panama, Puerto Rico, and Nicaragua — won one title. The competition was canceled after the 1964 tournament because of lack of fan interest in some countries.

Finally, in 1972, the Caribbean World Series was resurrected and has continued uninterrupted ever since. The participants have included Puerto Rico, Venezuela, the Dominican Republic, and Mexico. Through 1996, Puerto Rico and the Dominican Republic have each captured nine titles. Venezuela has been crowned champion five times, and Mexico has walked off with three championships.

Alejandro Carrasquel, as noted earlier, pitched in the major leagues. He was, in fact, the first Venezuelan to break into the big time, signing with the Washington Senators in 1939. The 6'1" right hander compiled a record of 50–39 over an eight-year career. He was followed into the majors by outfielder Chucho Jesus Ramos, who appeared in four games for the Cincinnati Reds in 1944. They were the only two Venezuelans to play major league baseball prior to the elimination of the color barrier. Between 1947 and 1990, 60 Venezuelan natives entered major league baseball, including Chico Carrasquel, Vic Davalillo, and Hall of Famer Luis Aparicio. Andres Gallaraga, Ossie Guillen, and Cleveland's sensational shortstop, Omar Visquel, are carrying on the Venezuelan tradition in the major leagues today.

Baseball came to Panama around the turn of the century. It was brought to the country by the American laborers who were building the Panama Canal. The first organized baseball league began in 1912. The Canal Zone league, a winter league, was formed two years later.

In 1936, Panama hired Negro league shortstop Bill Yancey to train their amateur athletes for the 1936 Berlin Olympics. As noted earlier, Panama was a participant in the Caribbean World Series and the Interamerican Series from 1949 to 1964. They withdrew from competition after 1964, as political upheaval and lack of fan support made it economically unfeasible to continue. Although they are a small country, they were never intimidated by the other entries in international tournaments. In fact, they won the World Series in 1950, with Negro league ace Chet Brewer winning the deciding game, defeating Puerto Rico's Dan Bankhead 9–3. They also won the 1963 Interamerican Championship.

Panama did not have any major league players prior to the 1950s. Pitcher Humberto Robinson, of the Milwaukee Braves, was the first Panamanian to play in the big leagues. Robinson compiled a record of 8–13 over a five-year career. Since 1955, more than 30 Panamanian nationals have played major league ball, including Hector Lopez, Hall of Famer Rod Carew, Manny Sanguillen, and Roberto Kelly.

Nicaragua, another Central American country, was indoctrinated into the fine points of baseball by American visitors in the late 1880s. The first recorded baseball club was the Boer Club of Managua, formed in 1888. The next year, the first baseball game was played in Bluefields, according to *Beisbol*.

Nicaragua had a fleeting association with the Caribbean tournaments when they joined the Interamerican Series in 1961. They participated in the tournament during its four years of operation and, in fact, captured the last title in 1964. They have not participated in the Caribbean competition since that time.

There have been very few Nicaraguan major league baseball players up to this time. The first and by far the best player to represent Nicaragua in the majors was Dennis Martinez, who joined the Baltimore Orioles in 1976. The 6'1" right handed pitcher enjoyed a 23-year career in the big leagues before retiring in 1998. His 245–193 won-loss record should entitle him to a place in the Baseball Hall of Fame in Cooperstown, New York, by 2004. With his four victories in 1998, Martinez became the winningest Latin American pitcher in history, topping Juan Marichal's 243 victories. In all, only five Nicaraguan natives have broken into the major leagues since 1876.

Baseball has also been played regularly in such countries as Colombia, Honduras, Curacao, Belize, and the Virgin Islands, although with much less support and enthusiasm than in the countries discussed previously. Colombia has had a total of three major league players, including Luis Castro, who played 42 games for the Philadelphia Athletics in 1902. Honduras has had one major leaguer, Curacao two, Belize one, and the Virgin Islands eight.

The Ultimate Other
All-Star Team

Over the previous chapters, the most outstanding professional baseball players ever to set foot on a diamond from the old Negro leagues as well as leagues in Japan, Mexico, Cuba, Puerto Rico and the Dominican Republic have been reviewed. The strengths and weaknesses of the various players were probed, in an attempt to locate the greatest of the great.

This chapter will present the ultimate baseball all-star team, from around the world. Unfortunately, these players are not competing on a level playing field with major league players when all-star teams are selected. Very few fans in the United States ever saw any of these players in action. Most of the players, with the exception of the Negro leaguers, never played baseball in the United States. Their exploits are known to us only through second or third hand accounts. The quality of their opposition is sometimes unknown. Very few articles have been written about them in English. In some cases there is even a lack of statistics on which to make intelligent comparisons.

We do not know the true greatness of baseball players who spent their professional careers outside the umbrella of organized baseball. We can never know, for sure, the level of pitching excellence of Masaichi Kaneda, "Bullet Joe" Rogan, or Jose Mendez; the home run prowess of Josh Gibson, Sadaharu Oh, or Hector Espino; or the hitting mastery of Tetsuharu Kawakami, Chino Smith, Francisco Coimbre, or Alejandro Oms. There are almost no movies or videos of these baseball immortals available to review. As the years pass, the second and third hand accounts, as unreliable as they may be, become fewer and fewer.

It is true there are indirect ways to measure the skills of the players in other leagues, and these methods have been utilized to the fullest. League-to-league comparisons give some idea as to the relative capabilities of the players outside organized baseball. The statistical comparison of players who participated in both the major leagues and the Japanese Leagues, for instance, provides an indication of the offensive performance that could be expected of players from the Japanese Leagues, if they played in the majors. Other comparisons between the Negro leagues and the major leagues, and the Negro leagues and leagues in Cuba, Puerto Rico, and the Dominican Republic, provide similar insights into the relative skills of the various players.

Still, it is an inexact and unsatisfactory method of determining the best baseball players in the world. Unfortunately, it is the only tool available at the present time. Therefore, in order to minimize an unfair situation, and to recognize the many great baseball players who have performed around the world over the past century, the ultimate all-star team will consist of 57 players from the old Negro leagues, Japan, Cuba, Mexico, Puerto Rico, and the Dominican Republic.

All-World All-Star Team — Non Major League

CATCHER:

Over the past 98 years, there have been many great catchers around the world, including outstanding receivers from the Negro leagues, the Japanese Leagues, and the Cuban Winter League. Unfortunately, some of the greatest catchers from the Dominican Republic, Puerto Rico, Mexico, and other countries, prior to 1940, have disappeared from the pages of history.

Josh Gibson. (Noir Tech Research, Inc.)

Of those catchers who were studied, the legendary Josh Gibson towers over his competition. He was, by all accounts, a capable defensive catcher with a rifle arm. Although not as strong defensively as some catchers, he far outdistanced all other catchers with a bat in his hand. His uncanny bat control (a .362 batting average with less than 50 strikeouts a year) and awesome power (48 homers a year) make him baseball's greatest catcher. He is ably supported by Louis Santop, Katsuya Nomura, and Koichi Tabuchi. Louis "Big Bertha" Santop was the most fearsome power hitter in the Negro leagues during the dead ball era, as well as being a steady defensive catcher. Nomura, who hit 657 career home runs in Japan, was the most durable catcher in professional baseball history. Moose, as he was called, holds the world record for the most years played (28) and the most games played (2918) by a catcher, an unbelievable total for such a demanding position. Tabuchi was outstanding, both offensively and defensively. His average of 44 home runs a year is #2 behind Sadaharu Oh, in Japanese baseball history.

PITCHER:

There are 15 pitchers on the all-star team, five from the Negro leagues, four from Cuba, three from Japan, two from Mexico, and one from the Dominican Republic. The staff is led by the legendary Satchel Paige, who entered the major leagues at the advanced baseball age of 42, after a 20-year career in the Negro leagues, and who pitched his last game in professional baseball at the age of 60. One source estimated his total career victories, against all opposition, at 602.

The other Negro league pitchers are "Smokey Joe" Williams, "Cannonball" Dick Redding, Willie Foster, and the great "Bullet Joe" Rogan. Jose Mendez leads the Cuban contingent, followed by Luis Padron, Eustaquio Pedroso, and Dolf Luque. Luque pitched in both Cuba and the major leagues for 22 years, recording a total of 287 victories, 194 of them in the majors. In addition to 400-game winner Masaichi Kaneda, the other Japanese pitchers are Tetsuya Yoneda (350

Left: "Bullet Joe" Rogan. (Noir Tech Research, Inc.) *Right:* Masaichi Kaneda. (Gary Engel.)

wins), and Dennis Eckersley's counterpart, Yutaka Enatsu, who racked up 206 victories as well as 193 saves over a dazzling 18-year career. Mexican aces Ramon Arano (334 victories) and Alfredo Ortiz (225 wins), and the Dominican legend Diomedes Olivo round out the staff.

FIRST BASE:

The greatest first basemen in the world, outside the major leagues, are Sadaharu Oh and Tetsuharu Kawakami of Japan, Buck Leonard and Mule Suttles of the Negro leagues, Hector Espino of Mexico, Julian Castillo of Cuba, and Alonzo Perry, a Negro league player who was an all-star in both the Dominican Republic and Mexico. Oh is the only man in the world to hit more than 800 career home runs, a record that could last forever. Tetsuharu Kawakami was Japan's most prolific hitter during the 1940s and '50s. When he retired, he had the highest career batting average in Japan. He still holds the record for the most doubles and triples on a frequency basis. Buck Leonard, called the "black Lou Gehrig," was a tough clutch hitter who helped the Homestead Grays win nine consecutive Negro league championships from 1937 to 1945. Mule Suttles was a world class slugger who hit more career home runs than any other Negro league batter. He was projected to have hit an average of 43 home runs a year in the major leagues. Hector Espino, a .300 hitter with good power, could have been a formidable major league slugger. Instead, he chose to play baseball in his own country. When he retired after 23 years, he had a .335 batting average and a career record of 453 home runs (763 home runs, including his winter record in the Mexican Pacific League). Julian Castillo was the premier power hitter in Cuba during the first decade of the twentieth century. Perry pounded the ball at a .300+ pace with 20 homers and 100 RBIs, wherever he played.

SECOND BASE:

Martin Dihigo was unquestionably one of the greatest all around players in baseball history. "El Maestro" could do it all. He played second base with a graceful motion that seemed effortless. He had excellent range, good hands, and a strong arm. He was also a standout center fielder and one of the top pitchers of his era, with over 250 career victories. He was deadly with a bat in his hands, a long ball hitter and consistent 100 RBI man. His backups were Morimichi Takagi, Bill Monroe, Sammy T. Hughes, and Manuel Cueto. Takagi, who played 21 years with the Chunichi Dragons of Japan's Central League, was a superb defensive second baseman, an offensive threat who averaged 16 home runs per year, and a dangerous base runner. Bill Monroe was a flashy fielding and .300 hitting infielder in the Negro leagues for 19 years. Sammy T. Hughes, another Negro leaguer, was one of the greatest defensive second basemen ever to step on a field: a master of the double play. Cueto, "The Devil Man," starred in Cuba for 22

Left: Tetsuharu Kawakami. (Gary Engel.) *Right:* Hector Espino. (Leo W. Banks Collection.)

years. He was a good glove man, and a dangerous hitter who won three Cuban League batting titles.

SHORTSTOP:

Brilliant defense defines the shortstop position. John Henry Lloyd, Perucho Cepeda, Yoshio Yoshida, Silvio Garcia, Dobie Moore, and Willie Wells were all outstanding fielders. Lloyd, known as "The Shovel" in Cuba because of his method of scooping up ground balls, was the epitome of perfection. In the field, Lloyd covered ground like a greyhound, with sure hands and a rifle for an arm. At the plate, he pounded the ball at a .359 clip with more than his share of extra base hits. He could have captured several batting championships if he had played in the major leagues. Cepeda was a dangerous .325 hitter, who could deliver the long ball when needed. He was one of the top RBI men in the Puerto Rican Winter League. Yoshida, Japan's "Mr. Shortstop," is generally considered to be the greatest defensive short fielder in the history of Japanese baseball. His great speed helped him win two stolen base crowns, en route to 350 career stolen bases. Garcia played baseball all over the western hemisphere for 18 years. He was a career .323 hitter in six countries, and possessed good long ball power. Moore, another veteran of the Negro leagues, was outstanding in the field and a .365 hitter who could have been expected to slam 15 home runs a year in the majors.

John Jenry Lloyd. (Noir Tech Research, Inc.)

Wells covered the infield like a blanket, while batting .328 with 20 home runs a year.

THIRD BASE:

Third base is well protected by Shigeo Nagashima and Ray Dandridge. Nagashima, Japan's most popular player and the leader of the famed Yomiuri Giants, was an outstanding all-around player. He had quick reflexes, a sure glove, a dynamite arm, and a bat that sent pitchers diving for cover. Japan's most famous clutch hitter had a reputation for making the big hit at the right time. The right handed slugger had a career batting average of .305, with 444 home runs, and 1522 runs batted in. The bandy-legged Dandridge was a impenetrable barrier at third. With his quick reflexes and steady glove, it was almost impossible to put a ball past him. He was also a dependable hitter who pounded Negro league pitching for a .322 average. He also hit well in AAA Minneapolis (.318), as well as in Mexico (.347) and Cuba (.282). Judy Johnson and Oliver Marcelle were other all-around Negro league third basemen, like Dandridge, who could beat you either with a glove or with a bat. Canena Marquez was a superb defensive third baseman who carried a .300+ bat with good power. He hit .306 over an 18-year career in Puerto Rico, Mexico, the Negro leagues, and the AAA minor leagues, averaging 14 home runs a year.

OUTFIELD:

The All-World All-Star team carries 15 outfielders from six different countries. The starting unit is comprised of Negro leaguer Oscar Charleston, Cuban Leaguer Cristobal Torriente, and Puerto Rican star Pancho Coimbre. Charleston was a

Yoshio Yoshida. (Gary Engel.)

true superstar, who was the equal of Willie Mays on the field. He was a brilliant flychaser who anchored some of the best outfields in baseball history. He was also a powerful right handed slugger who batted at a .350 clip in the Negro leagues and a .361 clip in Cuba. Based on conversion factors, he could have been expected to hit about .320 with 30 home runs a year in the major leagues. Torriente was considered to be a franchise player by many baseball experts. The husky Cuban was a powerful hitter in both Cuba and the United States. He was a .335 hitter in the Negro leagues and a .353 hitter in Cuba. Coimbre was another superstar who hit .361 in the Negro leagues and .337 in the Puerto Rican Winter League. He was a carbon copy of the great Roberto Clemente, his countryman. In fact, he outhit Clemente by 14 points in Puerto Rico.

Left to right: **Unidentified, Josh Gibson, Ray Dandridge, Leroy Matlock. (John B. Holway.)**

Other outfielders include Willard Brown, Turkey Stearnes, "Cool Papa" Bell, Isao Harimoto, Bernardo Baro, Bob Thurman, Tetelo Vargas, Yutaka Fukumoto, Koji Yamamoto, Alejandro Oms, Chino Smith, and Andres Mora. Several of the players, such as the aforementioned Charleston, Torriente, and Coimbre, as well as Stearnes, Brown, Yamamoto, Smith, and Oms, were five point players who could hit for average, hit with power, run, field, and throw. Bell, Fukumoto, and Vargas were speedsters who covered the outfield like frightened fawns, bunted and slashed their way to a .300 average, and raced around the bases in record time. Thurman and Mora were solid .300 hitters who were capable of hitting 30 or 40 home runs a year. Harimoto was Japan's greatest hitter, retiring with a record .319 career average. He is the only player in Japan to accumulate more than 3000 base hits. Baro was a brilliant outfielder, with world class speed, a .300 bat, and a penchant for stealing bases.

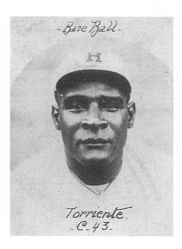

Cristobal Torriente. (Yuyo Ruiz.)

All-World All-Star Team — Non Major League

Catcher	Josh Gibson*	Louis Santop
	Katsuya Nomura	Koichi Tabuchi
Pitcher	Satchel Paige*	Joe Williams
	Bullet Joe Rogan	Willie Foster
	Jose Mendez	Dick Redding
	Masaichi Kaneda	Ramon Arano
	Adolfo Luque	Diomedes Olivo
	Alfredo Ortiz	Tetsuya Yoneda
	Eusatquio Pedroso	Yutaka Enatsu
	Luis Padron	
First Base	Sadaharu Oh*	Buck Leonard
	Tetsuharu Kawakami	Julian Castillo
	Hector Espino	Mule Suttles
	Alonzo Perry	
Second Base	Martin Dihigo*	Sammy T. Hughes
	Morimichi Takagi	Manuel Cueto
	Bill Monroe	
Shortstop	John Henry Lloyd*	Perucho Cepeda
	Yoshio Yoshida	Silvio Garcia
	Dobie Moore	Willie Wells
Third Base	Shigeo Nagashima*	Ray Dandridge
	Canena Marquez	Judy Johnson
	Oliver Marcelle	
Outfield	Oscar Charleston*	Tetelo Vargas
	Cristobal Torriente*	Cool Papa Bell
	Francisco Coimbre*	Willard Brown
	Turkey Stearnes	Isao Harimoto
	Bernardo Baro	Bob Thurman
	Yutaka Fukumoto	Alejandro Oms
	Chino Smith	Andres Mora
	Koji Yamamoto	

Note: An asterisk (*) denotes one of the nine starting players.

     The All-World All-Star team should not be considered to be a minor league squad. It is major league all the way and could be expected to be competitive with any representative major league team. Baseball's great slugger Babe Ruth would more than meet his match in the Negro league bomber Josh Gibson. A pitching duel between Walter Johnson and Satchel Paige would be a toss-up, as would a matchup between Grover Cleveland Alexander and Smokey Joe

Williams, or Sandy Koufax and Jose Mendez. The power of Lou Gehrig and Jimmie Foxx could be offset by the slugging of Sadaharu Oh and Buck Leonard. The infield genius of Brooks Robinson would have its counterpart in Ray Dandridge. Shortstops Honus Wagner and John Henry Lloyd were considered to be mirror images of each other by their peers. In the outfield, a major league combination of Willie Mays, Ted Williams and Babe Ruth would have a hard time outperforming a trio of Oscar Charleston, Cristobal Torriente and Pancho Coimbre. Ty Cobb, Tris Speaker, and Joe DiMaggio would be evenly matched by Turkey Stearnes, Cool Papa Bell, and Alejandro Oms.

Francisco Coimbre. (Yuyo Ruiz.)

Baseball's All-World All-Star team may be a composed of baseball's forgotten all-stars, but it is the equal of any professional baseball team anywhere.

Today, the American Baseball Hall of Fame includes Satchel Paige, Josh Gibson, Buck Leonard, Martin Dihigo, John Henry Lloyd, Ray Dandridge, Rube Foster, Monte Irvin, Judy Johnson, Oscar Charleston, Cool Papa Bell, Leon Day, Willie Wells, Willie Foster, Bullet Joe Rogan, and Smokey Joe Williams. Hopefully, Turkey Stearnes will join his comrades next year. Perhaps in the future a few Japanese stars, like Sadaharu Oh and Shigeo Nagashima will also be enshrined.

For the most part, these great players will go unrecognized in the United States. Not so, in their own countries, and other countries around the world. Most of them are already members of the Baseball Hall of Fame in their homeland. Many of them are also enshrined in other countries. Martin Dihigo is in the Hall of Fame in four countries, Josh Gibson in three countries, and Ray Dandridge, Satchel Paige, John Henry Lloyd, Oscar Charleston, Judy Johnson, and Tetelo Vargas in two countries.

In terms of universal interest, the author has selected the ultimate baseball all-star team, which consists of the greatest players in the world, including major leaguers and non–major leaguers. The ultimate all-star team can be found in the Table XXVII.

In future years, hopefully many more of these legends will be honored by the duly recognized baseball organizations around the world. The 57 men on this team are some of the world's greatest baseball players.

They should not be forgotten.

Statistical Tables

TABLE I

Comparison of Professional Leagues

League	AB	H	D	T	HR	BA
Major Leagues	550	143	25	6	19	.260
Cuban W.L. (1930–60)	550	152	–	–	14	.276
Puerto Rican W.L. (1958–94)	550	152	–	–	15	.276
Japanese Leagues	550	153	21	1	42	.278
Dominican W.L. (1955–97)	550	155	–	–	16	.281
Cuban W.L. (1920–60)	550	158	–	–	12	.284
AAA Minor Leagues	550	159	26	6	20	.287
Puerto Rican W.L. (1938–57)	550	161	–	–	16	.293
AA Minor Leagues	550	168	–	–	29	.306
Negro Leagues (1930–50)	550	169	24	8	15	.308
Mexican League (1938–97)	550	167	–	–	20	.310
Class C League (1948–54)	550	177	–	–	32	.321
Panama W.L. (1940–59)	550	181	–	–	24	.329
Venezuela W.L. (1930–59)	550	201	–	–	23	.365

Note: A previous study provided the data for the Class C league. A small sampling of data indicates the Panama Winter League, during the period of interest, to 1959, might have been about a Class C league or lower. The Venezuelan Winter League, from 1930 to 1959, might have been equivalent to an amateur league.

Legend: AB (at-bats); H (hits); D (doubles); T (triples); HR (home runs); BA (batting average).

TABLE II

Comparison of Home Run Totals—
Dead Ball Era to Lively Ball Era

	Average Number of Home Runs Per Year	
Player	**Pre 1920**	**After 1920**
Rogers Hornsby	7	25
Zack Wheat	6	12
Cy Williams	10	29
Ken Williams	7	24
Ty Cobb	5	7
Frank Baker	8	16
George Burns	6	6
Jack Fournier	6	18
Harry Hooper	3	9
Baby Doll Jacobson	5	9
Stuffy McInnis	2	1
Emil Meusel	9	13
Ed Roush	4	6
Babe Ruth	24	50
George Sisler	4	7
Tris Speaker	4	9
Bobby Veach	3	5
Max Carey	4	5
Tilly Walker	7	23
Harry Heilmann	6	16
Totals	130	290
Avg. no. home runs per year	7	15

The home run factor, from this table, to convert home runs hit in the dead ball era to projected home runs in the lively ball era is 2.14.

The actual number of home runs hit by both the National and American Leagues, from 1910 through 1919, was 4007.

The actual number of home runs hit by both the National and American Leagues, from 1920 through 1929, was 10,042.

The home run factor, based on the total number of home runs hit by both leagues, was 2.51.

TABLE III

Comparison of Negro Leagues
to Major Leagues

Name	Negro League Averages					Major League Averages				
	AB	H	HR	HR1	BA	AB	H	HR	HR2	BA
Luke Easter	434	146	23	29	.336	1725	472	93	30	.274
Sam Jethroe	1331	453	20	8	.340	1763	460	49	15	.261
Roy Campanella	629	211	18	16	.334	4205	1161	242	32	.276
Gene Baker	617	161	5	4	.261	2230	590	39	10	.265
Willie Mays	460	141	5	14	.307	10881	3283	660	33	.302
Bob Thurman	632	222	24	21	.351	663	163	35	29	.246
Monte Irvin	850	293	33	25	.345	2499	731	99	22	.293
Junior Gilliam	432	114	2	2	.264	7119	1889	65	5	.265
Hank Thompson	641	220	21	19	.343	3003	801	129	24	.267
Larry Doby	513	194	25	26	.378	5348	1515	253	26	.283
Elston Howard	495	143	3	10	.289	5363	1471	167	17	.274
Bob Boyd	1129	409	11	11	.362	1936	567	19	5	.293
Al Smith	431	126	8	10	.292	5357	1457	164	17	.272
Pancho Herrera	509	154	19	21	.303	975	264	31	17	.271
Curt Roberts	774	216	3	2	.279	575	128	1	1	.223
Average	550	175		15	.319	550	149		19	.271

Major league averages from Total Baseball, *edited by John Thorn and Pete Palmer.*

Negro league averages for Easter, Mays, Irvin, Gilliam, Thompson, Doby, Howard, and Boyd, © 1995 John B. Holway and Dick Clark, used with permission.

Negro league averages for Baker, Campanella, Thurman, Herrera, C. Roberts, and A. Smith, compliments of SABR, from The Negro Leagues Book, *edited by Dick Clark and Larry Lester.*

Legend: *HR1— Home runs per 550 at-bats, in the Negro leagues. HR2 — Home runs per 550 at-bats, in major leagues.*

The averages were arrived at by converting each player's statistics to a 550 at-bat basis, then obtaining an average for batting average and for home runs.

Note: *Requirements were for a minimum of 400 at-bats in the Negro leagues, and 575 at bats in the major leagues.*

TABLE IV

Negro League Averages —
Batting Statistics per 550 At-Bats

Name	AB	H	D	T	HR	BA
Josh Gibson	550	199	29	11	48	.362
Roy Campanella	550	184	31	3	16	.334
Buck Leonard	550	186	30	12	24	.339

Name	AB	H	D	T	HR	BA
Mule Suttles	550	181	31	12	34	.329
Ed Wesley	550	178	28	7	28	.324
Willie Wells	550	180	33	8	20	.328
Dobie Moore	550	201	35	15	16	.365
Jud Wilson	550	191	30	6	13	.347
Oscar Charleston	550	192	32	12	26	.350
Turkey Stearnes	550	194	33	18	30	.352
Martin Dihigo	550	174	21	8	25	.319
Chino Smith	550	235	50	8	33	.428
John Beckwith	550	194	33	8	30	.356
Frog Redus	550	176	27	9	21	.319
Heavy Johnson	550	200			20	.363
Monte Irvin	550	189	28	5	21	.345
Larry Doby	550	200	27	15	27	.363
Luke Easter	550	185	42	10	29	.336
Willard Brown	550	194	26	7	20	.352
Biz Mackey	550	177	22	8	11	.322
Louis Santop	550	176	21	8	10	.364
Dick Lundy	550	174	21	5	12	.324
Ray Dandridge	550	177	26	8	6	.322
Cool Papa Bell	550	185	29	10	9	.337
Cristobal Torriente	550	184	33	10	13	.335
Bullet Joe Rogan	550	189	30	15	16	.343
Pete Hill	550	174	27	8	9	.317
Spot Poles	550	191	16	0	4	.348
Artie Wilson	550	207	24	11	3	.376
Willie Mays	550	169	29	5	14	.307
Ernie Banks	550	164	40	4	12	.298
Jackie Robinson	550	212	47	14	17	.387
Bob Boyd	550	200	13	8	5	.362
Bill Wright	550	185	22	12	12	.336
Hank Thompson	550	188	30	12	18	.343
John Henry Lloyd	550	194	26	6	7	.353

Note: *Negro league averages for Campanella, A. Wilson, Doby, and Banks, compliments of SABR, from the book,* The Negro Leagues Book, *edited by Dick Clark and Larry Lester. Negro league averages for Santop, Hill, and Poles were derived from several sources.*

All other Negro league averages, c. 1995 John B. Holway and Dick Clark, used with permission.

TABLE V

Negro League Averages Adjusted to Major Leagues

Name	AB	H	D	T	HR	BA	
Josh Gibson	550	170	30	8	61	.312	
Roy Campanella	550	158	33	3	20	.286	(Proj.)
	550	152	23	3	32	.276	(Actual)
Buck Leonard	550	150	26	8	30	.291	
Mule Suttles	550	152	32	8	43	.279	
Ed Wesley	550	149	29	5	36	.274	
Dobie Moore	550	169	32	10	20	.317	
Oscar Charleston	550	163	33	9	33	.300	
Turkey Stearnes	550	164	34	13	38	.302	
Martin Dihigo	550	146	22	6	32	.269	
Chino Smith	550	204	52	6	42	.378	
John Beckwith	550	167	34	6	38	.306	
Larry Doby	550	173	28	12	34	.315	(Proj.)
	550	156	24	5	25	.283	(Actual)
Monte Irvin	550	163	29	4	27	.297	(Proj.)
	550	161	21	8	22	.293	(Actual)
Luke Easter	550	158	44	8	37	.288	(Proj.)
	550	151	17	4	30	.274	(Actual)
Jud Wilson	550	165	31	5	16	.300	
Frog Redus	550	155	28	7	28	.281	
Heavy Johnson	550	173			25	.315	
Willard Brown	550	167	27	5	25	.304	
Biz Mackey	550	151	23	6	13	.274	
Louis Santop	550	174	22	6	32	.316	
Dick Lundy	550	152	22	4	15	.276	
Ray Dandridge	550	151	27	6	8	.274	
Cool Papa Bell	550	159	30	7	11	.289	
Cristobal Torriente	550	158	32	7	16	.287	
Bullet Joe Rogan	550	162	31	12	19	.295	
Pete Hill	550	148	28	6	28	.269	
Spot Poles	550	165	17	0	5	.300	
Artie Wilson	550	180	25	9	4	.328	
Willie Mays	550	142	30	4	18	.259	(Proj.)
	550	166	26	7	33	.302	(Actual)
Ernie Banks	550	138	42	3	15	.250	(Proj.)
	550	151	24	5	30	.274	(Actual)
Jackie Robinson	550	186	49	10	21	.339	(Proj.)
	550	171	31	6	15	.311	(Actual)

Name	*AB*	*H*	*D*	*T*	*HR*	*BA*	
Bob Boyd	550	173	14	6	6	.314	(Proj.)
	550	161	23	7	5	.293	(Actual)
Bill Wright	550	158	23	9	16	.288	
Hank Thompson	550	162	31	9	23	.295	(Proj.)
	550	147	19	6	24	.267	(Actual)
John Henry Lloyd	550	168	27	4	9	.305	

TABLE VI

Negro League Players — League to League Batting Average & Home Runs Per 550 At-Bats

Name	*NL*		*CWL*		*PRWL*		*MEX*		*AA*		*AAA*		*ML*		*Proj.*
	HR	*BA*	*HR*	*BA*	*HR*	*BA*	*HR*	*BA*	*HR*	*BA*	*HR*	*BA*	*HR*	*BA*	*BA*
S. Amoros	16	.338	10	.300			18	.305			24	.319	18	.255	.282
S. Bankhead	7	.285	7	.297	4	.311	11	.335							.274
B. Boyd	12	.362	8	.302	7	.328					5	.318	5	.293	.294
R. Dandridge	3	.322	3	.282			7	.347			6	.316			.278
A. Wilson	6	.376	5	.328							8	.312			.303
M. Minoso	8	.282	12	.279							19	.312	16	.298	.257
S. Jethroe	10	.340	8	.290							17	.295	15	.261	.288
R. Noble	-	.270	16	.272							20	.274	20	.218	.246
E. Banks	12	.299											30	.274	.251
H. Rodriguez	ins			1	.269						4	.286	1	.265	.251
M. Smith	0	.163	9	.269							9	.277	16	.196	.202
W. Mays	14	.307			38	.395					30	.477	33	.302	.259
H. Thompson	19	.343	8	.319							25	.277	24	.267	.279
S. Garcia	5	.322	5	.282			13	.335							.269
E. Howard	10	.289									18	.308	17	.275	.266
L. Pearson	16	.308	12	.262											.248
B. Wilson	12	.332	12	.303							11	.312			.282
G. Baker	4	.261			7	.287					11	.271	10	.265	.242
W. Brown	20	.352			29	.350	13	.325	24	.309			ins		.307
J. Burgos	1	.232			1	.216									.192
R. Campanella	16	.334			13	.276	19	.291			22	.287	32	.276	.260
B. Clarkson	18	.335			26	.301	27	.316	17	.318	19	.314	ins		.278
C. Harmon					6	.311			14	.311	9	.295	7	.238	.275
M. Irvin	25	.345	17	.266	18	.359	46	.397			31	.356	22	.293	.323
L. Marquez	11	.371			16	.298	26	.337			14	.306			.285
F. Pedroso	4	.258	4	.244	21	.325	13	.329							.252
A. Smith	10	.292			15	.274					24	.288	17	.273	.254
P. Davis	8	.322			15	.297					11	.281			.269
B. Thurman	21	.351			22	.323					16	.276	29	.246	.286

Name	NL		CWL		PRWL		MEX		AA		AAA		ML		Proj.
	HR	BA	HR	BA	HR	BA	HR	BA	HR	BA	HR	BA	HR	BA	BA
L. Easter	29	.336			39	.359					36	.296	30	.274	.300
L. Doby	26	.363											26	.284	.315
J. Robinson	17	.387									4	.349	16	.311	.339
B. Leonard	24	.339					20	.325							.274
W. Wells	20	.328	8	.320	-	.378	11	.330							.281
M. Suttles	34	.329													.281
E. Wesley	28	.324													.276
J.H. Lloyd	7	.353	2	.329											.305
O. Charleston	26	.350	11	.361											.322
J. Gibson	48	.362	34	.353	27	.355	54	.373							.318
J. Beckwith	30	.356													.308
T. Stearnes	30	.352													.304
C.P. Bell	9	.338	11	.292			11	.398							.307
D. Moore	16	.365	3	.356											.324
Chino Smith	33	.428	3	.335											.345
J. Rogan	15	.343													.295
O. Marcelle	5	.304	3	.305											.268
J. Johnson	4	.301	3	.334											.281
R. Lundy	13	.324	4	.341											.296
P. Hill	9	.308	2	.307											.274
S. Poles	4	.292	2	.319											.270
J. Wilson	13	.347	13	.372											.324
M. Dihigo	25	.319	10	.293			10	.319							

Legend: *NL — Negro Leagues; CWL — Cuban Winter League; PRWL — Puerto Rican Winter League; MEX — Mexican League; AA — AA Minor Leagues; AAA — AAA Minor Leagues; ML — Major Leagues; Proj. — Projected major league average based on adjustment factors from other leagues.*

TABLE VII

Comparison of Negro Leagues to High Minor Leagues (AAA)

	Negro Leagues				AAA Leagues			
Name	AB	H	HR	BA	AB	H	HR	BA
Artie Wilson	1046	393	6	.376	5152	1609	8	.312
Bill Wright	908	305	21	.336	3438	1146	78	.333
Luke Easter	434	146	23	.336	4150	1227	269	.296
Ray Dandridge	878	263	5	.322	2699	852	27	.316
Sam Jethroe	1331	453	20	.340	3750	1108	119	.295
Roy Campanella	631	211	18	.334	959	275	39	.287
Willie Mays	460	141	5	.307	455	179	12	.393
Monte Irvin	850	293	33	.345	581	207	33	.356
Junior Gilliam	432	114	2	.264	1126	331	16	.294

Name	AB	Negro Leagues			AAA Leagues			
	AB	H	HR	BA	AB	H	HR	BA
Hank Thompson	641	220	21	.343	505	140	23	.277
Minnie Minoso	287	84	4	.293	1309	408	46	.312
Elston Howard	495	143	3	.289	994	306	32	.308
Bob Boyd	1129	409	11	.362	2113	672	20	.318
Frank Austin	689	229	2	.332	4607	1236	30	.268
Gene Baker	617	161	5	.261	2393	647	48	.270
Bus Clarkson	668	225	23	.337	1057	329	37	.311
Piper Davis	1507	485	22	.322	2524	709	49	.281
Sam Hairston	1283	435	52	.339	965	254	2	.263
Pancho Herrera	509	154	19	.303	3933	1140	187	.290
David Hoskins	616	186	6	.302	381	96	5	.319
Luis Marquez	577	214	11	.371	5640	1724	144	.306
Jim Pendleton	302	91	6	.301	4302	1265	112	.294
Curt Roberts	774	216	3	.279	3804	1130	63	.297
Bob Thurman	631	222	25	.352	2194	602	65	.274
Jesse Williams	850	213	3	.251	474	119	0	.251
Bob Wilson	575	191	13	.332	4433	1381	88	.312
Average Per 550 At-bats								
	550	176	11	.320	550	166	14	.301

Note: *Negro League averages for Wright, Easter, Dandridge, Jethroe, Mays, Irvin, Gilliam, Thompson, Doby, Minoso, Howard, and Boyd, c. 1995 John B. Holway and Dick Clark, used with permission.*

Other Negro League averages, and all minor league averages, compliments of SABR, from the book, The Negro Leagues Book, *edited by Dick Clark and Larry Lester.*

TABLE VIII

Comparison of Major Leagues to High Minor Leagues (AAA)
Home Runs & Batting Averages Per 550 At-bats

Name	Major Leagues		AAA Leagues	
	HR	BA	HR	BA
Elston Howard	17	.275	18	.308
Junior Gilliam	5	.265	8	.294
Sandy Amoros	18	.255	24	.319
Bob Boyd	5	.293	5	.318
Minnie Minoso	16	.298	19	.312
Sam Jethroe	15	.261	17	.295
Hector Rodriguez	1	.265	4	.286
Hank Thompson	24	.267	25	.277
Gene Baker	10	.265	11	.271
Roy Campanella	32	.276	22	.287

Name	Major Leagues		AAA Leagues	
	HR	BA	HR	BA
Chuck Harmon	7	.238	9	.295
Monte Irvin	22	.293	31	.356
Al Smith	17	.273	24	.288
Bob Thurman	29	.246	16	.276
Luke Easter	30	.274	36	.296
Richie Allen	30	.292	33	.289
Matty Alou	3	.307	12	.307
Earl Averill	21	.318	20	.342
Don Baylor	23	.260	22	.315
George Burns	6	.307	14	.335
Orlando Cepeda	26	.297	25	.309
Ron Cey	24	.261	30	.328
Ben Chapman	8	.302	26	.336
Rocky Colavito	32	.266	36	.280
Earl Combs	6	.325	9	.365
Willie Davis	11	.279	11	.346
Joe DiMaggio	29	.325	22	.361
Bobby Doerr	17	.288	2	.320
Ron Fairly	16	.266	27	.302
Rick Ferrell	3	.281	3	.291
Jack Fournier	14	.313	11	.310
Ralph Garr	8	.306	6	.356
Charlie Gehringer	11	.320	22	.325
Joe Gordon	24	.268	25	.284
Stan Hack	4	.301	4	.329
Johnny Frederick	15	.308	9	.323
Babe Herman	18	.324	16	.325
Ted Williams	37	.344	33	.325
George Kelly	14	.297	19	.317
Willie McCovey	35	.270	27	.337
Bill Terry	13	.341	24	.363
Average	17	.288	18	.315
Adjusted to base point	19	.260	20	.287

Note: *This table was used to determine the relative difference between the AAA leagues and the major league base point.*

TABLE IX

Comparison of the U.S. Major Leagues to Cuban Winter League

Name	AB	Major League H	HR	BA	AB	Cuban Winter League H	HR	BA
Rafael Almeida	285	77	3	.270	1273	322	8	.253
Armando Marsans	2273	612	2	.269	1632	426	2	.261
Mike Gonzalez	2829	717	13	.253	1679	487	12	.290
Adolfo Luque	1043	237	5	.227	671	169	2	.252
Sam Jethroe	1763	460	19	.261	663	192	10	.290
Hank Thompson	3003	801	129	.267	789	252	12	.319
Minnie Minoso	6579	1963	186	.298	3102	836	66	.270
Sandy Amoros	1311	334	43	.255	1613	484	30	.300
Bob Boyd	1936	567	19	.293	648	196	10	.302
Manuel Cueto	379	86	1	.227	1652	492	8	.298
Merito Acosta	436	111	0	.255	1094	315		.288
Napolean Reyes	931	264	13	.284	1018	277	5	.273
Roberto Ortiz	659	168	8	.255	1998	552	51	.276
Monte Irvin	2499	731	99	.293	358	95	11	.266
Curt Roberts	575	128	1	.223	560	143	7	.255
Jim Cooney	1575	413	2	.262	123	47	0	.382
Eddie Brown	2902	878	16	.303	167	54	2	.323
Charlie Dressen	2215	603	11	.272	287	90	1	.313
Dick Sisler	2606	720	55	.276	293	80	10	.274
Bob Allison	5032	1281	256	.255	342	75	10	.219
Ken Boyer	7455	2143	282	.287	234	71	6	.304
Bert Haas	2440	644	22	.264	1034	269	24	.260
Brooks Robinson	10654	2848	268	.267	266	55	9	.207
Bill Virdon	5980	1596	91	.267	253	86	6	.340
Dick Williams	2959	768	70	.260	283	72	6	.254
Don Zimmer	3283	773	91	.235	369	98	8	.266
Hector Rodriguez	407	108	1	.265	3420	921	9	.269
Average per 550 at-bats			10	.266			9	.282
Adjusted to M.L. base point			19	.260			17	.276
Prior to 1930			3	.260			3	.296
After 1930			19	.260			16	.268

Note: *Cuban Winter League averages compliments of Jorge S. Figueredo.*

TABLE X

Comparison of AAA Minor Leagues to Cuban Winter League

Name	AAA				Cuban Winter League			
	AB	*H*	*HR*	*BA*	*AB*	*H*	*HR*	*BA*
Minnie Minoso	1309	408	46	.311	3102	836	66	.270
Sandy Amoros	2229	710	98	.318	1613	484	30	.300
Artie Wilson	5152	1609	8	.312	746	245	5	.328
Bob Boyd	2113	672	20	.318	648	196	10	.302
Ray Dandridge	2699	852	27	.316	2042	575	11	.282
Sam Jethroe	3750	1108	119	.295	663	192	10	.290
Ray Noble	3593	986	130	.274	1940	527	55	.272
Hector Rodriguez	4899	1399	40	.286	3420	921	9	.269
Milt Smith	3644	1011	59	.277	705	189	11	.269
Hank Thompson	505	140	23	.277	789	252	12	.319
Bob Wilson	4433	1381	88	.312	495	150	7	.303

Name	*Averages Per 550 At-Bats*							
	AB	*H*	*HR*	*BA*	*AB*	*H*	*HR*	*BA*
Minnie Minoso	550	171	19	.311	550	148	12	.269
Sandy Amoros	550	175	24	.318	550	165	10	.300
Artie Wilson	550	172	1	.312	550	180	12	.328
Bob Boyd	550	175	5	.318	550	166	8	.302
Ray Dandridge	550	174	6	.316	550	155	3	.282
Sam Jethroe	550	162	17	.295	550	159	8	.290
Ray Noble	550	151	20	.274	550	149	16	.272
Hector Rodriguez	550	157	4	.286	550	148	1	.269
Milt Smith	550	152	9	.277	550	148	9	.269
Hank Thompson	550	152	25	.277	550	176	8	.319
Bob Wilson	550	172	11	.312	550	167	8	.303
Average	550	164	13	.298	550	167	9	.291
Adjusted to M.L. base point			20	.289			14	.282

TABLE XI

Comparison of Negro Leagues to Cuban Winter League

Name	Negro Leagues				Per 550 AB		Cuban Winter League				Per 550 AB	
	AB	*H*	*HR*	*BA*	*H*	*HR*	*AB*	*H*	*HR*	*BA*	*H*	*HR*
John Henry Lloyd	2231	788	27	.353	194	7	1378	456	5	.329	181	2
Oscar Charleston	3217	1125	150	.350	193	26	832	304	13	.361	199	11

Name	AB	H	HR	BA	Per 550 AB H	Per 550 AB HR	AB	H	HR	BA	Per 550 AB H	Per 550 AB HR
		Negro Leagues						*Cuban Winter League*				
C. Torriente	2311	774	53	.335	184	13	1410	498	18	.353	197	7
Dick Lundy	2017	654	47	.324	178	12	876	299	7	.341	188	4
Judy Johnson	2617	789	19	.301	166	4	499	165	6	.331	182	6
Dobie Moore	1393	509	41	.365	201	16	281	100	2	.356	196	3
Chino Smith	610	261	37	.428	235	33	565	189	3	.335	184	3
Sam Jethroe	1331	453	20	.340	187	8	663	192	10	.290	159	8
Hank Thompson	641	220	21	.343	188	18	789	252	12	.319	176	8
Artie Wilson	1046	393	6	.373	207	3	746	245	16	.328	180	12
Bob Boyd	1129	409	11	.362	200	5	648	196	10	.302	166	8
Ray Dandridge	878	263	5	.322	177	3	2049	575	11	.282	155	3
Jud Wilson	2763	960	63	.347	191	13	769	286	18	.372	204	13
Martin Dihigo	1363	435	62	.319	174	25	2158	632	34	.293	161	10
Willie Wells	3455	1133	126	.328	180	20	1121	358	16	.319	175	8
Sam Bankhead	1594	455	19	.285	157	7	802	238	10	.297	163	7
Lennie Pearson	1853	570	55	.308	169	16	1299	340	28	.262	144	12
Silvio Garcia	363	117	5	.322	176	8	3328	946	32	.284	156	5
Lorenzo Cabrera	349+	124+	10	.354	195	10	2004	616	12	.307	169	3
Bob Wilson	225	61	5	.332	183	12	495	150	11	.303	150	5
Fernando Pedroso	595	154	4	.250	142	4	450	110	3	.244	134	4
Pelayo Chacon	819	231	3	.282	155	2	1879	463	6	.246	135	2
Bernardo Baro	945	278	8	.302	166	5	936	293	3	.313	172	2
Alejandro Oms	913	279	29	.332	183	17	1531	537	15	.351	193	6
Valentin Dreke	1525	509	11	.334	184	4	1015	312	5	.307	169	3
Frank Warfield				.282	155			583	177	4	.304	167	4
Chaney White				.308	169			337	117	2	.347	191	3
Oliver Marcelle	1455	443	12	.304	167	5	957	292	6	.305	168	4
Cool Papa Bell	3952	1335	56	.338	186	8	569	166	10	.292	117	10
Pete Hill	1025	316	16	.308	169	9	661	203	2	.307	169	2
Spot Poles	271	79	2	.292	161	4	383	123	1	.319	175	2
Claro Duany	262	78	9	.298	164	19	1696	487	40	.277	152	13
Ray Brown	212	67	3	.316	174	8	353	94	6	.266	146	9
Josh Gibson	1679	607	146	.362	199	48	224	79	14	.353	194	34
Monte Irvin	850	293	33	.345	190	21	358	95	11	.266	146	17
Curt Roberts	774	216	2+	.279	153	2	560	143	7	.255	140	7
Bonnie Serrell	1068	329	9+	.308	169	7	342	92	2	.269	148	4
Quincy Trouppe	632	197	16	.312	172	18	307	78	5	.254	140	9
Harry Williams	850	213	2+	.251	138	2	597	186	6	.312	172	6
Average				.326	179	11				.306	168	7
Adjusted to M. L. base point				.308	169	15				.288	158	9
Adj. to M. L. b. p.—After 1930										.278	152	11

TABLE XII

Cuban Winter League All-Star Team Career Statistics

Name	Pos	Years	G	AB	H	D	T	HR	BA	ML Adj HR	ML Adj BA
Antonio Garcia	C	1882–1912	216	831	263	25	12	5	.316	27	.309
Mike Gonzalez	C	1910–1936	370	1679	487	55	20	12	.290	6	.266
Julian Castillo	1B	1901–1913	320	1201	372	55	32	8	.310	31	.303
Jud Wilson	1B	1925–1935		769	286	38	27	18	.372	25	.348
Manuel Cueto	2B	1912–1933	401	1652	492	66	19	8	.298	6	.274
Bienvenido Jiminez	2B	1913–1929	196	845	225	30	10	6	.266	9	.242
Silvio Garcia	SS	1937–1954	671	3328	946	89	26	19	.284	7	.260
John Henry Lloyd	SS	1906–1932		1378	456	45	33	5	.331	6	.307
Rafael Almeida	3B	1904–1925	361	1273	322	23	11	8	.253	7	.281
Ray Dandridge	3B	1933–1955		2129	601	68	14	10	.282	6	.258
Cristobal Torriente	OF	1913–1928		1410	498	62	41	18	.353	17	.329
Oscar Charleston	OF	1920–1928		832	304	48	19	13	.365	27	.341
Bernardo Baro	OF	1915–1929	204	936	293	30	14	3	.313	4	.289
Jacinto Calvo	OF	1913–1927	265	1110	344	41	30	6	.310	7	.286
Valentin Dreke	OF	1919–1928	254	1015	312	32	15	5	307	6	.283
Alejandro Oms	OF	1922–1946	254	1531	537	74	28	15	.351	13	.327
Alfredo Arcano		1887–1909	313	1273	352	22	24	11	.276	30	.270
Martin Dihigo	Util	1923–1945		2158	632	134	34	38	.293	28	.269

(Dihigo won 261 games and lost 138 games as a pitcher in Cuba, Mexico, and the Negro leagues)

| Lazaro Salazar | Util | 1931–1948 | | 1796 | 525 | | | | .292 | | .264 |

(Salazar won 154 games and lost 109 games as a pitcher in Cuba, Mexico and the Negro leagues)

Name	Pos	Years	G	W	L	PCT
Jose Mendez	P	1903–1927	157	74	25	.747
Luis Padron	P	1900–1926		39	23	.629
		1909–1926		26	18	.591 (Negro Leagues)

(Padron was a career .251 hitter W/6HR Adj. ML 35 HR/yr. Led league in doubles, 3 times, triples 4 times, home runs 4 times, batting average once —.463 in 1902. Led in wins 3X)

Adolfo Luque	P	1912–1946	216	93	62	.600
				194	179	.520 (Major Leagues)
Eustaquio Pedroso	P	1910–1930		65	46	.581 led in wins twice (13 & 11)
Jose Munoz	P	1904–1916		81	57	.587
Carlos Royer	P	1890–1911		87	40	.685
Manuel Garcia	P	1926–1948		91	60	.603
				96	68	.585 (Mexico)

Note: *The extra base hit totals for S. Garcia, M. Dihigo, and O. Charleston were incomplete. The extra base hit totals were adjusted to agree with the total at-bats. S. Garcia's total games played is incomplete.*

TEAM TWO

Name	Pos	Years	G	AB	H	D	T	HR	BA	ML Adj HR	ML Adj BA
Jose Fernandez	C	1915–1943	322	1879	520	35	15	3	.277	1	.253
Ray Noble	C	1942–1958	532	1940	527	63	23	55	.272	22	.248
Jose Rodriguez	1B	1913–1939	349	1597	400	39	20	7	.250	6	.226
Lorenzo Cabrera	1B	1942–1956	539	2004	616	99	30	12	.307	7	.283
Rogelio Crespo	2B	1918–1933		385	109	12	3	3	.283	3	.259
Willie Wells	2B	1928–1940		1121	358	48	20	16	.319	22	.295
Dick Lundy	SS	1920–1930		876	299	36	11	7	.341	13	.317
Luis Bustamante	SS	1901–1912	243	864	190	11	6	2	.220	5	.219
Eugenio Morin	3B	1910–1923		300	94	6	0	0	.313	0	.289
Hector Rodriguez	3B	1942–1959	880	3515	951	88	60	9	.271	2	.247
Carlos Moran	OF	1900–1916	314	1115	316	24	7	0	.283	0	.263
Alejandro Crespo	OF	1939–1954		2881	806	116	34	34	.280	15	.256
Emilio Palomino	OF	1904–1912		805	229	12	9	2	.284	4	.260
Pablo Mesa	OF	1921–1927		558	185	18	4	2	.332	3	.308
Armando Marsans	OF	1905–1928	455	1632	426	36	22	2	.261	1	.261
Claro Duany	OF	1942–1955		1696	487	103	12	40	.277	21	.253
Estaban Montalvo	Util	1923–1928		652	195	26	21	7	.299	8	.275
Pedro Formenthal	Util	1945–1955		2660	796	98	38	56	.280	19	.256

PITCHING

Name	Pos	Years	G	W	L	PCT	
Jose Acosta	P	1914–1929		140	119	.541	(U.S. minor leages, + 10-10 in majors)
Rodolfo Fernandez	P	1931–1944		50	38	.568	
Adolfo Lujan	P	1882–1891	48	34	9	.791	
Agapito Mayor	P	1938–1953		68	64	.515	
Jose Pastoriza	P	1888–1895	100	59	40	.596	
Ray Brown	P	1936–1948		46	20	.697	
				116	34	.77	(Negro Leagues)
				51	36	.586	(Mexico)
				22	8	.733	(Puerto Rico)
				12	10	.545	(U.S. minor leagues)
Ray Brown Totals				247	108	.699	

Note: ML Adj *is an approximation of the number of home runs and the batting average that could be expected if the player played in the major leagues.*

TABLE XIII

Comparison of Japanese Leagues to Major Leagues

Name	Japanese League Averages				Major League Averages			
	AB	H	HR	BA	AB	H	HR	BA
Matty Alou	913	258	15	.283	5789	1777	31	.307
George Altman	3183	985	205	.309	3091	832	101	.269
Mike Andrews	389	90	12	.231	3116	803	66	.258
Ken Aspromonte	943	257	31	.273	1483	369	19	.249
Don Blasingame	1356	371	15	.274	5296	1366	21	.258
Clete Boyer	1486	382	71	.257	5780	1396	162	.242
Don Buford	1779	480	65	.270	4553	1203	93	.264
Warren Cromartie	2961	951	171	.321	3796	1063	60	.280
Willie Davis	797	237	43	.297	9174	2561	182	.279
Wayne Garrett	606	146	28	.241	3285	786	61	.239
Dave Johnson	660	159	39	.241	4797	1252	136	.261
Cecil Fielder	384	116	38	.302	2870	743	191	.259
Willie Kirkland	2323	559	126	.246	3494	837	148	.240
Leron Lee	4934	1579	283	.320	1617	404	31	.250
Jim Lefebvre	1098	289	60	.263	3014	756	74	.251
Norm Larker	727	194	14	.267	1953	538	32	.275
Jim Lyttle	3319	945	166	.285	710	176	9	.248
Jim Marshall	1501	402	78	.268	852	206	29	.242
Felix Millan	1139	348	12	.306	5791	1617	22	.279
Bobby Mitchell	1718	429	113	.250	617	150	3	.243
Steve Ontiveros	2458	768	82	.312	2193	600	24	.274
Roger Repoz	1787	469	122	.262	2145	480	82	.224
Dave Roberts	2774	764	183	.275	194	38	2	.196
Reggie Smith	494	134	45	.271	7033	2020	314	.287
Daryl Spencer	2233	615	152	.275	3689	901	105	.244
Dick Stuart	685	176	49	.257	3997	1055	228	.264
Terry Whitfield	1407	406	85	.289	1913	537	33	.281
Walt Williams	952	264	44	.277	2373	640	33	.270
Bump Wills	633	164	16	.259	3030	807	36	.266
Roy White	1229	348	54	.283	6650	1803	160	.271
Randy Bass	2208	743	202	.337	325	69	9	.212
Boomer Wells	3482	1137	231	.327	127	29	0	.228
Ralph Bryant	1173	323	112	.275	1997	515	30	.258
Mike Diaz	943	288	72	.305	683	169	31	.247
Kent Hadley	2825	727	131	.257	363	88	14	.242
Ken Macha	1699	516	82	.303	380	98	1	.258
Carlos May	1397	431	70	.308	4120	1127	90	.274
Larry Parrish	874	227	70	.260	6792	1789	256	.263
Tony Solaita	1786	479	155	.268	1316	336	50	.255
Gordy Windhorn	1966	501	86	.255	108	19	2	.176

Name	Japanese League Averages				Major League Averages			
	AB	H	HR	BA	AB	H	HR	BA
Dick Davis	1703	564	117	.331	1217	323	27	.265
Mike Easler	517	156	26	.302	3677	1078	118	.293
Vic Harris	968	245	35	.253	1610	349	13	.217
Willie Upshaw	653	160	39	.245	4203	1103	123	.262
George Vukovich	754	193	32	.256	1602	430	27	.268
Chuck Essegian	300	79	15	.263	1018	260	47	.255
Ben Oglivie	805	246	46	.306	5913	1615	235	.273
Bob Nieman	355	107	13	.301	3452	1018	125	.295
Bombo Rivera	541	130	37	.240	831	220	10	.265
Gary Thomasson	477	119	20	.249	2373	591	61	.249
Bobby Tolan	360	96	6	.267	4230	1121	86	.265
Lee Walls	343	82	14	.239	2550	670	66	.262
Jim Trabor	495	150	24	.303	819	186	27	.227
Brian Dayett	481	126	21	.262	426	110	14	.258
Orestes Destrade	1655	436	154	.263	635	157	21	.247
Adrian Garrett	1302	338	102	.260	276	51	11	.185
Woody Jones	3182	762	246	.239	137	34	2	.248
Stan Palys	1525	419	66	.275	333	79	10	.237
Jack Pierce	291	66	13	.227	199	42	8	.211
Jose Vidal	122	27	2	.221	146	24	3	.164
George Wilson	624	161	27	.258	209	40	3	.191
Kevin Reimer	470	140	26	.298	1455	376	52	.258
Glenn Braggs	712	232	54	.326	2336	601	70	.257
Tom O'Malley	1721	548	74	.318	1213	310	13	.256
Mel Hall	939	269	52	.286	4212	1168	134	.277
Jack Howell	1146	336	86	.293	2268	535	84	.236
	90332	25539	5096	.283	170380	45200	4412	.265
Avg. per 550 AB	550	156	31	.283	550	146	14	.265

Note: *Japanese league averages compliments of Office of the Baseball Commissioner, Japan. Major League averages from* Total Baseball, *edited by John Thorn and Pete Palmer.*

TABLE XIV

Comparison of Japanese Leagues to Lower Minor Leagues (AA)

Name	Japanese Leagues				AA Leagues			
	AB	H	HR	BA	AB	H	HR	BA
Orestes Destrade	1655	436	154	.263	3051	779	137	.255
Adrian Garrett	1302	338	102	.260	5182	1344	280	.259
Woody Jones	3182	762	246	.239	3830	1068	211	.279
Stan Palys	1525	419	66	.275	4919	1586	189	.322

Name	Japanese Leagues				AA Leagues			
	AB	**H**	**HR**	**BA**	**AB**	**H**	**HR**	**BA**
Jack Pierce	291	66	13	.227	6926	2039	395	.294
Dave Roberts	2774	764	183	.275	6582	1858	244	.282
Jose Vidal	122	27	2	.221	5337	1486	251	.278
George Wilson	624	161	27	.258	6105	1901	275	.311
Totals	11475	2973	793	.259	41932	12061	1982	.288
Average	550	143	38	.259	550	158	26	.288

Note: *Minor league averages from SABR's* Minor League Baseball Stars.

TABLE XV

Japanese Leagues All-Star Team Personnel

Name	Position	Primary Club	Years Played
Katsuya Nomura	Catcher	Fukuoka Daiei Hawks	1954–1980
Koichi Tabuchi	Catcher	Hanshin Tigers	1969–1984
Sadaharu Oh	First Base	Yomiuri Giants	1959–1980
Tetsuharu Kawakami	First Base	Yomiuri Giants	1938–1958
Morimichi Takagi	Second Base	Chunichi Dragons	1960–1980
Shigeru Chiba	Second Base	Yomiuri Giants	1938–1956
Yoshio Yoshida	Shortstop	Hanshin Tigers	1953–1969
Yasumitsu Toyoda	Shortstop	Nishitetsu Lions	1953–1969
Shigeo Nagashima	Third Base	Yomiuri Giants	1958–1974
Futoshi Nakanishi	Third Base	Nishitetsu Lions	1953–1969
Isao Harimoto	Outfield	Toei Flyers	1959–1981
Koji Yamamoto	Outfield	Hiroshima Carp	1969–1986
Hiromitsu Ochiai	Outfield	Lotte Orions	1979–1998
Hiroshi Oshita	Outfield	Toei Flyers	1946–1959
Yutaka Fukumoto	Outfield	Hankyu Braves	1969–1988
Hiromitsu Kadota	Outfield	Fukuoka Daiei Hawks	1970–1990
Tsutomu Wakamatsu	Utility	Yakult Swallows	1971–1989
Sachio Kinugasa	Utility	Hiroshima Carp	1965–1987
Masaichi Kaneda	Pitcher	Yakult Swallows	1950–1969
Tetsuya Yoneda	Pitcher	Hankyu Braves	1956–1976
Keishi Suzuki	Pitcher	Kintetsu Buffaloes	1966–1985
Victor Starffin	Pitcher	Yomiuri Giants	1936–1955
Kazuhisa Inao	Pitcher	Seibu Lions	1956–1969
Takehiko Bessho	Pitcher	Yomiuri Giants	1942–1960
Yutaka Enatsu	Pitcher	Hanshin Tigers	1967–1984

TEAM TWO

Name	Position	Primary Club	Years Played
Masaaki Mori	Catcher	Yomiuri Giants	1955–1974
Takeshi Doigaki	Catcher	Hanshin Tigers	1940–1957

Name	Position	Primary Club	Years Played
Katsuo Osugi	First Base	Toei Flyers	1965–1983
Kihachi Enomoto	First Base	Tokyo Orions	1955–1972
Yutaka Takagi	Second Base	Taiyo Whales	1981–1994
Toshio Shinozuka	Second Base	Yomiuri Giants	1976–1994
Yoshihiko Takahashi	Shortstop	Hiroshima Carp	1975–1992
Takehiro Ikeyama	Shortstop	Yakult Swallows	1984–
Masayuki Kakefu	Third Base	Hanshin Tigers	1974–1988
Fumio Fujimura	Third Base	Hanshin Tigers	1936–1958
Kazuhiro Yamauchi	Outfield	Lotte Orions	1952–1970
Wally Yonamine	Outfield	Yomiuri Giants	1951–1962
Kenichi Yazawa	Outfield	Chunichi Dragons	1970–1986
Masahiro Doi	Outfield	Taiheiyo Club Lions	1962–1981
Yoshinori Hirose	Outfield	Nankai Hawks	1955–1977
Shinichi Eto	Outfield	Chunichi Dragons	1959–1976
Michio Nishizawa	Utility	Nagoya Dragons	1937–1958
LeRon Lee	Utility	Lotte Orions	1977–1987
Masaaki Koyama	Pitcher	Hanshin Tigers	1953–1973
Hisashi Yamada	Pitcher	Hankyu Braves	1969–1988
Minoru Murayama	Pitcher	Hanshin Tigers	1959–1972
Shigeru Sugishita	Pitcher	Chunichi Dragons	1949–1961
Tadashi Wakabayashi	Pitcher	Osaka Tigers	1936–1950
Jiro Noguchi	pitcher	Hankyu Braves	1939–1953
Hideo Fujimoto	Pitcher	Yomiuri Giants	1942–1955

TABLE XVI

Japanese Leagues All-Star Team Career Statistics

Name	G	AB	R	H	D	T	HR	RBI	SB	BA
Katsuya Nomura	3017*	10472*	1509	2901	397	23	657	1988	117	.277
Koichi Tabuchi	1739	5892	909	1532	167	12	474	1135	18	.260
Sadaharu Oh	2831	9250	1967*	2786	422	25	868*	2170*	18	.301
Tetsuharu Kawakami	1979	7500	1028	2351	408	99	181	1319	220	.313
Morimichi Takagi	2282	8367	1121	2274	346	55	236	843	369	.272
Shigeru Chiba	1512	5643	981	1605	194	52	96	691	155	.284
Yoshio Yoshida	2007	6980	900	1864	273	70	66	434	350	.277
Yasumitsu Toyoda	1814	6134	980	1699	269	47	263	888	215	.277
Shigeo Nagashima	2186	8094	1270	2471	418	74	444	1522	190	.305
Futoshi Nakanishi	1388	4116	673	1262	207	38	244	785	142	.307
Isao Harimoto	2752	9666	1523	3085*	420	72	504	1676	319	.319
Koji Yamamoto	2284	8052	1365	2339	372	21	536	1475	231	.290
Hiromitsu Ochiai	2236	7627	1335	2371	371	15	510	1564	65	.311
Yutaka Fukumoto	2401	8745	1656	2543	449*	115*	208	884	1065*	.291
Hiroshi Oshita	1547	5500	763	1667	293	66	201	861	146	.303

Name	G	AB	R	H	D	T	HR	RBI	SB	BA
Hiromitsu Kadota	2571	8868	1319	2566	383	19	567	1678	51	.289
Tsutomu Wakamatsu	2062	6808	1015	2173	355	43	220	884	151	.319
Sachio Kinugasa	2677	9404	1372	2643	373	23	504	1448	266	.270

PITCHING STATISTICS

Name	G	IP	W	L	S	SO	CG	SHO	ERA
Masaichi Kaneda	944	5526*	400*	298*	-	4490*	365	82	2.34
Tetsuya Yoneda	949*	5130	350	285	-	3388	262	64	2.41
Keishi Suzuki	703	4600	317	238	2	3061	340	71	3.11
Victor Starffin	586	4075	303	175	-	1950	350	83*	2.09
Kazuhisa Inao	756	3599	276	137	-	2574	179	43	1.98
Takehiko Bessho	622	4350	310	178	-	1934	335	72	2.18
Yutaka Enatsu	829	3196	206	158	193*	2987	154	45	2.49

TEAM TWO

Name	G	AB	R	H	D	T	HR	RBI	SB	BA
Masaaki Mori	1884	5686	392	1341	196	14	81	582	29	.236
Takeshi Doigaki	1413	4783	551	1351	220	52	79	654	87	.282
Katsuo Osugi	2235	7763	1080	2228	306	19	486	1507	32	.287
Kihachi Enomoto	2222	7763	1169	2314	409	47	246	979	153	.298
Yutaka Takagi	1628	5782		1716			88	545	321	.297
Toshio Shinozuka	1651	5572	739	1696	278	32	92	628	55	.304
Takahiro Ikeyama	1253	4312		1137			239	669	87	.264
Yoshihiko Takahashi	1722	6510	1003	1526	280	57	163	604	477	.280
Masayuki Kakefu	1625	5673	892	1656	250	31	349	1019	49	.292
Fumio Fujimura	1558	5648	871	1694	339	63	224	1126	103	.300
Kazuhiro Yamauchi	2251	7702	1218	2271	448	54	396	1286	117	.295
Wally Yonamine	1219	4298	707	1337	238	45	82	480	162	.311
Kenichi Yazawa	1931	6818	847	2062	348	25	273	969	42	.302
Masahiro Doi	2449	8694	1105	2452	309	11	465	1400	78	.282
Yoshinori Hirose	2190	7631	1205	2157	394	88	131	705	596	.282
Shinichi Eto	2084	7156	924	2057	274	15	367	1189	78	.287
Michio Nishizawa	1704	5999	750	1716	271	24	212	940	56	.286
LeRon Lee	1315	4934	786	1579	220	13	283	912	33	.320*

PITCHING STATISTICS

Name	G	IP	W	L	S	SO	CG	SHO	ERA
Masaaki Koyama	856	4899	320	232	-	3158	290	74	2.45
Hisashi Yamada	654	3865	284	166	43	2058	283	31	3.18
Minoru Murayama	509	3050	222	147	-	2271	192	55	2.09
Hideo Fujimoto	367	2628	200	87	-	1177	227	63	1.90*
Shigeru Sugishita	525	2841	215	123	-	1761	170	31	2.20

Tadashi Wakabayashi	528	3559	240	141	–	1000	263	57	1.99
Jiro Noguchi	517	3448	237	139	–	1396	259	65	1.96

Note: *An asterisk (*) denotes the all-time career leader. Hideo Fujimoto career winning percentage of .697 is #1.*

TABLE XVII

Japanese Leagues All-Star Team Statistics
Based on a 550 At-Bat Season

Name	G	AB	R	H	D	T	HR	RBI	SB	BA
Katsuya Nomura	154	550	79	152	21	1	35	104	6	.277
Koichi Tabuchi	154	550	85	143	16	1	44	106	2	.260
Sadaharu Oh	154	550	117*	166	25	2	52*	129*	5	.301
Tetsuharu Kawakami	154	550	75	172	30*	7*	13	97	16	.313
Morimichi Takagi	154	550	74	150	23	4	16	53	24	.272
Shigero Chiba	154	550	93	156	19	5	9	67	15	.284
Yoshio Yoshida	154	550	71	147	22	6	5	26	28	.267
Yasumitsu Toyoda	154	550	88	152	24	4	23	79	19	.277
Shigeo Nagashima	154	550	86	168	28	5	30	103	13	.305
Futoshi Nakanishi	154	550	90	169	28	5	33	105	19	.307
Isao Harimoto	154	550	87	175	24	4	29	95	18	.319
Koji Yamamoto	154	550	93	160	25	1	37	101	16	.290
Hiromitsu Ochiai	154	550	96	171	27	1	37	112	5	.311
Hiroshi Oshita	154	550	76	167	29	7	20	86	15	.303
Yutaka Fukumoto	154	550	104	160	28	7	13	56	67*	.291
Hiromitsu Kadota	154	550	82	159	24	1	37	110	3	.289
Tsutomu Wakamatsu	154	550	82	176	29	3	18	71	12	.319
Sachio Kinugasa	154	550	80	155	22	1	29	85	19	.270

TEAM TWO

Name	G	AB	R	H	D	T	HR	RBI	SB	BA
Masaaki Mori	154	550	38	130	19	1	8	56	3	.236
Takeshi Doigaki	154	550	63	155	25	6	9	75	10	.282
Katsuo Osugi	154	550	77	158	22	1	34	107	2	.287
Kihachi Enomoto	154	550	83	164	29	3	17	69	11	.298
Toshio Shinozuka	154	550	73	167	27	3	9	62	5	.304
Yutaka Takagi	154	550		163			8	52	31	.297
Yoshihiko Takahashi	154	550	85	154	24		14	51	40	.280
Takehiro Ikeyama	154	550	78	145	26	2	30	85	11	.264
Masayuki Kakefu	154	550	87	161	24	3	34	99	5	.292
Fumio Fujimura	154	550	85	165	33	6	22	110	10	.300
Kazuhiro Yamauchi	154	550	87	162	32	3	28	92	8	.295
Wally Yonamine	154	550	91	171	30	6	10	61	21	.311

Name	G	AB	R	H	D	T	HR	RBI	SB	BA
Kenichi Yazawa	154	550	68	166	28	2	22	78	3	.302
Masahiro Doi	154	550	70	155	20	1	29	89	5	.282
Yoshinori Hirose	154	550	86	156	28	6	9	51	43	.282
Shinichi Eto	154	550	71	158	21	1	28	91	6	.287
Michio Nishizawa	154	550	69	157	25	2	19	86	5	.286
LeRon Lee	154	550	88	176*	25	1	32	105	6	.320*

Note: *An asterisk (*) denotes the all-time career leader.*

TABLE XVIII

Comparison of Negro Leagues to Puerto Rican Winter League from 1938 to 1958 — Based on a 550 At-Bat Season

Name	Negro League			PRWL		
	H	HR	BA	H	HR	BA
Josh Gibson	200	48	.362	195	27	.355
Bob Boyd	200	12	.362	180	7	.328
Roy Campanella	184	16	.334	152	13	.276
Luke Easter	185	29	.336	198	39	.359
Monte Irvin	188	25	.345	198	18	.359
Piper Davis	177	8	.322	163	15	.297
Gene Baker	143	4	.261	158	7	.287
Willard Brown	194	20	.352	192	29	.350
Al Smith	161	10	.292	150	15	.274
Bob Thurman	193	21	.351	178	22	.323
Sam Bankhead	157	7	.285	171	4	.311
Bus Clarkson	184	18	.335	153	27	.301
Fernando Pedroso	142	4	.258	179	21	.325
Pancho Coimbre	198	11	.361	185	7	.337
Tetelo Vargas	188	1	.342	176	5	.320
Canena Marquez	204	11	.371	165	15	.300
Silvio Garcia	177	8	.322	164	5	.298
Average	182	15	.331	174	16	.316

Note: *The above statistics are based on a minimum of 431 at-bats in the Negro leagues, and a minimum of 389 at-bats in the Puerto Rican Winter League.*

TABLE XIX
Major League vs. Puerto Rican
Winter League Averages, 1950–1997

| Name | Years | Major League Statistics | | | | | PRWL Statistics | | | |
		AB	H	HR	BA	HR1	Yrs.	HR	BA	HR2
V. Power	54–65	6046	1716	126	.284	10	16	55	.296	10
R. Alomar	85–98	6048	1825	127	.302	12	10	21	.301	10
C. Baerga	86–98	4670	1367	121	.293	12	9	26	.294	12
J. Rivera	52–61	3552	911	83	.256	13	7	43	.279	18
C. Rojas	62–77	6309	1660	54	.263	5	5	7	.272	4
J. Beniquez	71–88	4651	1274	79	.274	9	22	73	.274	10
C. Martinez	79–91	2906	713	108	.245	20	13	63	.269	19
K. Bevaqua	71–85	2117	499	27	.236	7	4	25	.285	18
B. Bonilla	81–94	4637	1161	189	.278	22	5	14	.297	11
R. Campanella	46–57	4205	1161	242	.276	32	4	11	.276	13
O. Cepeda	58–74	7927	2351	379	.297	26	13	89	.323	21
R. Clemente	55–72	9454	3000	240	.317	14	15	35	.323	7
H. Cotto	80–94	2178	569	44	.261	11	12	32	.289	11
R. Sierra	83–94	5200	1421	201	.273	21	7	27	.268	15
J. Cruz	70–88	7917	2251	165	.284	11	21	119	.296	17
J. Dwyer	73–88	2463	633	73	.257	16	4	34	.295	26
J. Gilliam	53–66	7119	1889	65	.265	5	4	3	.278	4
J. Gonzalez	86–94	2237	613	140	.274	34	7	34	.267	19
E. Hendricks	68–79	1885	415	62	.220	18	15	105	.275	21
A. Howe	74–85	2626	682	43	.260	9	4	16	.297	12
M. Irvin	49–56	2499	731	99	.293	22	4	20	.359	18
J. Lopez	92–94	309	80	14	.259	25	7	11	.259	6
C. Maldonado	78–94	3916	992	137	.253	19	13	88	.272	24
D. Thon	79–88	4449	1176	71	.264	9	13	21	.292	5
B. Thurman	55–59	663	163	35	.246	29	12	120	.323	21
E. Martinez	83–98	4374	1389	174	.318	22	9	8	.286	4
W. Montanez	66–82	5843	1604	139	.275	13	18	86	.266	14
J. Morales	69–83	4528	1173	95	.259	11	18	63	.267	11
Jose Morales	73–84	1305	375	26	.287	11	19	84	.302	13
L. Olmo	43–51	1629	458	29	.281	10	16	40	.290	10
T. Perez	64–86	9778	2732	379	.279	21	10	59	.308	18
Averages per 550 at-bats:										
		550	150	372	.272	16	13	288	.288	13

Legend: *Years—1900+ ex: R. Clemente played in the major leagues from 1955 through 1972. Yrs.— Number of years played in the Puerto Rican Winter League. HR1— The average number of home runs per 550 at-bats in the major leagues. HR2— The estimated number of home runs in PRWL, per 550 at-bats. In many cases, the actual number of career at-bats for a player is not known. In those cases, the at-bats have been estimated based on the number of seasons an individual played in the PRWL, and the length of each season.*

TABLE XX

Puerto Rican Winter League All-Star Team — The Pioneers (to 1958)

Name	Pos.	Years	HR1	BA	Years Played
Josh Gibson	C	3	27	.355	1939–1945
Luis Villodas		13			1938–1950
Jacinto Hernandez	1B				1920s to '39
Jose Santana					20s to mid–40s
Millito Navarro	2B	6			1922–1943
Fernando Pedroso		7	21	.325	1944–1950
Menchin Pesante					1938–1948
Jose Seda					1930s
Pito Alvarez de la Vega					1930s
Perucho Cepeda	SS	11	6	.325	mid–20s to 1950
Bus Clarkson		11	27	.301	1940–1955
Pedro Caratini					1900–1930
Coco Ferrer					1940s
Canena Marquez	3B	20	15	.300	1945–1962
Tingo Daviu					1930s
Nenene Rivera					1930s
Pancho Coimbre	OF	13	7	.337	1930–1951
Willard Brown		10	30	.350	1941–1957
Bob Thurman		12	21	.323	1947–1960
Tetelo Vargas		16	5	.320	1938–1953
Nino Escalera		17	4	.275	1948–1964
Carlos Bernier		19	10	.268	1946–1964
Juan Sanchez					1940s
Manolo Garcia					1920–1946
Monchile Concepcion					1930s
Monte Irvin	Util	4	18	.359	1940–1947
Luis Olmo		16	10	.290	1938–1953

PITCHERS

Name	Years	Record	Years Played
Cefo Conde	12	32–24 Inc.	1938–1949
Juan Guilbe	10	19–6 Inc.	1939–1948
Jose A. Figueroa	10	14–13 Inc.	1938–1947
Carmelito Fernandez		11–5 Inc.	1938–?
Luis Raul Cabrera	18	105–99	1939–1950
Roberto Vargas	13	51–24	1947–1960

Name	Years	Record	Years Played
Rafaelito Ortiz	11	38–9 Inc.	1938–1949
Tomas Quinones	13	82–38	1941–1951
Raymond Brown	5	40–20	1938–1945
Satchel Paige	2	19–6	1939–1948
Leon Day	4	35–28	1939–1950

TABLE XXI

Puerto Rican Winter League All-Time All-Star Team, 1938 to 1997

Name	Pos.	Puerto Rican W. L.				Major Leagues			ML Est.	
		Yrs	HR1	BA	Yrs	HR2	BA	HR	BA	
Jose Morales	C	19	13	.302	73–84	11	.287	16	.285
Elrod Hendricks		15	21	.275	68–79	18	.220	26	.258
Orlando Cepeda	1B	13	21	.323	58–74	26	.297	26	.306
Vic Power		16	10	.296	54–65	10	.284	13	.279
Tony Perez		10	18	.308	64–86	21	.279	23	.291
Willie Montanez		18	19	.266	66–82	13	.275	24	.249
Roberto Alomar	2B	10	10	.301	85–98	12	.302	13	.285
Carlos Baerga		9	12	.294	86–98	12	.293	15	.277
Perucho Cepeda	SS	11	6	.325				7	.285
Bus Clarkson		11	27	.301				25	.271
Dickie Thon		13	5	.292	79–88	9	.264	6	.275
Canena Marquez	3B	20	15	.300	44–64	(143 AB)	.182	17	.290
Edgar Martinez		9	4	.286	83–98	22	.318	5	.269
Roberto Clemente	OF	15	7	.323	55–72	14	.317	9	.306
Pancho Coimbre		13	7	.337				11	.305
Willard Brown		10	30	.350	47	(67 AB)	.179	23	.291
Bob Thurman		12	21	.323	55–59	29	.246	23	.293
Jose Cruz		21	17	.296	70–88	11	.284	19	.279
Tetelo Vargas		16	5	.320				4	.286
Juan Beniquez		22	13	.274	71–88	9	.274	16	.258
Carlos Bernier		19	10	.268	–53	6	.213	11	.228
Nino Escalera		17	4	.275		(69 AB)	.159	5	.258
Gil Flores		13	3	.278	78–79	2	.261	3	.238
Carmelo Martinez		13	19	.269	79–91	20	.245	24	.252

PITCHERS

Name	Yrs	PRWL Record	Yrs	ML Record
Ruben Gomez	29	174–119	53–67	76–86
Juan Pizzaro	22	157–110	57–74	131–105

| Name | PRWL | | ML | |
	Yrs	Record	Yrs	Record
Luis Arroyo	19	111–93	55–63	40–32
Jose G. Santiago	16	107–96	54–56	3–2
Jose R. Santiago	16	60–52	63–70	34–29
Luis Cabrera	18	105–99		
Tomas Quinones	13	82–38		
Julio Navarro	22	98–84	62–70	7-9

Legend: HR1— Home runs in PRWL, per 550 at-bats. HR2 — Home runs in ML, per 550 at-bats. Yrs.— In PRWL, number of years played. In ML, 1900+. ex: Vic Power played from 1954 to 1965. ML Est.— Estimated home runs and batting average, per 550 at-bats, in major leagues, based on conversion factor from PRWL

TABLE XXII

Dominican League All-Time All-Star Team, 1951 to 1997

| Name | Pos | Major League | | | Dominican League | | |
		HR	HR1	BA	HR	HR1	BA
Tony Pena	C	106	9	.263	41	12	.283
Federico Velasquez		0	0	.256	24	8	.248
Ramon Lora		-	-	-	12	7	.283
Gilbert Reyes		0	0	.202	9	5	.217
Alonzo Perry	1B	-	-	-	49	19	.310
Rafael Batista		0	0	.280	45	8	.257
Tito Fuentes	2B	45	4	.268	4	2	.281
Pedro Gonzalez		8	11	.244	22	5	.272
Felix Fermin	SS	4	1	.259	0	0	.274
Alfredo Griffin		24	2	.249	3	1	.268
Winston Llenas	3B	3	3	.230	50	9	.244
Manuel Castillo		3	2	.242	6	2	.264
Felipe Alou	OF	206	15	.286	31	9	.310
Jesus Alou		32	4	.280	20	4	.302
Matty Alou		31	3	.307	14	4	.326
Miguel Dilone		6	2	.265	8	2	.299
Manny Mota		31	5	.304	9	2	.332
Rico Carty		204	20	.299	59	17	.301
Ralph Garr		75	8	.306	5	4	.412
Tetelo Vargas		-	-	-	2	2	.322
Cesar Geronomo		51	7	.258	17	4	.282
Pedro Guerrero		215	22	.300	21	13	.290
Rufino Linares	Util	11	11	.270	32	9	.285
Rafael Landestoy		4	2	.237	2	1	.270

Name	Pos	Major League HR	HR1	BA	Dominican League HR	HR1	BA
Mario Guerrero		7	2	.257	1	1	.288
Teodoro Martinez		7	3	.240	9	2	.266

PITCHERS

Name	Pos	Major League W	L	Pct.	Dominican League W	L	Pct.
Juan Marichal	P	243	142	.631	36	22	.621
Arturo Pena	P	0	0	.000	24	21	.533*
Joaquin Andujar	P	127	118	.518	50	42	.543
Diomedes Olivo	P	5	6	.455	86	46	.652
Federico Olivo	P	7	6	.538	79	69	.534
Danilo Rivas	P	-	-	-	52	36	.591
Arnulfo Espinosa	P	44	55	.444	48	39	.552
Pascual Perez	P	67	68	.496	44	33	.571
Mickey Mahler	P	14	32	.304	40	17	.702

*Artura Pena holds the career record for saves, with 80. He led the league in saves five times.

Key: Pos — Position played. HR — Total number of home runs, hit in league. HR/550AB — Average number of home runs per 550 at-bats. BA — Batting average. W — Wins. L — Losses. Pct. — Winning percentage. HR1 — Home runs per 550 at-bats.

TABLE XXIII

Comparison of Major Leagues to Mexican League Batting Averages and Home Runs

Name	AB	Major Leagues H	HR	HR1	BA	AB	Mexican League H	HR	HR1	BA
Sandy Amoros	1311	334	43	18	.255	408	123	13	18	.305
Rico Carty	5606	1677	204	20	.299	401	142	11	15	.354
R. Avila	4620	1296	80	10	.281	2262	744	20	5	.329
Lou Klein	1037	269	16	8	.259	638	186	10	9	.292
G. Hausmann	1136	304	3	1	.268	928	263	2	1	.283
M. Hayworth	430	91	1	1	.212	540	143	1	1	.265
M. Minoso	6579	1963	186	16	.298	2254	715	56	14	.317
R. Ortiz	659	168	8	7	.255	1895	576	106	31	.304
H. Rodriguez	407	108	1	1	.265	3476	1040	19	3	.299
R Campanella	4205	1161	242	32	.276	423	123	14	18	.291
H. Simpson	2829	752	73	14	.266	757	241	35	25	.318
Bernie Carbo	2733	722	96	19	.264	306	85	6	11	.278
Dan Driessen	5479	1464	153	15	.267	436	153	12	15	.351

Name	AB	Major Leagues H	HR	HR1	BA	AB	Mexican League H	HR	HR1	BA
Dan Gardella	543	145	24	24	.267	378	104	13	19	.275
LeRon Lee	1617	404	31	11	.250	400	110	15	21	.275
J. Tartabull	1857	484	2	1	.261	336	85	5	8	.253
W. Aikens	2492	675	110	24	.271	2328	867	170	40	.372
Vin Castilla	1644	488	84	28	.297	613	177	15	13	.289
W. Crawford	3435	921	86	14	.268	556	171	13	13	.308
V. Davalillo	4017	1122	36	5	.279	2190	782	35	9	.357
Mike Guerra	1581	382	9	3	.242	432	132	8	10	.306
Von Joshua	2234	610	30	7	.273	1285	386	20	9	.300
Cesar Tovar	5569	1546	46	5	.278	539	185	2	2	.343
H. Villanueva	473	109	25	29	.230	606	209	42	38	.345
Average Per 550 At-bats										
	550	146		13	.266	550	170		15	.309
Adjusted to Major League Base Point										
	550	143		19	.260	550	167		22	.303

Note: *HR1 is the number of home runs hit per 550 at-bats.*

TABLE XXIV

Comparison of Negro Leagues to Mexican League Home Runs and Batting Averages Per 550 At-Bats

Name	Negro Leagues H	HR	BA	Mexican Leagues H	HR	BA
Roy Campanella	184	16	.334	160	18	.291
Bill Wright	177	15	.322	184	13	.335
Ray Dandridge	164	3	.322	191	7	.347
Martin Dihigo	174	25	.319	171	16	.311
Gene Collins	156	7	.283	163	18	.298
Leon Kellman	163	6	.297	170	14	.309
Buck Leonard	178	24	.339	179	20	.325
Luis Marquez	214	11	.371	185	26	.337
Fernando Pedroso	143	4	.258	181	13	.329
Alonzo Perry	173	24	.316	193	24	.351
Bonnie Serrell	170	7	.308	171	7	.311
Harry Simpson	134	9	.244	175	25	.318
Lonnie Summers	167	-	.304	150	9	.273
Earl Taborn	172	7	.313	156	21	.284
Jesse Williams	138	2	.251	152	4	.276
Marvin Williams	178	15	.324	189	22	.343

Name	H	Negro Leagues HR	BA	H	Mexican Leagues HR	BA
Willie Wells	180	20	.328	182	11	.330
Bus Clarkson	184	18	.335	174	27	.316
Josh Gibson	199	48	.362	216	54	.393
Cool Papa Bell	185	9	.337	202	12	.367
Average	172	14	.313	177	17	.322
Adjusted To Major League Base Point						
	169	15	.308	174	18	.317

TABLE XV

Mexican League All-Time All-Star Team, 1938 to 1997

Name	POS	YEAR	AB	H	D	T	HR	BA	HR1
Francisco Estrada	C	1966–94	7583	2089	297	34	84	.275	6
Orlando Sanchez		1985–93	3136	1078	190	3	134	.344	24
Carlos Soto		1973–91	5788	1743	237	23	264	.301	25
Roberto Herrera		1965–75	3238	1013	131	13	111	.313	19
Hector Espino	1B	1962–84	8205	2752	373	45	453	.335	30
Jesus Sommers		1970–95	10133	2958	481	64	240	.292	13
Angel Castro		1938–57	6249	1914	355	83	230	.306	20
Alonzo Perry		1955–63	3122	1107	203	58	138	.355	24
Mario Ariosa	2B	1947–72	5968	1836	271	48	113	.308	10
Moises Camacho		1951–75	7262	2110	350	58	185	.291	14
Arnoldo Castro		1960–83	7579	2224	355	54	85	.293	6
Vinicio Garcia		1944–70	4953	1601	284	49	82	.323	9
Roberto Mendez		1965–84	7201	2091	260	62	21	.290	2
Juan Navarette		1970–90	6056	1979	218	47	35	.327	3
Juan Rodriguez		1977–95	6658	1948	231	38	34	.293	3
Silvio Garcia	SS	1938–48	2344	786	132	30	52	.335	12
Ray Dandridge		1940–48	2714	943	172	26	34	.347	7
Francisco Rodriguez		1965–85	8099	2186	330	61	61	.270	4
Beltran Herrera		1980–94	5279	1515	214	67	18	.287	2
Rigoberto Mena		1964–76	5918	1777	237	34	75	.300	7
Enrique Aguilar	3B	1974–95	7811	2389	372	37	295	.306	21
Luis Garcia		1956–65	4181	1348	229	14	171	.322	22
Oscar Rodriguez		1957–69	5586	1808	334	66	195	.324	19
Alfred Pinkston	OF	1959–65	3233	1204	227	40	108	.372	18
Jimmie Collins		1978–87	4506	1596	280	75	59	.354	7
Andres Mora		1972–95	7167	2247	324	32	419	.314	32

Name	POS	YEAR	AB	H	D	T	HR	BA	HR1
Matias Carrillo		1982–	3364	1150	197	48	156	.342	26
Miguel Suarez		1971–87	7573	2444	262	86	23	.323	2
Lazaro Acosta		1968–76	3973	1371	166	73	35	.345	5
Ramon Montoya		1962–83	5349	1692	216	80	44	.316	5
Daniel Fernandez		1983–95	5288	1511	305	93	185	.286	19
Martin Dihigo	Util	1937–50	1917	607	110	29	55	.317	16

(Dihigo also pitched 213 games. He recorded a won-loss mark of 119-57, with an earned run average of 2.84)

Name	POS	YEAR	AB	H	D	T	HR	BA	HR1
Lazaro Salazar		1938–52	2103	703	117	32	31	.334	9

(Salazar also pitched 270 games. He recorded a won-loss mark of 112-78, with an earned run average of 3.43)

Key: HR1— *Number of home runs hit for every 550 at-bats.*

PITCHERS

Name	Pos	Years	W	L	Pct.	
Ramon Arano	P	1959–95	334	264	.559	
Alfredo Ortiz	P	1963–87	255	210	.548	
Antonio Pollorena	P	1965–85	233	170	.578	
Jose Pena	P	1962–84	214	154	.582	
Ramon Bragana	P	1938–55	211	162	.566	
Cesar Diaz	P	1969–89	208	184	.531	
Vincente Romo	P	1963–86	182	106	.632	
Salome Barojas	P	1976–94	115	58	.665	plus 152 saves
Miguel Solis	P	1972–89	202	140	.591	
Angel Moreno	P	1975–95	182	103	.639	
Andres Ayon	P	1964–79	169	98	.633	
Ernesto Escarrega	P	1970–89	192	141	.577	
Francisco Ramirez	P	1950–70	184	161	.533	

TABLE XXVI

Other Leagues Batting Average and Home Runs Per 550 At-Bats

Name	NL		AAA		Mexico		Major Lge		Panama		Venezuela	
	HR	BA	HR	BA	HR	BA	HR	BA	HR	BA	HR	BA
Frank Austin	2	.332	4	.268					3	.309		
Leon Kellman	6	.297			14	.309			10	.297		
Jonathon Parris	4	.234	18	.298					19	.318		
Pablo Bernard	-	.242	4	.252	8	.312			4	.262		
A. Braithwaite					4	.270			5	.307		
Happy Gladstone	12	.240	13	.247	22	.293			11	.289		

Name	NL HR	NL BA	AAA HR	AAA BA	Mexico HR	Mexico BA	Major Lge HR	Major Lge BA	Panama HR	Panama BA	Venezuela HR	Venezuela BA
Lou Johnson			16	.303			13	.258	15	.295		
Milt Smith	0	.217	9	.277					4	.279		
Joe Taylor			28	.286			17	.249	34	.381		
Charlie White	0	.256	7	.267			4	.236	4	.313		
Gene Collins	7	.283			18	.297					0	.356
Sam Hairston	22	.339	1	.263							0	.380
David Hoskins	5	.302	7	.252							-	.323
Jim Pendleton	11	.301	13	.295					11	.255	25	.387
David Pope			18	.262			12	.265			17	.336
Bob Wilson	12	.332	11	.311							12	.350
Parnell Woods	7	.315	12	.275							4	.354
Ramon Bragana					12	.243					-	.318
Wilmer Fields	0	.294									5	.336
Buck Leonard	24	.339			20	.325					-	.425

Key: *NL — Negro League. AAA — Class AAA minor league. Mexico — Mexican League. Major Lge — major leagues. Panama — Panama Winter League. Venezuela — Venezuela Winter League. HR — Home Runs Per 550 At-bats. BA — Batting Average*

Note: *The averages listed above were derived from statistics presented in* The Negro Leagues Book, *edited by Dick Clark and Larry Lester.*

TABLE XXVII

All-Time All-Star Teams

NEGRO LEAGUES ALL-TIME ALL-STAR TEAM
Selected by Negro League Hall of Fame Outfielder Monte Irvin

Catcher:	Josh Gibson
	Roy Campanella
	Biz Mackey
Pitcher:	Satchel Paige
	Bullet Rogan
	Joe Williams
	Leon Day
	Slim Jones
	Willie Foster
First Base:	Buck Leonard
	George Giles
Second Base:	Sammy T. Hughes
	Newt Allen
	Jackie Robinson

Shortstop:	Willie Wells
	John Henry Lloyd
	Dick Lundy
Third Base:	Ray Dandridge
	Oliver Marcelle
Outfield:	Willie Mays
	Cristobal Torriente
	Oscar Charleston
	Turkey Stearnes
	Cool Papa Bell
	Bill Wright
Utility:	Martin Dihigo
	Raymond Brown
Manager:	Rube Foster
	C.I. Taylor

NEGRO LEAGUE ALL-TIME ALL-STAR TEAM
Selected by Negro League Baseball Historian Normal "Tweed" Webb

Catcher:	Biz Mackey
Pitcher:	Smokey Joe Williams
	Satchel Paige
First Base:	Ben Taylor
Second Base:	Bingo DeMoss
Shortstop:	John Henry Lloyd
Third Base:	Judy Johnson
Outfield:	Oscar Charleston
	Cool Papa Bell
	Turkey Stearnes
Utility:	Pete Hill
Manager:	Rube Foster

CUBAN WINTER LEAGUE ALL-TIME ALL-STAR TEAM
Selected by Cuban Baseball Historian Jorge S. Figueredo

	First Era 1878–1909	Second Era 1910–1939	Third Era 1940–1961
Catcher	Antonio Garcia	Mike Gonzalez	Rafael Noble
Pitcher	Carlos Royer	Adolfo Luque	Camilo Pascual
	Jose Munoz	Martin Dihigo	Pedro Ramos
	Jose Mendez	Manuel Garcia	Conrado Marrero
	Eustaquio Pedroso	Jose Acosta	Adrian Zabala
	Juan Pastoriza	Emilio Palmero	Mike Fornieles
	Luis Padron	Ramon Bragana	Agapito Mayor

First Base:	Julian Castillo	Jose Rodriguez	Lazaro Salazar
Second Base:	Carlos Moran	Manuel Cueto	Heberto Blanco
Shortstop:	Luis Bustamante	Pelayo Chacon	Silvio Garcia
Third Base:	Rafael Almeida	Bienvenido Jiminez	Hector Rodriguez
Outfield:	Armando Marsans	Cristobal Torriente	Orestes Minoso
	Heliodoro Hidalgo	Alejandro Oms	Santos Amaro
	Emilio Palomino	Bernardo Baro	Claro Duany
	Juan Viola	Jacinto Calvo	Roberto Ortiz
	Roman Calzadilla	Merito Acosta	Edmundo Amoros

CUBAN WINTER LEAGUE ALL-TIME ALL-STAR TEAM
Selected by Cuban Baseball Historian Angel Torres

First Era
1878–1950

Catcher:	Gervasio Gonzalez
	Fermin Guerra
	Andres Fleitas
Pitcher:	Jose Mendez
	Adolfo Luque
	Martin Dihigo
	Ramon Bragana
	Rodolfo Fernandez
	Agapito Mayor
	Adrian Zabala
	Cocaina Garcia
	Lazaro Salazar
First Base:	Julian Castillo
	Lorenzo Cabrera
Second Base:	Bienvenido Jimenez
	Heberto Blanco
Shortstop:	Silvio Garcia
	Willie Miranda
Third Base:	Hector Rodriguez
	Rafael Almeida
Outfield:	Alejandro Oms
	Cristobal Torriente
	Alejandro Crespo
	Roberto Ortiz
	Pedro Formenthal
Manager:	Mike Gonzalez

CUBAN WINTER LEAGUE ALL-TIME ALL-STAR TEAM
Selected by Cuban Baseball Historian Ralph Maya

Catcher:	Gervasio Gonzalez
	Antonio Garcia
Pitcher:	Jose Mendez
	Bombin Pedroso
	Carlos Royer
	Adolfo Luque
First Base:	Julian Castillo
Second Base:	Bienvenido Jimenez
Shortstop:	Pelayo Chacon
Third Base:	Manuel Cueto
Outfield:	Alejandro Oms
	Cristobal Torriente
	Jacinto Calvo
	Bernardo Baro
Utility:	Martin Dihigo

JAPAN LEAGUE ALL-TIME ALL-STAR TEAM
Selected by Japanese Baseball Historian Dan Johnson

Catcher:	Katsuya Nomura
	Koichi Tabuchi
Pitcher:	Kazuhisa Inao
	Masaichi Kaneda
	Minoru Murayama
	Hisashi Yamada
	Yutaka Enatsu
	Takehiko Bessho
	Keishi Suzuki
First Base:	Sadaharu Oh
	Tetsuharu Kawakami
Second Base:	Morimichi Takagi
	Shigeru Chiba
Shortstop:	Yoshio Yoshida
	Yasumitsu Toyoda
Third Base:	Shigeo Nagashima
	Futoshi Nakanishi
Outfield:	Isao Harimoto
	Yutaka Fukumoto
	Koji Yamamoto
	Hiroshi Oshita

	Kazuhiro Yamauchi
	Wally Yonamine
Utility:	Hiromitsu Ochiai
	Sachio Kinugasa

Note: *Dan Johnson's selections concentrated on retired players who had long, distinguished careers. Outstanding players whose careers were brief were not considered, nor were active players like Ichiro Suzuki, who will most likely become a member of the team after he retires.*

JAPAN LEAGUE ALL-TIME ALL-STAR TEAM
Selected by Japanese Baseball Historian Fumihiro "Fu-chan" Fujisawa

Catcher:	Katsuya Nomura
	Masaaki Mori
Pitcher:	Masaichi Kaneda
	Kazuhisa Inao
	Takehiko Bessho
	Shigero Sugishita
	Masaaki Koyama
	Hisashi Yamada
	Yutaka Enatsu
First Base:	Sadaharu Oh
	Hiromitsu Ochiai
Second Base:	Morimichi Takagi
	Shigeru Chiba
Shortstop:	Yoshio Yoshida
	Tatsuro Hirooka
Third Base:	Shigeo Nagashima
	Futoshi Nakanishi
Outfield:	Isao Harimoto
	Koji Yamamoto
	Yutaka Fukumoto
	Kazuhiro Yamauchi
	Tokuji Nagaike
	Ichiro Suzuki

PUERTO RICAN WINTER LEAGUE ALL-TIME ALL-STAR TEAM
Selected by Puerto Rican Baseball Historian Luis Alvelo

Catcher:	Luis Villodas
	Jose E. Montalvo
Pitcher:	Jose Antonio Figueroa
	Rafaelito Ortiz
	Marcelino Blondet
	Tomas Quinones
	Carmelito Fernandez
	Tite Figueroa

First Base:	Pepe Santana
	Jacinto Hernandez
	Saturnino Escalera
Second Base:	Millito Navarro
	Gacho Torres
Shortstop:	Millito Martinez
	Coco Ferrer
	Artie Wilson
Third Base:	Tingo Daviu
	Nenene Rivera
Outfield:	Perucho Cepeda
	Francisco Coimbre
	Luis Marquez
	Juan Sanchez
	Alfonso Gerald
	Tetelo Vargas
	Willard Brown
	Manolo Garcia
Utility:	Vicente Villafane
	Geraldo Rodriguez
	Monchile Concepcion
Manager:	Jose Seda
	Felle Delgado
	George Scales

PUERTO RICAN WINTER LEAGUE ALL-TIME ALL-STAR TEAM
Selected by Puerto Rican Baseball Historian Yuyo Ruiz

Catcher:	Jose E. Montalvo
	Ellie Rodriguez
Pitcher:	Cefo Conde
	Juan Guilbe
	Carmelito Fernandez
	Roberto Vargas
	Luis Raul Cabrera
	Rafaelito Ortiz
First Base:	Tingo Daviu
	Sammy Cespedes
Second Base:	Mechin Pesante
Shortstop:	Perucho Cepeda
	Coco Ferrer
Third Base:	Millito Navarro
	Canena Marquez

Outfield: Pedro Miguel Caratini
                     Luis Olmo
                     Felo Guilbe
                     Francisco Coimbre
                     Juan Sanchez
                     Tetelo Vargas
                     Roberto Clemente

Manager: Pepe Seda
                     Monchile Concepcion

BASEBALL'S ULTIMATE ALL-WORLD ALL-STAR TEAM
Selected by William F. McNeil

	Team #1	Team #2
Catcher:	Josh Gibson	Johnny Bench
	Roy Campanella	Katsuya Nomura
Pitcher:	Walter Johnson	Bullet Joe Rogan
	Christy Mathewson	Eddie Plank
	Sandy Koufax	Cy Young
	Satchel Paige	Warren Spahn
	Lefty Grove	Grover Alexander
	Smokey Joe Williams	Jose Mendez
	Bob Feller	Masaichi Kaneda
First Base:	Lou Gehrig	Sadaharu Oh
	Jimmie Foxx	Buck Leonard
Second Base:	Rogers Hornsby	Jackie Robinson
	Charlie Gehringer	Nap Lajoie
Shortstop:	Honus Wagner	Dobie Moore
	John Henry Lloyd	Luis Aparicio
Third Base:	Brooks Robinson	Mike Schmidt
	Ray Dandridge	Shigeo Nagashima
Outfield:	Babe Ruth	Turkey Stearnes
	Joe DiMaggio	Cool Papa Bell
	Ted Williams	Mickey Mantle
	Willie Mays	Hank Aaron
	Joe Jackson	Stan Musial
	Ty Cobb	Cristobal Torriente
Utility:	Martin Dihigo	Ernie Banks
	Oscar Charleston	Willie Wells

Bibliography

Alvelo, Luis. Correspondence. Caguas, P.R., 1996.

Bak, Richard. *Turkey Stearnes and the Detroit Stars*. Detroit: Wayne State University Press, 1994.

The Ballplayers. Mike Shatzkin, editor. New York: William Morrow, 1990.

Bankes, James. *The Pittsburgh Crawfords*. Dubuque, Iowa: Wm. C. Brown, 1991.

Baseball America's Almanac, 1986, 1988, 1989, 1990, 1991, 1992, 1993, 1994, 1997. Allan Simpson, editor. Durham, N.C.: Baseball America.

The Baseball Encyclopedia. Joseph L. Reichler, editor. New York: Macmillan, 1979.

The Baseball Research Journal, 1975 through 1996. Cleveland: Society for American Baseball Research.

Baseball's First Stars. Ivor-Campbell, Frederick, Robert L. Tiemann, and Mark Rucker, editors. SABR, Cleveland: Society for American Baseball Research, 1996.

Baseball's Hall of Fame: Cooperstown Where the Legends Live and Die. Joe Hoppel, editor. New York: Arlington House, 1988.

Benson, Michael. *Ballparks of North America*. Jefferson, N.C.: McFarland, 1989.

Bruce, Janet. *The Kansas City Monarchs*. Wichita: University Press of Kansas, 1985.

Chadwick, Bruce. *When the Game Was Black and White*. New York: Abbeville, 1997.

Couzens, Gerald Secor. *A Baseball Album*. New York: Lippincott & Crowell, 1980.

Cult Baseball Players. Danny Peary, editor. New York: Simon & Schuster, 1990.

Daguerreotypes, 8th edition. Craig Carter, editor. St. Louis: The Sporting News, 1990.

Dodger yearbooks, Brooklyn and Los Angeles, 1950 to 1993.

Durant, John. *The Story of Baseball in Words and Pictures*. New York: Hastings House, 1973.

Enciclopedia del Béisbol Mexicano. Pedro Treto Cisneros, editor. S.A. De C.V. Redsa: Revistas Deportivas, 1996.

The Encyclopedia of Minor League Baseball. Lloyd Johnson and Miles Wolff, editors. Durham, N.C.: Baseball America, 1993.

Figueredo, Jorge S. Correspondence. Tampa, Fla., 1996.

Goldstein, Richard. *Superstars, and Screwballs*. New York: Penguin, 1991.

Grayson, Harry. *They Played the Game*. New York: A.S. Barnes, 1945.

Gregorich, Barbara. *Women at Play*. New York: Harcourt and Brace, 1993.

Holway, John B. *Black Diamonds*. New York: Stadium Books, 1991.

_____. *Blackball Stars*. Westport, Conn.: Meckler Books, 1988.

_____. *Josh and Satch*. New York: Carroll & Graf, 1991.

_____. *Voices from the Great Black Baseball Leagues*. New York: Da Capo, 1992.

Honig, Donald. *The Brooklyn Dodgers*. New York: St. Martin's Press, 1981.

Japan Pro Baseball Fan Handbook and Media Guide. Compiled by Wayne Graczyk. Tokyo: 1991 and 1995.

Jiminez, Dr. José de Jesús. Correspondence. Santiago, D.R., 1996.

Johnson, Daniel. Correspondence. Woodacre, Calif., 1996.

Johnson, Susan E. *When Women Played Hardball*. Seattle, Wash.: 1994.

Krich, John. *El Béisbol*. New York: Prentice Hall, 1989.

Los Angeles Dodger Media Guide, 1996. Los Angeles Dodgers, 1996.

Lowry, Philip J. *Green Cathedrals*. Reading, Mass.: Addison-Wesley, 1992.

Maitland, Brian. *Japanese Baseball: A Fan's Guide*. Rutland, Vt.: Charles E. Tuttle, 1991.

Maya, Ralph. Correspondence. Coral Gables, Fla., 1996.

McNary, Kyle P. *Ted "Double Duty" Radcliffe*. Minneapolis: McNary, 1994.

McNeil, William F. *The Dodgers Encyclopedia*. Champaign, Ill.: Sports Publishing, 1997.

Minor League Baseball Stars. Cleveland: Society for American Baseball Research. *Volume I*, 1984; *Volume II*, 1985; *Volume III*, 1992.

Minor League History Journal. Cleveland: Society for American Baseball Research. *Vol. 1*, 1992; *Vol. 2*, 1993; *Vol. 3*, 1994.

Mooreland, George L. *Balldom*. New York: Balldom, 1914.

The National Pastime. John Thorn, editor. New York: Bell, 1987.

The National Pastime. 1982 through 1996. Cleveland: Society for American Baseball Research.

Navarro, Victor, and Armada Navarro. *Angel*. Béisbol Profesional de Puerto Rico. Inter Island Spring Corp., 1995.

The Negro Leagues Book. Dick Clark and Larry Lester, editors. Cleveland: Society for American Baseball Research, 1994.

Nineteenth Century Stars. Robert L. Tiemann and Mark Rucker, editors. Cleveland: Society for American Baseball Research, 1989.

Oh, Sadaharu, and David Falkner. *Sadaharu Oh*. New York: Random House, 1984.

Okkonen, Marc. *Baseball Memories 1900–1909*, New York: Sterling, 1992.

Oleksak, Michael M., and Mary Adams Oleksak. *Beisbol*. Masters, 1996.

La Pelota Nuestra. Osvaldo Rodriguez Suncar, editor. Santo Domingo, D.R., 1995.

Perez, Louis A., Jr. "Between Baseball and Bullfighting: The Quest for Nationality in Cuba, 1868–1898." *The Journal of American History*, September 1994.

Peterson, Robert. *Only the Ball Was White*. New York: McGraw-Hill, 1970.

Riley, James A. *The Biographical Encyclopedia of the Negro Baseball Leagues*. New York: Carroll & Graf, 1994.

Ritter, Lawrence S. *The Glory of Their Times*. New York: William Morrow, 1984.

Rogosin, Donn. *Invisible Men*. New York: Macmillan, 1987.

Ruiz, Yuyo. Correspondence. San Juan, P.R., 1997

Seymour, Harold. *Baseball: The Early Years*. New York: Oxford University Press, 1960.

Spalding, Albert G. *America's National Game*. San Francisco: Halo, 1991.

Torres, Angel. *La Leyenda del Béisbol Cubano 1878–1997*, Miami: Review Printers, 1996.

Total Baseball. John Thorn and Pete Palmer, editors. New York: Warner, 1989.

Van Hyning, Thomas E. *Puerto Rico's Winter League*. Jefferson, N.C.: McFarland, 1995.

Whiting, Robert. *You Gotta Have Wa*. New York: Vintage, 1990.

Who's Who in Baseball, 1916–1994. New York: Who's Who in Baseball Magazine.

Index

227